Building the City of Spectacle

Building the City of Spectacle

Mayor Richard M. Daley and
the Remaking of Chicago

*Costas Spirou
and Dennis R. Judd*

Cornell University Press

Ithaca and London

First published 2016 by Cornell University Press

Printed in the United States of America

Library of Congress Cataloging-in-Publication Data

Names: Spirou, Costas, author. | Judd, Dennis R., author.
Title: Building the city of spectacle : Mayor Richard M. Daley and the remaking of Chicago / Costas Spirou and Dennis R. Judd.
Description: Ithaca : Cornell University Press, 2016. |
    Includes bibliographical references and index.
Identifiers: LCCN 2016013032 | ISBN 9781501700477 (cloth : alk. paper)
Subjects: LCSH: Chicago (Ill.)—Politics and government—1951– |
    Tourism and city planning—Illinois—Chicago—History. |
    Urban renewal—Illinois—Chicago—History. | Daley, Richard M.
    (Richard Michael), 1942–
Classification: LCC F548.52 .S65 2016 | DDC 977.3/11—dc23
LC record available at http://lccn.loc.gov/2016013032

Cornell University Press strives to use environmentally responsible suppliers and materials to the fullest extent possible in the publishing of its books. Such materials include vegetable-based, low-VOC inks and acid-free papers that are recycled, totally chlorine-free, or partly composed of nonwood fibers. For further information, visit our website at www.cornellpress.cornell.edu.

Cloth printing   10 9 8 7 6 5 4 3 2 1

We dedicate this book to our lovely wives,
Patrice Spirou and Nan Kammann-Judd

Contents

Preface

The genesis of this book goes back almost fifteen years, to a lively discussion between the authors about the almost unbelievable pace of physical construction that was occurring along Chicago's lakefront and in and around the Loop. Costas Spirou's office on Michigan Avenue overlooked the museum of the Art Institute of Chicago and Lake Michigan beyond, and from this bird's-eye view he could witness the remarkable changes that were taking place in Grant Park and along the lakefront—what people have long called the city's front door. Dennis Judd had recently moved into a town house near the huge Museum Campus project; from his balcony he could see thirteen construction cranes dotting the downtown skyline. We loved the city and thought it was, day by day, becoming a more exciting and interesting place. At the same time, since both of us had previously written about tourism-led urban development, we knew all too well that it was a double-edged sword that generally ushered physical revitalization and jobs but also, all too often, a questionable use of public resources. Like so many of our fellow citizens, we had mixed feelings about tourists and the changes they bring to the places they visit. Before long our conversations led us to the notion that we should write a book that would not only help us to take a firm position about the historic urban transformation unfolding right before our eyes but also, ideally, stimulate useful debate among scholars and other interested readers. Finally, more than ten years later, we have completed this vexatious labor of love.

In the years before and after we started this book, Chicago officials announced spectacular entertainment and tourist projects at every turn, and office towers and residential buildings sprouted like mushrooms on a damp prairie. All this bustling activity in and near the downtown and the lake created a heady atmosphere of optimism and energy in the city, and an adoring local and national press stoked the ebullient mood. Flower planters and hanging baskets lined the main thoroughfares, and more appeared each summer. Potholed streets were resurfaced, performance venues and concerts were filled, and visitors from all over the world jammed the tour buses. By the mid-1990s Navy Pier was already attracting crowds, and in the next few years the Museum Campus, a redesigned Soldier Field, improvements to Grant Park, and the new Millennium Park brought millions of tourists. However, a phrase like "the tourist economy" describes only one dimension of a multifaceted process. Young professionals and a rising number of college students filled the dozens of condominium towers shooting up everywhere, or so it seemed, as did empty nesters lured by the enriching possibilities of an exciting urban lifestyle. The U.S. Census identified Chicago's downtown as the fastest-growing city center in the nation, but the bureau's statistical tables could not possibly convey how fast and how thoroughly this great American city was being remade.

All this made a mayor with the legendary last name Daley a darling of the local and national press. Like his father, Richard J., who ruled postwar Chicago as the boss of America's last great party machine, Richard M. won one election after another by overwhelming margins. His love for his job and the city was on display at every press conference; his style, speech, and bearing were reminiscent of a bygone era, grounded on values associated with Chicago's working class and ethnic neighborhoods. Yet while he was clearly very powerful, Richard M. Daley did not project the persona of a machine politician in the Chicago tradition. It was obvious that he fully embraced the political necessities of the global era, which required him to reach out to a broad assortment of political groups. He was a consummate politician who seemed to love politics not for its own sake but for what it allowed him to do in making Chicago into a prosperous and beautiful city.

Daley was not the first mayor to employ tourism, leisure, culture, and spectacle as an urban growth strategy. Years before he came into office, other mayors had identified the development of tourism and its associated sectors as perhaps the only viable path to urban recovery. In a very brief time, however, Daley managed to craft a model of revitalization that urban leaders in cities all over the world strove to emulate. This accomplishment reflected Daley's exceptional political skills and his clear vision, but it was not always recognized that he owed much of his success to something he did not control: a man-made geography and cultural inheritance that truly sets Chicago apart from any other American city. Daniel Hudson Burnham served as the director of works for the 1893 Columbian Exposition, and his firm, Burnham and Root, designed arguably the most historically significant buildings in the city (architecture tours devoted solely to his works are very popular). In the 1909 *Plan of Chicago*, Burnham entered into the city's psyche with his dictum "Make no little plans." The aspirations expressed in that famous phrase inspired successive generations of Chicago's political leaders and civic groups, but Daley tied himself more closely to Burnham's legacy than any previous mayor in

Chicago's history. Unlike Burnham, Daley did not devise a formal blueprint for the city's future; nevertheless, he was motivated by a consistent vision of the twenty-first-century city he wanted to bring into being.

A story tracing the rise of Chicago's City of Spectacle cannot be told without recognizing that Richard M. Daley was its chief architect and builder. During his more than twenty years as mayor, Daley took care to cultivate close relationships with the city's many ethnic and racial factions. He also forged an unbreakable bond with Chicago's business and civic elites, corporations, and philanthropic community. This alliance made it possible for him to pursue an extraordinarily ambitious and coherent revitalization program, and his efforts produced demonstrable economic benefits. For the first time in decades, major corporations began to leave the suburbs and move their offices to the city center. Companies such as Boeing, ADM, Exelon, Hyatt, RR Donnelly, and United Continental were persuaded to stay home in Chicago or move their global headquarters from elsewhere to gleaming skyscrapers in the Loop. Nineteen of the thirty tallest buildings in downtown Chicago today were completed during the Daley years.

As the longest-serving mayor in the history of the city, Daley seemed to love every part of his job, but what he enthused about most often were his plans for transforming the lakefront. He drew on a combination of public and private sources to raise billions of dollars in investments for an infrastructure to support a tourist- and leisure-based economy. Every summer millions of visitors poured into the city to enjoy its entertainment and cultural attractions and fabulous lifestyle. The bundle of policies that changed neighborhoods, the Loop, and the lakefront made Daley into a popular mayor, but—especially in hindsight—it has become obvious that he left an ambiguous legacy. Daley took on every challenge he could find, but some of them did not yield to ready solutions. The education reforms he so enthusiastically championed shifted resources to middle-class neighborhoods and weakened the schools located in struggling neighborhoods. His public housing policies displaced low-income residents, transferred valuable land to private developers, and energized gentrification. As the years went by, accumulating controversies over education and housing prompted a rising chorus of opposition.

Despite the frequent disputes over his education and housing policies, on the whole these policies were regarded as positive initiatives by many of the mayor's supporters because they encouraged the revival of deteriorated neighborhoods. Practically no one, however, gave him passing marks for the corruption scandals that dogged him year after year, or for the constant reports of police brutality, or for the city's deteriorating financial condition. He did not help his cause either, with a leadership style that became progressively more impatient and autocratic as the time rolled on. Near the end of his last term in office, Daley sold valuable city assets in privatization deals to fill year-to-year shortfalls in the city budget. One of these involved an agreement to sell the Chicago Skyway (a 7.8-mile, elevated toll-road) to private investors in exchange for a ninety-nine-year lease. Many observers thought the deal was not bad for the city, but another transaction, which sold the revenues from more than thirty-six thousand metered parking spaces for seventy-five years to a private corporation, excited public anger that endures to the present day. Daley promised that the proceeds from these deals would secure the city's financial health for years to come, but by the time he left office most of the money had been spent. And thus, in one disastrous decision, Daley badly compromised his legacy.

As we researched the rise of Chicago's City of Spectacle and the mayoralty of Richard M. Daley, we came to recognize that there were two sides of his personality and political style. On the one hand we saw a leader who managed to successfully craft and execute an incredibly ambitious vision to shape Chicago's future, one that won him widespread admiration and praise. His policies to bring Chicago into the global age fundamentally transformed its economy, changed its culture, and reconfigured the lakefront and neighborhoods throughout the city. Daley's enormous political authority allowed him to accomplish these grand goals. But on the other side of the ledger, as the years wore on he was increasingly willing to use his power to overreach and to crush all opposition.

In the conclusion to our book we consider a transcendentally important question: was the rise of Chicago's City of Spectacle worth the price? Trying to answer this question puts us squarely in the middle of recurring and often contentious debates about the recent strategies to revitalize America's central cities. Among planners and other academic critics, the word "neoliberalism" is often used as an epithet describing a style of urban redevelopment controlled by the private institutions that command large volumes of capital. According to detractors, privately led redevelopment benefits wealthy property owners and investors and middle-class gentrifiers but often displaces and ignores the needs of poorer residents.

Although we agree that the benefits flowing from the recent revitalization of American cities have been unevenly distributed, we nevertheless argue that the economic restructuring that has transformed urban economies in the last few years has been both necessary and, for most urban residents, beneficial. Chicago's future, like that of cities everywhere, is influenced by any number of forces that lie beyond the control of the civic leaders in any particular place: intense competition pitting one jurisdiction against the next; constantly changing demographic shifts; unpredictable economic pressures; and unexpected sociopolitical circumstances. Public leaders who are committed to both transformational economic change and to remedies for the social ills so deeply embedded in American society cannot alter the large-scale structural circumstances that constrain their actions. With this consideration in mind, we conclude the book by arguing that without the efforts of Richard M. Daley to remake Chicago, the city would be much poorer than it is, and possibly a basket case. Future scholars who assess Daley's impact on the city may well reach a different conclusion, but the difficulty of making a final judgment is exactly why this book has been so challenging but also so rewarding to write.

Acknowledgments

M any people have given generously of their time and talents to help us write a better book. We hope we have, in some measure, rewarded their efforts. We owe much gratitude to Michael McGandy, senior editor at Cornell University Press, who not only expressed early interest in the project but also devoted an extraordinary amount of time closely reading and critiquing the several versions of the manuscript. The attention he gave to this work reminded us of times we thought were long past, when editors expected to substantially shape the books they published. Karen Hwa, senior production editor at Cornell University Press, also helped strengthen the manuscript with insightful feedback. We want to express a special thanks to our colleague and friend Dick Simpson, with whom we shared many conversations about Chicago politics over the years. His close reading of the manuscript as it neared completion was especially valuable because, as is widely recognized, as both a former alderman and longtime scholar he knows more about Chicago's politics than just about anyone alive. We also thank Sam Bassett for his careful reading of manuscript drafts, and the press reviewers for their constructive feedback. Doug Otter aided us with the creation of the lakefront map, and Joe Mocnik and Jon Scott with the acquisition of photographs. The Georgia College & State University Foundation provided research assistance.

We thank a number of colleagues who over the years have contributed to our understanding of Chicago's unique urban environment. Mark Newman, David Perry, Terry Nichols Clark, Annette Steinacker, Yue Zhang, and Mike Pagano helped us gain a deeper understanding of the rapidly evolving city. Larry Bennett's extensive scholarship, exceptional insights and unique understanding of Chicago and urban change proved critical to our efforts. We would be remiss if we did not recognize our spouses, Nan Kammann-Judd and Patrice Spirou, who deserve special recognition for their continued support. They patiently and graciously endured the challenges of completing this project and, at various times, read drafts and listened to us bang on about our latest bright idea. We have dedicated this book to them.

Building the City of Spectacle

Introduction

BUILDING A CITY OF SPECTACLE

One of the most widely recognized views of Chicago's skyline appears in photos taken by someone standing on the Museum Campus; typically, it features a serene, panoramic view of Monroe Harbor and Grant Park, foregrounded against a crenellated wall of high-rise towers and skyscrapers looming in the distance. Anyone gazing at this scene on a book jacket or in a magazine article or visitors' brochure would likely not be surprised to learn that in Chicago, the leading industry is tourism and entertainment. What might be less obvious is that a large proportion of the more than fifty million tourists a year from all over the world are drawn to the city not because of its magnificent collection of historic architecture, its cultural treasures, or fortunate location on Lake Michigan. As essential as these assets might be, what draws the tourists in such numbers is a City of Spectacle that has been arisen along the lakefront, and most of it was constructed during a twenty-two-year period from April 4, 1989, when Richard M. Daley won his first mayoral race, to September 2010, when the papers ran stories that he would not run for a sixth term. By the time he left office, Navy Pier had become a popular downtown tourist attraction, and the Museum Campus had coalesced into a sprawling landscape containing the John G. Shedd Aquarium, the Adler Planetarium, the Field Museum of Natural History, the recently renovated Soldier Field, a nature preserve, and a network of bicycle paths, beaches, and boat basins (figure I.1). Over

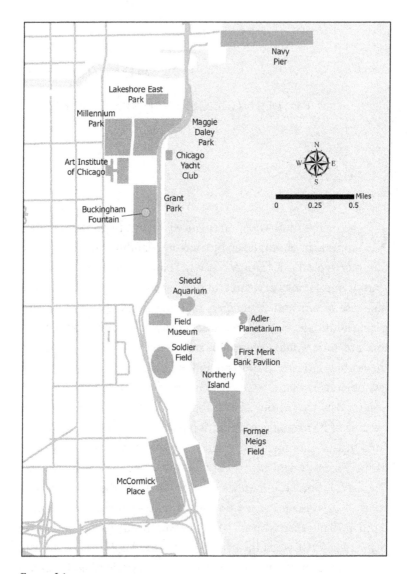

Figure I.1
Map of attractions on Chicago's lakefront. Data derived from the City of Chicago, Open Source Street Maps, and the U.S. Geological Survey. Courtesy of Doug Otter.

the years, constantly changing displays of public art appeared in the downtown and along the lakefront. From March until November, fireworks lit the skies above the Monroe Harbor at least twice each week. Open-air films, concerts, dancing, parades, and a round of festivals and celebrations turned Chicago's lakefront into a destination for millions of out-of-town tourists and local residents acting as if they, too, were tourists.[1]

Richard M. Daley, the Builder

The program of construction required to build Chicago's lakefront playground necessitated an investment of more than $5 billion of public money and much more in private resources. Most of it occurred on Daley's watch, and because of that he became a darling of the national press. A 2005 issue of *Time* magazine featured a story on the five best big-city mayors in the country. Daley led the list. According to the magazine's writers he had "presided over the city's transition from a graying hub to a vibrant boomtown."[2] In September 2010 the *New York Times* offered an equally enthusiastic assessment of Daley's accomplishments: "Mr. Daley oversaw a city that transformed its economy, making Chicago the vibrant hub of the Midwest. He remade the city's front yard. . . . He was ready to show it off on a global stage with an ambitious bid for the 2016 Summer Olympics."[3] In a companion article, the *Times* reporters, in breathless prose, called Daley a transformative leader who transcended even his own time: "All cities change over time, but Chicago may be in a class by itself. It took a measure of sheer willpower to transform the 'hog butcher for the world,' as Chicago was known around the middle of the last century, into one of the most forward-looking of cities, with an abundance of public art and green space alongside an ever-expanding skyline. The greater part of the transformation took place over the last two decades, under the command of Mayor Richard M. Daley."[4] Chicago had not received such an outpouring of glowing press since the 1893 World's Fair—the World's Columbian Exposition—closed its gates more than a century before.

Something the mayor's admirers often failed to note was that his success was intimately connected to his uncontested control of a disciplined political apparatus fueled by money, marketing, and media. Corporate CEOs and other influential players in Chicago's global economy provided the enormous resources required to fund a formidable and durable reelection operation that helped keep him in office for so many years. Even the most sophisticated and well-funded, elite-centered strategy might have floundered in the rough seas of Chicago's tumultuous politics, but Daley took care to cultivate close relationships with political and community leaders representing the city's racial, ethnic, and neighborhood groups. Voters responded by reelecting him five times, and by winning margins even more lopsided than those achieved by his legendary father, Richard J. Daley, who from 1955 to 1976 ran one of the most powerful big-city machines in American history.

Daley the son went to great pains to establish a persona as a visionary urban leader guided by lofty aims, and in this cause he constantly invoked the name of Daniel Burnham, the chief planner of the Chicago World's Fair of 1893 and author of the 1909 *Plan of Chicago*. Even before his first inauguration, the mayor-elect announced his intention to plant thousands of trees and install flower beds along the lakefront and in street medians, parks, and neighborhoods throughout the city. Twenty-two years later, near the end of his sixth term, the mayor employed a soaring rhetoric that linked the city's storied past to the last, and most audacious, of his many undertakings. An Olympic Games, he declared, would be comparable to the World's Colombian Exposition, a "once in a lifetime opportunity to redefine our city."[5]

In the years before he entered the mayor's office, the idea that Daley might someday fancy himself to be Daniel Burnham's rightful heir would likely have provoked gales of laughter. His penchant for verbal gaffes and malapropisms carried forward a family tradition firmly established by his father, and many observers considered him to be a political and intellectual lightweight. In an article on the younger Daley's losing bid to become mayor in 1983, a *U.S. News & World Report* article called him "Dumb Ritchie."[6] After his election six years later, however, the caustic comments gave way to admiring praise. Comparisons to Burnham became a regular feature in newspapers and the popular press and even, on occasion, in professional outlets. In 2007, the noted Chicago architect Stanley Tigerman wrote in the *Architectural Record* that "here in Chicago we have a great mayor, Mayor Daley, who is arguably the Daniel Burnham of the 21st century."[7]

The mayor clearly relished such flattering analogies, and he was not shy about offering his own. In a speech delivered to the Chicago Greening Convention in 2002, Daley exclaimed, "I am very proud of how Chicago's appearance has improved over the last decade or so. Visitors continually tell me the same thing they tell you: 'I had no idea Chicago was such a beautiful city.' . . . They expect Nelson Algren and they get Martha Stewart."[8] Blair Kamin, the architectural critic for the *Chicago Tribune*, once referred to the mayor as "Chicago's Johnny Appleseed, carrying out a simple (and politically popular) idea: The more trees the better."[9]

Daniel Burnham? Martha Stewart? Johnny Appleseed? This colorful collection of characters conjures up a startling image of Daley as an avuncular visionary who transformed Chicago into a twenty-first-century version of the City Beautiful (figure I.2).

FIGURE I.2

During his tenure as mayor of Chicago, Richard M. Daley presided over an ambitious construction plan along the city's lakefront. Visible in this aerial image of the north end of Grant Park is the Chicago Yacht Club, Millennium Park, and the under-construction Maggie Daley Park, which was completed in early 2015. Courtesy of user marchello74, Shutterstock Images.

One more name, however, should be added to this list. Kamin, among others, sometimes associated Daley's name with Robert Moses, one of the most iconic figures of twentieth-century urbanism. In 2002 one of Kamin's colleagues, also a columnist for the *Chicago Tribune*, found it impossible to resist a fanciful bit of hyperbole: "Think of the great city-building duets in world history. Think imperial Rome, built for eternity by Emperor Augustus and a cohort of architects led by Pollio Vetruvius. Or 19th Century Paris, redrawn in grand boulevards by Napoleon III and Baron Haussmann. Or mid-20th Century New York, reconnected in steel and concrete by Mayor Fiorello LaGuardia and public works czar Robert Moses."[10] In a 2007 retrospective on what Daley had wrought, Kamin asked, "Should every city have a strongman?"[11]

It is easy to understand why Daley was sometimes compared to Robert Moses. In his monumental, Pulitzer Prize–winning work *The Power Broker*, Robert Caro traces the story of how, over a four-decade period from the 1920s to the 1960s, Moses used his control over the most powerful development agencies of the New York metropolitan region to try to wipe the slate clean and utterly redraw the region's transportation and park systems and, in the process, level many of its neighborhoods.[12] Moses was often called both a power broker and a master builder, and his career illustrates how tightly these roles were yoked together. In 1924 Moses became the chairman of the Long Island Parks Commission and New York State Council on Parks, and over the next two decades he gained such a complete control over the largest transportation and development authorities in the New York region that "no housing, public buildings or roads were built without Moses."[13] The expressways and the parks that he built reshaped metropolitan New York, and his urban renewal and housing projects put vast swaths of land in the path of the bulldozer. Caro thought that Moses's vanity and lust for power drove him to ravage the urban landscape, but when Moses died in 1981, the *New York Times*'s obituary declared that "he hurt thousands, but he helped millions."[14]

Of course there are countless differences between Moses the career bureaucrat and Daley the elected official. As mayor, Daley was required to answer to an electorate every four years, and his lakefront building program, as ambitious as it was, displaced very few people. Still, the mayor's detractors accused him of exercising autocratic authority to get what he wanted. One critic charged that in "Daleyland, it's the mayor's way or the highway."[15] The urban affairs columnist for the *Chicago Tribune* once wrote, "Welcome to one of the great one-man shows in the history of American city planning."[16] Such appraisals reveal why it is useful to bring Moses's name into the conversation: it serves as a reminder that Daley, like Moses, managed to become his city's master builder only because, at the same time, he became a power broker capable of getting things done.

Daley built what some writers have called a "new machine" by playing a masterful inside as well as outside game. To win the inside game he needed to gain the upper hand with a fractious city council of fifty aldermen. This was a daunting challenge because he could not automatically rely on the disciplined party apparatus that had worked so well for his father. Early on, he bought the aldermen's loyalty by continuing a long-established practice of granting them autonomous control over key city services in their wards and, the biggest prize of all, the authority to veto decisions of the city's zoning board. In this way, he gained mastery over a "rubber stamp council" that proved to be even more compliant than his father's.[17] Alderman Joe Moore told an interviewer, "I often liken the City of Chicago [to] a feudal system, where the mayor is sort of a de facto king [and] each alderman is the lord—I guess, lady, for female aldermen—of their individual fiefdom."[18] If an alderman exercised an excessive degree of independence, Mayor Daley made sure that a good opponent was ready to run in the next election, and he threw money and political support to the contender. The mayor adroitly filled vacant aldermanic posts. By 1998, twenty of the fifty aldermen owed their jobs to the mayor, which is why, as a leading expert on Chicago politics put it, "They'll look at what comes across their desk, ask what the mayor wants, and vote 'yes.'"[19]

A compliant city council was crucial to Daley's policy goals because, year by year, he was obliged to ask the council to pass sometimes-controversial legislation he needed to advance his policy agenda. In 1997, for instance, the aldermen approved an ordinance that authorized the city's Housing Department to take control of more than fifteen hundred parcels in neighborhoods with high levels of tax-delinquent properties. The next year, the council passed a town-house ordinance requiring residential real estate developers to integrate substantial open space into their plans. In 1999, Daley expanded his beautification policies into the neighborhoods by pushing an ordinance calling for a comprehensive update of the city's landscaping ordinance, which stipulated that developers would be required, when appropriate, to install "ornamental" fencing and wrought-iron railings, and to plant trees, shrubbery, and even vines. Legislation like this discomfited some developers, but land clearance, the demolition of dilapidated buildings, and beautification supported the gentrification of neighborhoods and added momentum to Daley's program of downtown and lakefront development.

With the inside game in hand, Daley was in a position to attend to the two key strategies of his outside game—to build an electoral coalition that would keep him in office. To realize his ambitions to make Chicago into a global city he needed to secure the support of

Chicago's civic elite. This was a natural marriage because civic and corporate leaders stood to benefit from policies to revitalize the downtown and lakefront and to gentrify the neighborhoods. Contributions to his 1989 campaign showed that powerful civic leaders bought into his vision right from the beginning, and in subsequent elections the resources they provided the mayor allowed him to overwhelm his opponents with multimillion-dollar media campaigns.

The other strategy comprising Daley's outside game was more challenging because it required him to assemble a broad constituency of support in a city riven by racial and ethnic antagonisms. Daley lost his first bid for the mayor's office in 1983, in a three-way race that pitted him against Jane Byrne, the Democratic incumbent, and Harold Washington, a candidate backed by a coalition of community activists and leaders of the black community. Washington's election as Chicago's first African American mayor brought to the surface tensions that had been building for many years. All through the 1980s, ethnic and racial animosity had torn at the city's political fabric. When Daley beat two African American candidates in the 1989 election, it seemed doubtful that he, or any mayor, would be able to break the impasse, but within months he began forging close relationships with leaders of the African American and Hispanic communities. His overwhelming reelection victory two years later showed that he had built a base of support that extended into every corner of the city, and in the next four elections a serious challenger never emerged.

At What Price?

Today, a visitor to Chicago cannot help but notice that the city seems to converge around spaces along the lakefront and near the Loop devoted to spectacle and play. It is important to understand that this geographic configuration was established more than a century ago, and nearly everything Daley did was built on this physical foundation. The 1909 *Plan of Chicago* shaped a unique urban landscape that continues to distinguish Chicago from any other American city (figure I.3). Grant Park is a centerpiece; extending nearly two miles north to south, and more than a half mile wide, it prevents the densely built environment of the downtown from crowding the lakefront. The park provides space for the Buckingham Fountain, completed in 1926; the Art Institute of Chicago, completed in 1893; and formal flower gardens, ball fields, tennis courts, and sweeping expanses of trees and lawns. Its position has made it the logical location for community gatherings of every kind: jazz, blues, gospel, and country music festivals; the Taste of Chicago; Fourth of July fireworks; ethnic parades; outdoor movies,

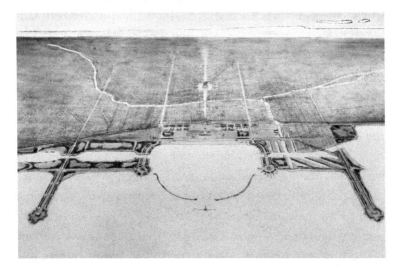

Figure I.3

View looking west over the city, showing the proposed Civic Center, the grand axis, Grant Park, and the harbor. "Plan of Chicago," pl. 87, Chicago, 1909. Daniel H. Burnham and Edward H. Bennett. Historic Architecture and Landscape Image Collection, Ryerson and Burnham Archives, The Art Institute of Chicago. Digital File # 80372.

dancing, and free concerts. Navy Pier is perched on the lakefront to the north of the park, and several blocks south is the sprawling McCormick Place. The city's image is closely identified with and even defined by what takes place on this three-mile stretch of lakefront.

There is much to like. Only a determined curmudgeon would fail to delight, for example, in Millennium Park. Children of every ethnic and racial identity splash and play in the waters of Jaume Plensa's Crown Fountain. Crowds cannot resist stroking the giant "bean" sculpture designed by Indian artist Anish Kapoor. Tourists and locals alike wander by the native prairie landscapes of Lurie Garden and then take a peripatetic stroll over Frank Gehry's serpentine pedestrian bridge to enter Maggie Daley Park. The vaulting aluminum curving surfaces of Gehry's band shell loom over the park and have become instant signifiers of Chicago's skyline. Because of its incredible success, the Millennium Park template is now being emulated by cities all over the world.

When one crosses the street and runs the gauntlet of homeless panhandlers on Michigan Avenue, though, troubling questions arise. Has all that pleasure come at too high a price? What should the city's priorities be? On countless occasions we, the authors, have experienced this combination of pleasure and discomfort as we travel around Chicago, and especially when we find ourselves passing through poverty-ridden neighborhoods with crumbling public infrastructure. Over the years many other observers have noticed something similar. Chicago's front door draws copious praise from sources in and far beyond the city, but it has come in for its share of criticism, too, from those who complain that the huge sums spent to improve aesthetics and urban amenities amount to an indefensible diversion of public resources from the pressing needs of the city's residents.

For these reasons we found it harder than we had imagined to arrive at our own position about Daley's legacy as a builder mayor. We wrote this book as a way of working through this dilemma, but feel compelled to confess that we have never fully resolved it. We came to understand that the City of Spectacle is so central to Chicago's history, image, and economy that is impossible to know what the city would be like without it. It would certainly be less prosperous, less attractive, and less diverse. It is likely that it would be a troubled city still coping with decline instead of the global city it has become. A price has been paid for this success, but the cost of failure would have been immeasurably higher.

The Plan of the Book

In the course of our research we saw Burnham's ghost hovering over almost every undertaking related to Chicago's lakefront. The Commercial Club, which provided the funding for the 1909 *Plan of Chicago*, still gives every new city council member a beautifully embossed version of the *Plan*, and the lavishly illustrated book is also the customary gift ceremoniously handed to visiting dignitaries or new city leaders—it was given, for example, to Blase Cupich when he became the archbishop of the Archdiocese of Chicago in November 2014. This gesture served as a reminder of how fixedly Chicago's culture and collective identity has pivoted around Burnham; Daley, in particular, made it clear that he thought of Burnham as his muse and main inspiration. Accordingly, we explore the meaning and influence of Burnham's legacy on Chicago, and on Daley's undertakings, in chapter 1.

The Burnham name typically inspires flights of rhetorical eloquence and provides guidance and benediction for new undertakings. Less obviously, though, it should be noted that on-the-ground structural conditions provided Daley with the urgent motivation to assert strong leadership to restructure Chicago's economy. As we detail in chapter 2, in the half century after World War II, Chicago grappled with the same economic and social crises that afflicted cities and urban regions sprinkled all along the arc of industrial production that became known as the Rust Belt. From the mid-1950s through the mid-1970s, Richard J. Daley's command of a powerful political machine gave him the ability to bring huge resources to the fight. He became known as "the builder mayor," but even his efforts were not enough to decisively turn the tide. When his son ran successfully for the mayor's office thirteen years after the father's death, it came at the end of a decade in which the city had lost 7 percent of its population. In his spring 1989 campaign, Daley the son kept returning to the theme that Chicago's economy had to change. Chicago was, he said, "going to be an international city."[20] He considered an economy revolving around tourism and leisure to be a key ingredient in that formula.

In chapter 3 we endeavor to describe how Daley's aggressive leadership shaped the six signature projects undertaken during his years in office: Navy Pier, the Museum Campus, Millennium Park, McCormick Place, Soldier Field, and Northerly Island (a remake made possible by the removal of an airport, Meigs Field). The scale and duration of this program of construction prompted some writers to compare Daley to Robert Moses, and the title of this chapter is a tip-off that we believe the comparison is apt.

It should be recognized that almost any mayor elected in the late 1980s would surely have taken steps to promote Chicago's tourist economy because other cities were already marching down that path. Chicago was already several years behind, and the volatile politics during the Daley to Daley interregnum showed how hard it would be for any mayor to form a political coalition stable enough or broad enough to sustain a consistent program of economic restructuring.

At the time of Daley's first election there was little reason for anyone to expect that the rancorous infighting that had come to characterize the city's politics would soon come to an end. Considered against this background, it is surprising that Daley could have become a popular mayor who would remain in office for so long (figure I.4). In chapter 4 we tell the tale of how Daley accomplished this daunting task.

While for many years Daley won widespread praise for making Chicago into a model of tourist-led urban regeneration, during his time in office he also did a lot of other things, and in those areas his legacy is decidedly mixed. As we show in chapter 5, for

FIGURE I.4
Richard M. Daley at a press conference, August 14, 2007. Courtesy of user dbking, Flickr.

many years Daley's mayoral tenure was marked by an unceasing stream of news accounts detailing often lurid scandals and revelations related to police corruption and misconduct, and by his last term in office the city's increasingly precarious fiscal position received a flood of negative press. Adding to the growing list of issues, intense disagreements over Daley's education and housing policies made many people question whether the mayor's actions in these two areas, which he held up as examples of creative leadership, had worsened rather than improved social conditions in the poorest neighborhoods. Near the end of his last term, Daley's ill-advised move to privatize the city's parking meters angered almost everyone and focused attention on questionable budgetary practices that continue, to this day, to compromise the city's fiscal health.

In the epilogue to this book we pose a concern we have encountered often in the course of this research: Has the City of Spectacle turned Chicago into a city of bread and circuses? To approach this question, we go back to criticisms leveled even in Burnham's time. As we discovered, the concerns expressed at the time of the World's Fair of 1893 still echo in today's debates. While the fair was in progress and for decades after, critics vilified Burnham for building his version of the city upon a hill in the midst of a metropolis wracked by massive social problems and a national depression. The startling contrasts between Burnham's White City and the festering immigrant slums practically at the fair's front gates gave his detractors powerful ammunition. A century on, similar complaints were expressed about the city that Daley built; according to his detractors, resources devoted to festival, spectacle, and play should have been used instead to address the serious social problems of the city.

Of course identical concerns have been aired in many other cities, too. Over the last quarter century, cities almost everywhere have invested heavily in the reconstruction of downtowns and waterfronts for tourist consumption. This strategy of economic revitalization brought an end to decades of central-city decline, and in our estimation, this was a necessary and important achievement. Today, cities are more pleasant, more fun, and more prosperous than they have ever been—for many, but not for all. At the end of our epilogue we wrestle with the intractable question of whether success on those terms has been sufficient and worthwhile.

1

The Founding City

Chicago is the founding City of Spectacle. To this day, much of its identity and collective memory revolves around Daniel Hudson Burnham and the 1893 World's Columbian Exposition. The dazzling centerpiece of the fair, the White City, morphed into the Emerald City of L. Frank Baum and William Wallace Denslow's children's novel, *The Wonderful Wizard of Oz* (published just seven years after the closing of the fair). Burnham's conception of what the White City represented was only slightly less fanciful than the one portrayed in the land of Oz. The fair had barely closed its gates when Burnham began promoting the White City, with its cluster of classicist Beaux-Arts structures, fountains, and manicured grounds, as the model for what soon became known as the City Beautiful. The idea that parks, open space, and beautification might serve as the much-needed antidotes to the social disorder and chaos of the industrial city quickly gained an enthusiastic following, and in the 1890s a movement devoted to the ideals of the City Beautiful swept the country. The philosophical premises and design features of the City Beautiful informed the 1909 *Plan of Chicago* and the plans adopted by many other cities in the coming decades.

The fair's Midway Plaisance exerted an equally enduring, though less often acknowledged, influence on twentieth-century city development. In stark contrast to the formal and ordered ambience of the White City, the displays at the mile-long Midway were titillating, garish, and risqué. Fairgoers strolling along the Midway encountered the entertainments typically available in today's theme parks, plus many that revealed a prurient fascination with exotic cultures and social customs (African villagers and dancing girls were especially popular). Within a decade of the closing of the fair, the several features of the Midway were resurrected in several themed areas of Luna Park on Coney Island (such as the "Eskimo Village"); in the next few years movie palaces and other venues offering carnival delights began to spread elsewhere.[1] Walt Disney (whose father worked as a carpenter at the World's Fair) incorporated the contradictory elements of the White City and the Midway into the nation's first theme park, Disneyland, which opened on July 17, 1955.[2]

Two decades later, some echoes of the Disney formula made a much-heralded appearance in downtown Boston, when, on August 26, 1976, the developer James Rouse (who said he was inspired by Disney) opened the renovated Quincy Market. Defying expectations, crushing crowds filled the aisles, boutique shops, and restaurants of the three renovated buildings of the long-abandoned 150-year-old market. It was "a gigantic, four-day party" with people "dancing into the night," a celebration of "the day the urban renaissance began."[3] The national press seemed utterly awestruck; overnight, it seemed, Boston's downtown had been transformed into a "Disney World with class," "a glittering rebuke to the notion that inner cities could not attract tourists and shoppers with their cameras, their appetites, and their money."[4]

Noting Boston's success, over the next decade a generation of "messiah mayors" campaigned on promises that they would lead similar urban revivals in their own cities.[5] Festival marketplaces, renovated waterfronts, new sports stadiums, convention centers, and luxury hotels began popping up all over the place, literally from coast to coast. Renaissance mayors became media superstars, with William Donald Schaefer receiving top billing. In his four terms as the mayor of Baltimore, Schaefer presided over the construction of Harborplace, a project that transformed the city's harbor from a collection of derelict docks to a waterfront complex anchored by a Rouse mall, the National Aquarium (with its glassed-over Amazon rain forest), and acres of plazas and open space. In 1984 he was hailed as the "Best Mayor in America" and rode the wave of positive press all the way into the governor's office. Success stories like this became infectious. Even sober and pessimistic scholars came to believe that the worst of the urban crisis had passed, prompting a professional journal to publish three articles in 1985 asking, "Where Has the Urban Crisis Gone?," "Whatever Happened to the Urban Crisis?," and "What Urban Crisis?"[6]

While other cities basked in the breathless prose employed by journalists to announce the renaissance of America's inner cities, Chicago was receiving a less than favorable press. The racially charged invective that preceded and followed the election of the city's first African American mayor in 1983 supplied a reliable stream of juicy media stories about Chicago's bitter racial divisions. Year after year Chicago managed to produce plenty of spectacle, but it was not the kind that seemed likely to raise the city out of its economic malaise. It came as an unexpected surprise to almost everyone when Daley managed to calm the political waters while also placing Chicago at the center of the late-twentieth-century national narrative of urban recovery and transformation. To do so, he relied on a template fashioned in Chicago a century before.

Fashioning the Original Template

On the eve of the 1893 Columbian Exposition, Chicago was led by an energetic group of entrepreneurs and aristocrats eager to counter any impression that the city and its residents were, in a phrase used by A. G. Stephens, "a hustling horde of pig-killers."[7] Rudyard Kipling wrote that Chicagoans were always in a "blind hurry" that gave rise to "their grand ignorance of things beyond their immediate interests."[8] Confident that such wrongheaded perceptions endangered their own prospects, the city's business and civic establishment cast about for ways to change Chicago's image, and the chance to host a world's fair presented a perfect opportunity. In previous decades London, Paris, New York City, Dublin, Philadelphia, and several other cities had hosted international exhibitions. Local boosters regarded the fairs as opportunities to project a sense of modernity and progress and improve future commercial opportunities. The people who attended them were looking for entertainment and cultural enlightenment; in this respect fairs and exhibitions may be regarded as precursors to modern tourism.[9]

The London World's Fair of 1851 established a model for the several fairs that opened over the next half century. Named the Crystal Palace Exhibition, after the main building that was constructed of nine hundred thousand square feet of glass held up by thirty-three hundred cast-iron columns, this international gathering was heralded as the "Exhibition of the Works of All Nations." The Crystal Palace and surrounding grounds contained fifteen thousand exhibits, sixty-five hundred of them from out-side Great Britain, and it covered almost twenty-six acres. The six million visitors who attended the London fair gawked at displays featuring inventions such as the telegraph, the steam locomotive, and the electric clock. Other exhibits showcased the world's largest organ and the first life-size reproductions of prehistoric dinosaurs. The Crystal Palace Exhibition included public art and new design forms in furniture. The five-shilling admission fee guaranteed that attendance would mainly be restricted to the more prosperous classes, which had the effect of highlighting the class divide that was becoming a defining feature of the industrial age. In the words of Karl Marx, it was a "Pantheon in which the bourgeoisie worship their gods."[10]

Only two years later New York City held the "Exhibition of the Industry of All Nations," and in 1855 Paris hosted the "Exposition Universelle." International expositions followed in London (1862), Paris (1867), Vienna (1873), and Philadelphia. Philadelphia's Centennial Exposition of 1876 sprawled over 450 acres in Fairmount Park, with close to forty thousand exhibitors scattered through 199 buildings and 250 pavilions. Referenced as the "International Exhibition of Arts, Manufactures and Products of the Soil and Mine," its displays featured motors, pneumatic and hydraulic equipment, railway engines, forest products, and educational and scientific exhibits. The exposition introduced Alexander Graham Bell's telephone and the first typewriter (Remington) and bottle of ketchup (Heinz).[11]

London's Crystal Palace Exposition celebrated England's industrial might and expanding empire, and the Exposition Universelle de Paris in 1855 came at a time when Napoleon III's Second Empire was undertaking a massive physical reconstruction of the French capital. New York's and Philadelphia's expositions were, in essence, rejoinders, conveying the message that the United States was now an industrial power equal to any European nation. It is within this historical context that the people involved in planning the Columbian Exposition worked. In the late 1880s Chicago's entrepreneurial elite seized on the idea that Chicago should enter the competition to host the Columbian Exposition, a prize plum being dangled by Congress to mark the four hundredth anniversary of Columbus's discovery of America.[12] In 1889, Mayor DeWitt C. Cregier assembled the city's civic leaders to begin the process of raising money. When Chicago won the competition, the fair's organizing committee selected Daniel Hudson Burnham, who had already made celebrated contributions to the Loop's development, as the fair's chief planner.

What made the Columbian Exhibition different from its predecessors was the seamless merger between Burnham's noble ideals of civic life and the crassest expressions of a rapidly emerging mass culture of consumption. In Burnham's White City, the nightly illumination of the elaborately ornamented neoclassical buildings created an unforgettable impression. Sepia photos from the period only faintly convey the magical realm of the White City. Visitors who had never experienced electricity were dazzled by the nightly drama of the floodlit buildings lining the Court of Honor, with rows of statues flanking both sides of the Grand Basin, thirteen hundred feet long and three hundred feet wide (roughly the size of eight football fields). At the basin's center, the Statue of the Republic, resplendently gilded, projected a perfect symbol of strength and wealth. The Columbian Fountain lofted its waters within the image of a boat oared by eight figures representing the arts and industry. Figures representing music, architecture, sculpture, and painting rowed on one side of the boat; agriculture, science, industry, and commerce lifted their oars on the other. It was an

FIGURE 1.1

Grant Park, with the towering buildings of the Loop looming up in the background, has emerged as the centerpiece of Chicago's contemporary quest for fantasy and spectacle. Concerts, festivals, celebrations, and various other events bring large crowds to the lakefront. Courtesy of user marchello74, Shutterstock Images.

imagined marriage of knowledge, progress, and prosperity. Visitors sometimes strolled for hours, barely able to take their eyes from this extraordinary ensemble.

Inside the White City's monumental structures an equally mesmerizing but very different kind of spectacle was put on display. The exhibits within the Manufactures Building, the Electricity Building, the Mines and Mining Building, the Machinery Hall, and the Agriculture Building, which were clustered around the Grand Basin, artfully melded utopian ideals, technological invention, and a rising consumer culture. Between 1870 and 1910, the number of clerical workers, salespersons, government employees, technicians, and salaried professionals in the United States multiplied 7.5 times, from 756,000 to 5.6 million.[13] The members of this burgeoning middle class provided a ready market for mass-produced industrial goods, and the exhibits in the White City spoke directly to their aspirations. In the Electricity Building, fairgoers got their first glimpse into the power of electricity: lightbulbs, lamps, carpet sweepers, electric doorbells, electric clocks, fans, stoves, irons, laundry machines, fire alarms, sewing machines, elevators, and much more. Visitors stared in amazement, disbelief, and expectant desire. Electric generators, phonographs, motion picture viewing stations, a model house filled with electric appliances—these and other astonishing wonders drew them from one display to the next. Sales representatives roved about, providing information on how to purchase the products the eager crowd now coveted.

Just to the north of this ensemble a short walk took strollers into an idyllic sanctuary, where a cluster of Beaux-Arts buildings surrounded Wooded Island. Included in this assemblage was the Transportation Building, filled with exhibits ranging from horse-drawn carriages to bicycles to steam-powered locomotive trains; the Fisheries Building, which displayed lighted aquariums containing sea mammals and other ocean specimens; the Horticulture Building, with its elaborate collection of exotic plants from the world over; the Fine Arts Palace—the fair's only permanent structure—which exhibited thousands of paintings of national and international acclaim. In addition, the Woman's Building highlighted the accomplishments and advancements of women; and several state and foreign buildings showcased products from around the world.

The White City's combination of soaring architecture and frenetic commerce may have conveyed a mixed message, but visitors to the mile-long, six-hundred-foot-wide Midway Plaisance encountered no such contradictions. At first the members of the fair's committee followed their instinct for solemn purpose by hiring a Harvard anthropology professor to design a "Street of All Nations" aimed at educating the visitor, but Chicago's mayor, Carter Harrison Jr., soon prevailed upon them to instead retain one of his confidants, Sol Bloom. Bloom, the founder of a music store, was known for his predilection for loud, profane, and even lewd entertainment. Under his guidance the Midway evolved into "a jumble of side shows, eateries, thrill rides, and 'villagers' and 'living museums' of exotic people from around the world . . . a carnival of consumption and commercial cosmopolitanism."[14] Placed at the center of the Midway was the giant (and newly invented and named) Ferris wheel, a spectacle that towered over everything else (figure 1.2). Visitors boarded the thirty-six luxury cars, each capable of carrying sixty people, to begin a twenty-minute, 260-foot climb that at its peak offered unforgettable views of the fairgrounds and the city beyond. A dining counter in each of the cars added an element of Gilded Age luxury. The exhibits in the White City were free, but most of the entertainments lining the Midway included entrance fees, in addition to the fifty cents general admission charge to enter the Plaisance. Fees ranged from ten cents for the Sliding Railway and the Libbey Glass Works to two dollars for the Balloon Ascension. Attractions like the Ferris wheel, the Persian Theater, the Chinese Theater, the Bernese Alps Panorama, the Kilauea Panorama, and the Javanese and German Villages charged fifty cents. The Turkish Village at $1.00 and the Street in Cairo at $1.10 charged higher rates but still attracted thousands of visitors. A few blocks from the fairgrounds, a crush of people crowded into the tents of Buffalo Bill's Wild West show,

FIGURE 1.2
The genesis of Chicago's contemporary quest for spectacle and entertainment can be traced to the World's Columbian Exposition and its Midway Plaisance. In contrast to the White City, the grounds of the Midway offered visitors an informal setting, with the Ferris wheel dominating the skyline. World's Columbian Exposition, Midway Plaisance, Chicago, 1891–1893. Daniel H. Burnham (architect), C. D. Arnold (photographer). Historic Architecture and Landscape Image Collection, Ryerson and Burnham Archives, The Art Institute of Chicago. Digital File # M525830.jpg.

a nightly extravaganza organized by Buffalo Bill Cody without sanction from the fair's organizers.

In his officially approved and officious account, *Book of the Fair*, Hubert Bancroft offered the naïve and mistaken assertion that "if to any class of visitors the Columbian Exposition was somewhat of a disappointment, it was to those who went there merely in search of amusement. Instruction rather than amusement, but instruction conveyed in its most attractive form, was the main purpose of the Fair."[15] This perspective was contradicted by popular accounts published while the fair was in progress. *Dial* magazine's September 1893 issue made the point that "amusement, of cheap and even vulgar sorts, is being substituted for education, because most people prefer being amused to being instructed."[16] The October 1893 issue of *Harper's Weekly* proclaimed, "One of the most comic things associated with the Midway is that . . . in the catalogue it is set as part of the department of Anthropology."[17] Plainly, "instruction rather than amusement" was an aim that the masses did not fully embrace.

For its backers, the Columbian Exposition was a smashing success. It put Chicago on the international map more firmly than even they might have imagined. A month before the fair's opening, a professional trade magazine declared "Chicago for the next six months will be the Mecca of the civilized world."[18] In 1894, the *Century Magazine* published a story claiming that Chicago's exposition had bested Paris's: "Had Chicago equaled Paris, it would be greatly to our credit; but it has surpassed Paris. Had it produced a beautiful exhibition in imitation of the Paris Exhibition, it would again be much; but it has conceived an entirely different ideal, and carried it out on entirely novel lines."[19] This outpouring of praise piqued curiosity about this energetic city located in a region of the United States little known to most foreigners. Even the European critics who panned the fair's neoclassical architecture as historicist and derivative expressed amazement at the creative thought that went into the fair's structures. Jacques Hermant, a noted Paris architect who wrote extensively about American architecture, admitted to a "truly magnificent impression which results from this dream so audaciously conceived and naively realized."[20]

While the visual impact of the White City was impossible to ignore, the real-life downtown that anchored Chicago—the Loop—received nearly as much attention. The Loop was composed of buildings that expressed an emerging American urbanism more accurately than did the White City (figure 1.1). In the Loop the architects were limited by space, which forced them to build up, and many of the buildings were constructed with little ornamentation. The cluster of skyscrapers and the business environment they nurtured prompted comments concerning the relationship between form and function. Arnold Lewis offered this assessment of the observations made by foreign architectural critics: "If the architecture of the White City disappointed restless European professionals in 1893, the architecture of the Black City of the Loop in 1893, did not."[21] No other event in Chicago's history has ever rivaled the scale or drama of the Columbian Exposition. Even so, the physical reminders of the fair are few. Aside from the neoclassical building occupied by the Museum of Science and Industry, only a few remnants of the Columbian Exposition are scattered about, like shards of pottery from an ancient civilization.

The World's Fair of 1893 became firmly lodged in Chicago's civic consciousness. The reason it achieved such iconic stature might be explained as much by what followed it as by the fair itself, which, after all, lasted only a few months. Within weeks of the fair's closing, Burnham found an enthusiastic audience poised to embrace the ideal of the City Beautiful (figure 1.3). Parks, ponds, formal gardens, bandstands, ball fields, tree-lined boulevards, and ornate public buildings began to appear in cities everywhere. For his part, Burnham authored a series of urban plans that eventually led to the 1909 *Plan of Chicago*. All his work, he often said, was inspired by the example of the White City.

FIGURE 1.3

The Santa Fe Building on Michigan Avenue. Also known as the Railway Exchange Building, this was one of the many projects along the historic thoroughfare designed by D.H. Burnham and Company. The firm operated for many years from its offices on the fourteenth floor. Courtesy of user Ken Lund, Flickr.

The City Beautiful and Urban Reform

After 1893, Burnham turned his attention to the task of elaborating on the principles of the White City. In 1901, he wrote a proposal that would complete important features of the original 1791 L'Enfant plan for Washington, D.C. Later, he declared, "The plans for the improvement of Washington were prepared by the same hands that guided the artistic development of the World's Columbian Exposition in Chicago. The dream city on Lake Michigan, people said, should take on enduring form in the capital of the nation."[22] And so it did. Burnham doubled the dimensions of the mile-long, four-hundred-foot-wide open space stretching west from the Capitol to create a mall befitting a national capital, intentionally separating the seats of government from the poverty and slum condition of its surrounding neighborhoods.[23]

In 1902, as head of the Board of Supervision for Public Buildings and Grounds in the City of Cleveland, Burnham embarked on a project to combat the uncontrolled industrialism obvious in unsightly physical spaces and congested environments on the shores of Lake Erie. His plan specified the construction of several government buildings—a County Court House, a City Hall, and a Public Library. Other smaller public structures included schools, branch libraries, and markets designed to complement his vision of a reorganized lakefront connected by an elaborately landscaped Lake Shore Boulevard. He incorporated a new railroad station into the plan as a first step in building a metropolitan transportation network. Influenced by the Court of Honor in the 1893 Columbian Exposition, Burnham also included a City Gate and a fountain.

Taken together, this elaborate composition was intended to create a harmonious and integrated physical environment. Arnold William Brunner, who won the competition for the design of the Cleveland Federal Building and who, along with Burnham and John Carrère, served on the three-member committee for the development of the civic center, expressed the essence of this perspective when he observed,

> In the turmoil of city life the clash of commercial interests, the fierce competition, the struggle for supremacy, have made our business streets ugly and chaotic. . . . The Civic Centre is where the city speaks to us, where it asserts itself. Here the streets meet and agree to submit to regulation. They resolve themselves into some regular form, the buildings stop swearing at each other, competition is forgotten, individuals are no longer rivals—they are all

citizens. Petty struggles for prominence, small successes and failures disappear. Here the citizens assume their rights and duties and
here civic pride is born.[24]

Similarly, in San Francisco, Burnham aimed to employ architectural beauty to inspire civic pride and to create a "hilly Paris by the
Golden Gate."[25] Commissioned in 1904 by Mayor James Phelan, a
self-proclaimed advocate of order and beauty, Burnham endeav-
ored to transform a chaotic urban layout into a place that would, he
said, appropriately reflect the city's name as "Chrysopylae" (Golden
Gate), the crossroads between the East and the West. His vision
for the city included broad boulevards converging on an imposing civic center; in this respect, he borrowed heavily from Baron
Georges-Eugène Haussmann's Second Empire reconstruction of
Paris, which replaced the warren of narrow and winding streets inherited from its medieval past with broad boulevards and urban
monuments. Burnham's goal was to reorganize the irregular and
unplanned streets of San Francisco with structures, avenues, parks,
and greenways that composed a "miraculous formal equilibrium."[26]

The main impediment Burnham faced was that, unlike Haussmann, he was not backed by the enormous resources and autocratic political authority of Napoleon III and the Second French
Empire. His plan would have required wealthy property owners to give up their properties to make way for open spaces and
allow several imposing public structures to be placed on top of
the Twin Peaks and Telegraph Hill. Because the proposal constituted such a radical dismantling of entire blocks, it ignited overwhelming opposition, and that the city's civic leadership rushed
to abandon it.

Not at all sobered by this experience, Burnham, in collaboration
with Edward H. Bennett, distilled the most audacious elements of

his series of city plans into his signature work, the 1909 *Plan of Chicago*. In 1901 a member of the Commercial Club and the Merchants Club had proposed the idea that something should be done to improve the physical environment of the city, and in October 1906 the Merchants Club approved a campaign to raise money to finance preparation of a specific plan to do so. With his customary dramatic flair, Burnham published the finished product on July 4, 1909. He was aware that his sponsors' energetic support was necessary if there was to be any hope of implementing a project as ambitious as the one he proposed. In this cause he took care to remind the civic and business leaders who supported him that there was a direct connection between his plan and their own prospects. As Carl Smith has observed, the *Plan* "appealed primarily to businessmen who had much at stake in Chicago's future, and therefore its authors went to some pains to make the connection between profits and more noble ideals clear."[27]

The future city sketched in the *Plan of Chicago* called for a reconstruction of the city and the surrounding urban area on a scale that, if faithfully followed, would have rivaled Haussmann's grand plan to remake Paris. Burnham made it clear that "the origin of the plan of Chicago can be traced directly to the World's Columbian Exposition. The World's Fair was the beginning, in our day and in this country, of the orderly arrangement of extensive public grounds and buildings."[28] It was also, he argued, a summation of the soundest principles of city planning inherited from ancient times. Burnham's infatuation with classical architecture showed through in florid language praising the monumental structures of ancient Rome and Athens. Signaling his intention to remake Chicago almost in its entirety, Burnham praised the design of post-Haussmann Paris, arguing that Paris's indisputable exquisiteness was due to its willingness to undertake bold projects. His

drawings of the proposed civic center draw the eye to a monumental building that looks nearly identical to the U.S. Capitol Building;
as in Haussmann's Paris, great boulevards radiate out like spokes
on a wheel to define an orderly metropolis. The civic center would
become, wrote Burnham, "what the Acropolis was to Athens, or
the Forum to Rome, and what St. Mark's Square is to Venice,—
the very embodiment of civic life."[29] Not surprisingly, he made
no mention of the social dislocation, rubble, and disruption that
years of clearance and construction would bring.[30]

Burnham proposed to situate Chicago at the center of a great
metropolis by building an integrated system of highways, upgrad-
ing passenger and freight transportation terminals, and introduc-
ing a planned network of streets and avenues to ease access to and
movement within the Loop. At the same time he proposed that
the living conditions of the city's residents would be improved by
combining two initiatives: the construction of an interconnected
park system built along the lakefront and beyond, and the building
of civic institutions such as libraries and museums to enrich the intellectual life of the city. On the one hand, he went to some pains to
appeal to the city's civic elite by noting that in Parisian cityscapes,
urban culture and economic progress combined in a perfect blend
in which "the convenience and beauty of Paris bring large returns
in money."[31] On the other hand, he also claimed, without missing a
beat, to be guided by a democratic vision that would bring benefits
to all the city's residents. His plan for the lakefront, he wrote, was
an expression of this promise: "The Lake front by right belongs
to the people. It affords their one great unobstructed view, where
water and clouds seem to meet. . . . These views of a broad expanse
are helpful alike to mind and body."[32] Such aspirations, Burnham
thought, put the *Plan* beyond politics and social division; instead,
it provided a blueprint for building a great city for all.

Daniel Burnham as a Civic Totem

As the Chicago historian Carl Smith has observed, for more than a century the sponsors of almost every major public endeavor in the city have invoked Burnham's name (figure 1.4). However, precisely because Burnham's *Plan of Chicago* has been treated as a "civic totem"[33] for so long, all claims to a blessing from beyond the grave must be regarded with a skeptical eye. In the first couple of decades after publication of the *Plan*, the city's civic leaders made a conscious effort to undertake and complete some of its most important features. Burnham's collaborator on the *Plan*, Edward H. Bennett, took charge of the task of reconstructing Grant Park, a project that extended through the 1920s; in the same period (and in some cases years later), the chain of parks along the city's lakefront was improved, and several nature preserves were set aside elsewhere in the metropolitan region.

Smith asserts that the general aims of the *Plan of Chicago* were, a few decades later, "revived considerably" under the first Mayor Daley. On behalf of this argument he mentions the building of the Chicago Civic Center and the State of Illinois Civic Center, the relocation of the University of Illinois campus, the construction of an expressway system, the expansion of O'Hare Airport, and several other major infrastructure projects. In addition, he makes mention of the *Lakefront Plan of Chicago* of 1972 and the *Chicago 21* plan of 1973 as important planning documents.[34]

Although we agree with Smith's point that the senior Daley's initiatives followed Burnham's famous injunction to "make no little plans," we doubt that Richard J. Daley was guided as much by Burnham's legacy as by the dire economic circumstances then facing the city. Like the mayors of other failing industrial cities, the senior Daley was driven more by a search for practical solutions than by

FIGURE 1.4

The American architect Daniel H. Burnham, 1910. Burnham has had a significant impact on Chicago, and his dictum "Make no little plans; they have no magic to stir men's blood" guided the city's planners, politicians, and business and civic leaders for over a century. Daniel H. Burnham Collection, Ryerson and Burnham Archives, The Art Institute of Chicago. Digital File # 194301_110614-009.jpg.

abstract ideals and lofty principles. Because of his aggressive program of urban reconstruction, Richard J. Daley managed to stem some of the worst effects of the postwar urban crisis in Chicago, although when he died in office in 1976, much was left to be done.

Richard J. Daley did not leave a significant imprint on the two lakefront features that constituted centerpieces for the *Plan of Chicago*—Grant Park and a ninety-one-acre peninsula named Northerly Island (indeed, Grant Park became famous, during his tenure, for the police riots outside the 1968 Democratic convention). Because Grant Park is between the lakefront and the Loop, Chicago's skyline can be observed from anyone standing in it as a sweeping panorama. Grant Park (until 1901 called Lake Park) is the essential link in a chain of parks stretching north and south along the lakefront. Here, at Chicago's front door, Burnham's footprint is more faithfully preserved than in any other single location in the Chicago region, but Richard J. Daley undertook few steps to enhance the park and its immediate environs.

Only a few months after the closing of the Columbian Exposition, civic leaders began proposing improvements to Lake Park, with the White City as the template. Although in 1893 the park had served as the jumping-off point for travel to the fair, once the exposition was over it was painfully clear that it was not much more than a flat, rather narrow strip of land, mostly devoid of trees and landscaping, bounded by railroad tracks running right along the lakeshore. In 1896 the Chicago City Council approved an ordinance authorizing a landfill project east of the tracks, and the Illinois Central Railroad lowered its tracks to facilitate access. Ultimately the landfill tripled the size of the park, and for the first time, park users had easy and direct access to the water.

Years earlier, in June 1895, Daniel Burnham and Charles Atwood (who served as an architect for the Columbian Exposition) had proposed that Lake Park should follow the "buildings in a park" principle established by the White City (and later enshrined as a cardinal principle of the City Beautiful movement):

> Using the White City's Court of Honor as a point of departure, Burnham and Atwood presented their vision for a park with fountains, playgrounds, flower beds, graveled walks, macadamized driveways, grass patches, statuary, trees, vine-covered walls, and a copy of the MacMonnies fountain from the World's Columbian Exposition, with a bronze statue of Columbus nearby. They recommended the construction of [a library]; a music hall; a National Guard Armory, and an exposition building. Reflecting the neoclassical style of the Art Institute and the Chicago Public Library, these new structures were depicted with long, horizontal lines.[35]

Grant Park did not end up as Burnham and Atwood envisioned. A series of three lawsuits initiated by Aaron Montgomery Ward stood in the way of the conception of the park as a mixture of landscape and neoclassical cultural and civic structures. In each of these cases (litigated against the South Park Commission) Ward argued that the original statute creating the park had prohibited the construction of permanent buildings. Only the Art Institute escaped the legal wrangling. The last of the court decisions was handed down in October 1909, only a few months after Burnham and Bennett had completed the final draft of the *Plan of Chicago*.

Burnham died in 1912. As consulting architect of the City Plan Commission, Bennett and his architectural firm influenced the subsequent design of Grant Park, although groups and donors also exerted major influence. It was, at every stage, a work in progress, with many spoons stirring the pot. Although permanent buildings were barred, the formal spaces and classicism were preserved in the geometric shapes and straight lines of the paths and plantings that, in effect, divided the park into formal "rooms" encouraging strolling and contemplation.

The exterior design of the White City reflected Burnham's ideal of an orderly and ennobling city, but the almost wild commercialism that went on in the interior of his buildings did not. Something similar happened in Grant Park. Historian Dennis Cremin has expressed doubts that Burnham intended that Grant Park would become the site of civic celebrations and spectacles, but, it turned out, the park proved to be an ideal space for such events.[36] In 1909, a two-week military encampment and tournament occupied the grounds, the first of many Fourth of July celebrations. The International Aviation Meet, first held in August 1911, drew two hundred thousand people on each of its nine days. That same summer the park was the place for sporting events, outdoor movies, band concerts, and parades.[37] And thus, like the White City, the classicist formalism of Grant Park could not restrain the exuberant energy of those who inhabited it.

Claiming the Burnham Legacy

Long before Richard M. Daley came onto the scene, Grant Park and its lakefront environs had become settings for mass entertainment and celebration. For decades the mayor of Chicago has led the annual Saint Patrick's Day parade down Columbus Drive, the street that runs through the center of the park. In the first decade of Daley's leadership, the development of Navy Pier and the Museum Campus brought renewed energy to the lakefront, but was this enough? The *Tribune*'s architectural critic, Blair Kamin, did not think so. In a Pulitzer Prize–winning, six-part series published in 1998, Kamin complained that despite the big projects undertaken on Daley's watch, Grant Park attracted crowds of people only when festivals drew them in. There was, he said, no unifying vision.[38] In a weeklong series of articles published the following

year, writers for the *Tribune* played upon a theme of "two eras and
two cities": "There is even a carryover symbol: a carnival ride. The
World's Columbian Exposition in 1893 featured the world's first
Ferris wheel. Today at Navy Pier, a Ferris wheel is a link to the
past and a symbol that the pier and the tourist-friendly amusement district that stretches to Michael Jordan's restaurant and
Planet Hollywood [in the Gold Coast] is a modern equivalent of
the fair's Midway Plaisance."[39] Perhaps what bothered Kamin was
an unresolved tension between Grant Park and the nearby tourist-
oriented venues—the same tension that had existed, more than a
century before, in the uncomfortable juxtaposition of the White
City and the Midway Plaisance. By 2004, however, when Millennium Park opened in Grant Park's northwest corner, much of this
tension was resolved. Daley accomplished this remarkable feat by
a sleight of hand rarely, if ever, noticed, by claiming Burnham's
vicarious blessings not only for those projects arguably inspired
by the century-old example of the White City, but also for those
undertakings that can be regarded as the offspring of the Midway
and its entertainments.

On numerous occasions Daley spoke of Burnham's influence
on the city and sometimes intimated that he was completing that
work. Writing in 1993, a commentator for the *Chicago Tribune*
noted: "Ask Daley about trees, and his face lights up like a Boy
Scout in the woods. 'Nature is what life is about,' Daley said on a
day that saw him taking a break from a thicket of school negotiations."[40] In 1998, while overlooking the acres of landscaped terraces, trees, and flower beds of the redesigned Museum Campus,
Daley concluded his dedication speech by saying, "Somewhere,
Daniel Burnham is smiling down on us and nodding his head in
approval."[41] At every turn, Daley appeared to go out of his way
to confirm such impressions, often by contrasting the grittier

Chicago of the past with the one that was emerging under his leadership. In a speech delivered to the Urban Parks Institute in 2001, the mayor reminded his audience that Chicago had two sides: "We have plenty of factories, railroads, and hard-working people who are responsible for one of our nicknames, City of Broad Shoulders. But there's a softer side of Chicago. . . . It's reflected in projects as small as the window boxes on City Hall and the play lots in our neighborhoods, and as large as our new Millennium Park."[42]

When Daley formally unveiled the Millennium Park project in 1998, his frequent allusions to Burnham moved Blair Kamin to comment, "The purpose of all this invoking, apparently, was to imply that the current administration is completing Burnham's vision for Grant Park. But in reality, the legendary planner's intention for this corner of the park is impossible to ascertain."[43] Kamin was on to something here, because the elements of entertainment and play so central to the conception of Millennium Park (and even more purely in Navy Pier) did not appear in Burnham's vision. In invoking Burnham's name, however, Daley was not striving for historical accuracy. As a public leader he was exceptionally skilled at mining Chicago's past for present purposes. This facility was put on bold display when, in his inaugural speech for a sixth term, the mayor claimed that an Olympic Games for Chicago would be equivalent to "rebuilding our city after the Great Chicago Fire. Embracing the visionary plans of Daniel Burnham. Hosting the World's Columbian Exposition."[44] And thus in one rhetorical burst, Daley managed to put all three of the most iconic images from Chicago's past to use in the present day.

2

Arresting Chicago's Long Slide

By the mid-1960s a narrative of decline was becoming fixed in the public's imagination, one that made American central cities "synonymous with poverty, crime, and general social decay."[1] A "deep angst" about the future of the old industrial cities took root,[2] and even Chicago, long an industrial powerhouse, fell into a funk. In 1983 the *New York Times* had referred to Chicago as "a troubled city of three million people"—and so it was.[3] In 1950 more than 70 percent of the population of the Chicago region lived in the city proper, but a four-decade suburban exodus reduced that proportion to 38 percent by 1990.[4] The number of manufacturing jobs in the city actually rose slightly from 1958 to 1972 but then went into a free fall, plummeting 34 percent from 1972 to 1983.[5] In September 1985 the *Chicago Tribune* offered a graphic description of the effects job losses had on the city's neighborhoods:

> The old Harvester site isn't Chicago's only economic ghost town. Drive west on the Eisenhower Expressway, out past the hospital complex, and look south. What you'll see is block after block of abandoned, gaping old factories. The West Side once lived off them. Residents now would be satisfied just to have the danger-ous, fetid carcasses torn down. Or walk under the "L" along 63d Street in Woodlawn, down what used to be, after State Street, the

second-busiest shopping street in Chicago. It's as much a ghost town as a Wild West set: Boards cover doors and windows, but the grime and decay only half cover the names of businesses that once thrived there—an A&P, a Hi-Lo, a Walgreens, the Kimbark Theater, the Empire Warehouse, the Pershing Hotel, the Southeast Chicago Bank. In all these places, and hundreds more throughout Chicago, the overwhelming sensation is emptiness. Not so many years ago, these factories and stores throbbed with people, jobs, money, goods, life. Now, all are gone. What's left is, literally, nothing.[6]

Reflecting their dismal assessment of the local economy, the *Tribune* writers called the series of articles on Chicago's troubles "Lost Jobs Leave a Legacy of Despair."

Chicago's fortunes continued to sag despite aggressive measures undertaken by the first Daley, Richard J., for the two decades from the mid-1950s to the mid-1970s. The elder Daley secured massive volumes of federal money and vastly expanded the city's revenue base through a series of new taxes and bond issues, which yielded resources for an expansion of O'Hare Airport, the construction of the McCormick Place convention center, a system of expressways, and capital improvement in the downtown. In his 1967 campaign for reelection the mayor proclaimed that "Chicago is well on its way to being the only city in the history of the civilization of the world to solve these [urban] problems."[7] Even judged by the liberal standards of the speechwriting craft, the mayor's rhetoric ("in the history of civilization"?) might have seemed excessive to an alert listener; in any case, it turned out to be premature. In his more than twenty years as mayor, Daley brought enormous resources and attention to the task of revitalization, but when he died in office in 1976, he had still not arrested Chicago's long postwar slide.

The only way Chicago could gain a firm footing again was to chart an entirely new and unfamiliar path forward. The four mayors who occupied the fifth floor of City Hall in the years after the death of the senior Daley did experiment and sometimes simply improvised, often in response to the press of dire necessity. By the time he came to office in the late 1980s, the second Daley, Richard M., appreciated that something different needed to be done. Daley was convinced that "this city is changing. You're not going to bring factories back. I think you have to look at the financial markets—banking, service industry, the development of O'Hare field, tourism, trade."[8] His program of economic restructuring, which depended on policies to promote services, tourism, and urban amenities, ended a half-century search for a formula to secure the city's economic future.

The False Hope

Although harbingers of Chicago's postwar future began to emerge as early as the 1930s, civic leaders generally regarded the Great Depression as a temporary aberration in a city long celebrated for its unbounded energy, ambition, and ceaseless growth. Chicago had morphed from a village of fewer than forty-five hundred people in 1840 to a city of more than 2.7 million by 1920, and though Congress passed legislation in 1920 and 1921 severely restricting foreign immigration, the city nevertheless grew by 25 percent in the 1920s. From 1910 to 1930 more than eighty thousand bungalows were built along a one- to four-mile-wide strip stretching from the northern to the southern borders of the city, forming tightly knit, working-class communities in what became known as Chicago's Bungalow Belt. Chain stores spread throughout the city to serve the rapidly expanding middle- and working-class neighborhoods. Thompson's Cafeterias, F. W. Woolworth, Walgreens Drugs, Central Cigar, United Cigar, and other chain outlets grew by the hundreds. By 1928, 19 Woolworth stores, 47 Thompson's Cafeterias (24 of them located in the Loop), and 101 Walgreens stores occupied storefronts.[9]

The Great Depression brought a century of prosperity to a screeching halt. By 1932, 750,000 workers were out of work in Chicago, and scarcely more, only 800,000, were employed. The city government could do little to help those who were destitute because it had already exhausted its fiscal resources.[10] Homelessness and hunger became common. The Joint Emergency Relief fund was formed by civic and charitable leaders, and by the end of 1931 it had neared its goal of $8.8 million. Individuals, philanthropic groups, banks, and even government officials were publicly scolded into contributing.[11] In the summer of 1932, the *Chicago Tribune* urged all the employed to support a campaign to raise additional emergency funds to supplement state and federal support.[12] Local officials opened summer playgrounds, such as Camp Algonquin, which served the mothers and children living in two thousand homes that had suffered the devastating effects of unemployment.[13]

Recovery of the local economy came only with a massive infusion of federal spending during World War II. More than $9.2 billion in war-related contracts poured into the region from 1940 to 1945, and by the end of the war the value of publicly financed industrial and manufacturing facilities reached $926 million, placing Chicago first among all U.S. metropolitan areas.[14] By 1950 the city's population reached 3.6 million residents, the highest in its history. Automobiles and trucks crowded the city's streets. The long arc of the city's past gave Chicago's civic elite ample reason to believe that the Depression had merely been an unfortunate aberration. Historically, Chicago's growth had been fueled by the products from a vast hinterland that extended throughout the Midwest and beyond, and since the 1860s, when it decisively passed St. Louis in population and economic production, Chicago had occupied a secure position in a national and international system of cities. The economic benefits of Chicago's hegemonic position in the region flowed into the city's downtown and its neighborhoods. It appeared that a city always destined for greatness was returning to its former glory.

Not everyone shared such a sanguine view. Perceptive observers noticed that some troubling social and economic changes were afoot. By the late 1950s a headlong flight to the suburbs had commenced in all the metropolitan areas of the nation's industrial belt. White middle-class families were leaving crowded neighborhoods in the inner cities for the new tract housing developments being aggressively marketed by real estate developers. Their quest for a suburban home was facilitated by the Federal Housing Administration, which underwrote loans with long amortization periods and small down payments. Massive investments in urban roads and expressways made it easier for workers to travel from the suburbs to their jobs in the city, and within a few years the expanding road network made it easier and easier for people to make the suburban move.

Even before Congress approved the Interstate Highway Act of 1956, a metropolitan highway system in the Chicago region began to take shape. In 1926, the Chicago Regional Planning Association produced a study titled *In the Region of Chicago*, which was aimed at addressing the notorious problem of traffic congestion. A map featured in the report displayed a network of "paved highways" and "suggested pavement" routes connecting the entire metropolitan area.[15] The Great Depression intervened to slow implementation of the report's recommendations, but the blueprint for the future metropolis was now drawn. Indeed, just one year after the conclusion of World War II, construction began on the Edens Expressway (North), and in 1949 work started on the Congress Parkway (West), later renamed the Eisenhower Expressway. The passage of the Highway Act thus accelerated what was already a frenzy of construction.

In 1954, 1958, and 1960, extensions of the Eisenhower Expressway into DuPage County, together with the closing of the Chicago Aurora and Elgin (CA&E) Railroad, signaled the start of a new era. Up until that time, most growth had occurred near rail depots, which sustained village centers. As the highway network matured, suburban subdivisions proliferated. By the 1960s a highway system was in place capable of handling the daily movement of millions of commuters, and by 1970 Cook County and surrounding jurisdictions were covered by a spiderweb of roads and transportation access points. By virtue of these far-reaching changes in infrastructure and demographics, the Chicago region was, year by year, becoming fundamentally reconfigured.

A review of the population changes in the five-county metropolitan area outside Chicago from 1920 to 1940 (see table 2.1) reveals that even before the war, Chicago's population growth had lagged behind the pace of suburban development. At the time these changes did not seem greatly consequential, but in the years after the war, when the exodus from Chicago to its suburbs picked up speed, for the first time since its founding the city of Chicago began to actually lose population. The data in table 2.1 provide a perspective on how fast this historic process unfolded. In the two decades following the 1950 census, Chicago's population shrank from 3,621,000 to 3,369,000, and in the twenty years from 1970 to 1990 it fell still more, to 2,784,000 people. Meanwhile, suburban populations outside Chicago exploded, growing by 72 percent in the 1950s and 35 percent in the following decade. The frenzied

Table 2.1

Population of Chicago and the suburbs, 1920–2010

	Chicago	% change	Metropolitan population outside city of Chicago	% change
1920	2,702,000	—	693,000	—
1930	3,376,000	+25	1,073,000	+55
1940	3,397,000	+1	1,173,000	+9
1950	3,621,000	+7	1,557,000	+3
1960	3,550,000	−2	2,671,000	+72
1970	3,369,000	−5	3,612,000	+35
1980	3,005,000	−11	4,097,000	+13
1990	2,784,000	−7	4,477,000	+9
2000	2,894,000	+4	5,225,000	+17
2010	2,695,000	−7	5,621,000	+8

Source: Robert Spinney, *City of Big Shoulders: A History of Chicago* (DeKalb: Northern Illinois University Press, 2000), 211; U.S. Census, 1980, 1990, 2000, 2010; Northeastern Illinois Planning Commission.

pace of suburban growth slowed somewhat in the 1970s, but by that time a new metropolitan pattern had been firmly established, one in which population and economic activity were dispersed throughout a sprawling metropolitan landscape.

During the war years the members of the Chicago Plan Commission had already begun thinking about how to entice people to stay in the city. The commissioners settled on a strategy of transforming inner-city neighborhoods into something resembling a romanticized version of suburban life. In a report issued in June 1943 titled *Building New Neighborhoods*, the commission proposed a development concept for a 1.8-square-mile tract on the city's southwest side. It presented two land-use layouts, A and

B, complete with illustrations on opposing pages. Plan A was designed "according to the rectilinear block arrangement, [making it] as uninteresting and lacking in character as any one of the oldest sections of Chicago." Plan B recommended curvilinear streets and cul-de-sacs radiating from a park at the center that included schools, a community building, a community park, and athletic fields, with access to shopping centers nearby. According to the commission's report, these design principles would "permit families to enjoy the benefits of urban life without its hazards—where they can have quiet and pleasant homes within the convenient walking distance of the neighborhood schools and parks."[16] Ironically, the unintended antiurban critique contained in this statement anticipated the themes that suburban developers would learn to fine-tune only a few years later.

By the late 1940s, the number of suburban subdivisions began multiplying. In 1951, Harold Moser launched the marketing for hundreds of homes in the Moser Highlands subdivision in Naperville, located about twenty miles from Chicago. Under the direction of Jack and Sam Hoffman, the Hoffman Group began its operations in 1954 with the development of a 160-acre farm called Hoffman Estates, about thirty miles out. Over the years, the firm completed subdivisions in Lombard, Glen Ellyn, Bolingbrook, Bloomingdale, Wheaton, and Glendale Heights.[17] As the number of municipalities grew, the Chicago region became one of the most fragmented metropolitan areas in the nation. As people moved into DuPage County, for instance, dozens of incorporated communities sprang up. From 1970 to 1980, the county added 171,000 residents, which was more new residents than any other county outside the Sunbelt during that period. Some cities within the county doubled and even tripled in population in little more than a decade.

Economic Restructuring

Chicago was a powerhouse of the industrial age, but as early as the 1920s a process of national economic restructuring that favored services over goods-producing sectors began to eat away at the city's economic foundation. By 1952, 35.5 percent of Americans held goods-producing jobs in such sectors as mining, construction, and manufacturing; at the same time 53.3 percent were employed in service-producing sectors. The processes of economic restructuring unfolded inexorably; only thirty years later, in 1982, 27.2 percent of the nation's workers were engaged in producing goods, but 69.2 percent held service-sector jobs. Deindustrialization on such scale devastated the economies of cities and urban regions all through the nation's industrial belt, and Chicago was no exception. In 1947, there were 668,000 manufacturing jobs in Chicago, but by 1963 the number of jobs in the city had fallen to 509,000.[18]

The decline of the old economic sectors was clearly evident in the sagging fortunes of the city's iconic industry, meatpacking. In the years after 1865, when the Union Stock Yards opened, they became a potent symbol of Chicago's economic might and political culture. "The Yards" emerged as a favorite stop of tourists visiting the 1893 World's Fair; a few years later Upton Sinclair's lurid exposé of the working conditions and filth on the killing floors helped to launch the Progressive movement. Despite the negative press and subsequent regulatory scrutiny, production roared on; between 1890 and 1933 the Yards processed an average of thirteen million animals annually, and employed, at their peak, sixty thousand workers.

The meatpacking industry began to change around the time of the Great Depression. Despite a modernization effort that included construction of a new hog house and an expanded rail-shipping facility, the earlier production volumes could not be sustained. In the 1930s, technological advancements and a union campaign launched by the Congress of Industrial Organizations (CIO) brought more efficient production methods. Later, the emergence of cross-country truck transportation and the construction of the interstate highway system undermined the economic advantages of bringing livestock to a central location. In 1952, Chicago-based meatpacker Wilson & Company opened a facility in Kansas City to replace its aging stockyards structure. Wilson's relocation was a harbinger of things to come, and the endgame unfolded rapidly. Three years later, the company ceased its Chicago operation altogether, and other companies began to leave as soon as a relocation was convenient. The Yards officially closed in 1971.[19]

Though the timing was different, the printing industry followed a similar trajectory. When businesses discovered the power of advertising in the late nineteenth century, these services became critical to corporate operations. Printing House Row, located at the southern edge of the Loop, emerged as a hub of publishing activity. The adjacent Dearborn Street Railway Station made it possible to ship supplies easily and to handle orders into and out of the district, and by 1962 more than forty-eight thousand workers were employed in printing in Chicago's central business district.

In 1970, 50 percent of the region's printing jobs were still located in Printing House Row, but that statistic masked a decline that had been unfolding in the district for some time.[20] By the 1950s the advantages of placing all the equipment on the same floor prompted a years-long exodus from the multistory warehouse buildings in and around Printer's Row. The Physicians' Record Company, which had located in Printer's Row in 1928, moved to Berwyn in 1959. Clyde Printing, founded in 1942 and originally located in

Printer's Row, stayed the longest, but in the 1980s the company moved south to newer buildings in the Bridgeport neighborhood. In 1960 almost one hundred thousand people in the city were employed in printing; by 1984, the number of jobs had fallen drastically, to just over nineteen thousand.[21]

Likewise, wholesaling, which had long been anchored in and near the Loop, began to leave. As with the printing industry, the vertical layout of the old lofts was not as efficient as horizontal production. As wholesaling moved out, the pace of teardowns picked up, connected in part to a rising volume of automobile traffic and a need for more garage and surface parking. In 1927, only 26 garages and 34 parking lots were located in and around the Loop, but by 1938 that number had increased to 40 garages and 161 lots. During the 1940s, one and a half million square feet of space of parking was added, and from 1950 to 1954 another million square feet became available. Wholesale employment in the Loop dropped from 138,000 jobs in 1948 to 101,000 by 1972; during the same period, the number of wholesale jobs in the suburbs rose from 17,000 to 98,000. Retail businesses of all kinds also deserted the crowded confines of the urban center. Appliance and furniture stores were the first to go because they required more space and found it beneficial to locate closer to customers; others, like music stores, relocated to suburban shopping centers.[22] The city's retail employment fell from 249,000 in 1948 to 193,000 by 1972, but over the same twenty-four-year period, the number of retail jobs in the suburbs more than doubled, from 105,000 to 260,000.[23]

This sector-by-sector decline redefined the geography of employment within the region. As late as 1960, less than 7 percent of the residents living in the city of Chicago worked in the suburbs, but more than 18 percent did so by 1980. Conversely, during the

FIGURE 2.1
Oakbrook Terrace Tower in Oakbrook Terrace, Illinois, is the tallest building in suburban Chicago. Designed by Helmut Jahn, the thirty-one-story structure was completed in 1987. Courtesy of user Joe+Jeanette Archie, Flickr.

same period the proportion of suburban workers commuting into the city fell from 34.6 percent to 22.5 percent.[24] The shift in the regional pattern of employment reinforced the detrimental effects already associated with the changing demography of the Chicago metropolis. Increasingly, suburban commuters found well-paying job opportunities closer to home. Oakbrook became the headquarters for fifteen large companies, including McDonald's and Chicago Bridge & Iron (figure 2.1). The high-tech corridor along I-88 (later named the Reagan Expressway) was transformed into one of the leading research and development centers in the United States. By the mid-1980s, thirty-eight industrial parks were located in DuPage County alone. Retail malls opened by the score, beginning with Oakbrook Mall in 1962.[25]

The migration of business activity altered commuting patterns fundamentally and, it seemed, irrevocably, with more workers traveling to their jobs from one suburban county to the next and fewer from the suburbs into the city of Chicago. The urban scholar Robert A. Beauregard has referred to the parallel processes of central-city decline and suburban growth as "parasitic urbanization,"[26] because suburban prosperity was directly connected to the emptying of the city. The relationship was deeply organic and structural. The old urban form was dissolving, and nothing was going to stop it or reverse the process.

By the 1980s, employment subcenters emerged in the suburbs, providing the economies of scale that came from clustering related activities in one location. As the economist Daniel P. McMillen has pointed out, a subcenter is "large enough to have significant effects on the overall spatial distribution of population, employment, and land prices. Large subcenters can look remarkably similar to a traditional central business district (CBD), with thousands of workers employed in a wide variety of industries."[27] In 1970, nine major clusters of this kind in the Chicago area were located outside the city limits, and by 1990 the number had risen to fifteen. While most of these subcenters were composed of manufacturing, some were diversified, and others were concentrated in the service sector.

Perhaps because it had historically relied so heavily on manufacturing and goods-producing industries, Chicago found it particularly difficult to offset the job losses with gains in service-sector employment. From 1967 to 1987, New York lost 459,200 manufacturing jobs in its core but added 302,294 taxable service jobs (a 66 percent replacement rate). Meanwhile, Baltimore managed to offset 61.3 percent of its manufacturing jobs with services, and even Milwaukee was able to recoup 44.6 percent of its job losses. By comparison, Chicago succeeded in replacing only 31.7 percent of its lost jobs, which put it barely ahead of St. Louis (29.1 percent).[28] In her late-1980s study of Chicago, Janet Abu-Lughod understated the gravity of the situation somewhat when she observed that "while expanding services have indeed taken up some of the slack in employment, in the Chicago economy this has been insufficient to replace all lost jobs."[29] Even after decades of effort to reverse the losses, Chicago still had not turned the corner.

"Dick the Builder"

When Richard J. Daley took office in April 1956, he confronted structural problems that threatened to rend the city's social and economic fabric. There was, on the one hand, a gathering awareness among the city's civic and business class that the exodus of people and jobs to the suburbs posed a serious threat to the city's economic health. Daley himself realized that if his own economic development policies were to succeed, he would need to forge a positive relationship with the members of that elite group. On the other hand, Daley was keenly aware that the rapidly changing racial makeup of the city posed potential problems. Since the 1920s, Chicago's successive political machines had managed to maintain the loyalty of black voters through a political arrangement that granted black leaders control over their own wards. Daley inherited this system and took measures to strengthen it.[30] In exchange for their loyalty to Daley, black politicians were able to control zoning decisions, distribute jobs, and operate independently.

Buying the peace in this way gave Daley the ability to focus his efforts on the downtown without risking an unacceptable level of political opposition. In 1966, when Martin Luther King Jr. joined the Chicago Freedom Movement to demand school reform, jobs, and improved services in black neighborhoods, the African American aldermen on the South Side opposed the campaign. The machine's hold over African American politicians remained in place even after the massive riots that broke out in the wake of King's assassination in April 1968. The political arrangements that kept the aspirations of Chicago's African American community in check helped support the centralized political apparatus that allowed the first Daley to become "Dick the Builder."[31]

All through the years of the Great Depression, Chicago had been beset by economic calamity, but, somewhat paradoxically, at the same time it had entered into a period of unprecedented political stability. For years, Democrats and Republicans had competed intensely in mayoral elections. "Big Bill" Thompson presided over a Republican machine that lasted for several years, but rather than a disciplined political organization, it more resembled a loose confederation of thieves and opportunists who thrived by forging close relationships with the key players in organized crime. Thompson's years as a notorious machine boss before and during the Prohibition era, from 1915 to 1923 and again from 1927 to 1931, left an indelible imprint on the city's self-image and official story. Thompson's 1927 election campaign was successful in large part because of support, financial and otherwise, he received from the infamous gangster Al Capone.[32] The city's special brand of wide-open vice, political corruption, and organized crime became a favorite cinematic and television theme that has endured right up to the present day.

Thompson's excesses and the devastation left by the Depression gave birth to one of the most powerful urban machines of the twentieth century. From 1931, when Anton J. Cermak defeated Thompson, to 1947, when the Democrats were forced to replace his successor, Edward J. Kelly, to avert a voter rebellion over corruption scandals, the machine became a finely tuned mechanism for distributing jobs and favors in exchange for the loyalty of voters. The machine managed to stay intact during the two terms of Martin H. Kennelly, a businessman who fancied himself to be a reformer, but there was relief all around when Richard J. Daley replaced him in 1955. The party insiders who selected Daley expected him to respect their exclusive spheres of influence, but were quickly disappointed.

Daley had honed his political skills as a party committeeman from the working-class Bridgeport neighborhood located in the shadow of the stockyards and as chairman of the Cook County Central Committee. These positions gave him the power to distribute thousands of patronage jobs, and his election as mayor gave him control over even more. Daley refashioned the machine into an organization guided by the principle "Don't make no waves, don't back no losers."[33] He vastly expanded the number of patronage jobs and imposed strict standards on the committeemen and precinct captains who were charged with getting out the vote. On its own, this would have given Daley formidable political authority, but he had bigger ambitions. He wanted to be the mayor who remade Chicago. As soon as he entered the mayor's office, Daley began to forge relationships with the downtown business community. At first, he received a lukewarm response. Corporate leaders, many of whom resided in wealthy suburbs on the North Shore, judged that Daley's working-class background and his roots in machine politics would clash with their own interests.[34] Daley won them over by modernizing and restructuring city government and hiring professional staff that worked for him, not for the machine.[35] To his business supporters he became known as a reformer and even a visionary, at least in those respects that mattered to them. The *New York Times* called him a "reformer at heart."[36]

When he created the Department of City Planning in 1957, Daley signaled his commitment to an aggressive downtown development plan and demonstrated it by "hiring some of the finest urban planners in the nation."[37] In 1958 the planners recruited by Daley looked on as the mayor, with much fanfare, released the *Development Plan for the Central Area of Chicago*. Media coverage made it appear that the plan was almost as ambitious as Daniel Burnham's 1909 *Plan of Chicago*. The mayor had worked closely with downtown corporate leaders, who organized their efforts through the Chicago Central Area Committee. The development plan represented "a new vision for the city emanating from the headquarters of Chicago's major corporations."[38] Ultimately, the plan catalyzed a $5 billion building boom in Chicago's central business core.

Until the mid-1950s, the Palmolive Building (1929) and the Board of Trade (1930) had been the last major projects undertaken in the Loop. The Prudential Building (1955) and the Inland Steel Building (1957) seemed to signal a turning point, but Daley and the downtown corporate community were eager to bring direction and momentum to development in the Loop. Tax levies, bond issues, and federal funding provided Daley the resources to construct several government buildings downtown and undertake giant infrastructure projects in and near the Loop. In 1964 the Dirksen Federal Building was completed, and a year later the Civic Center (later renamed the Richard J. Daley Center) opened adjacent to City Hall. These were followed a few years later by the Loop Post Office in 1973 and the Kluczynski Federal Building in 1974.

As a result of massive highway construction that had begun in the 1950s, the Eisenhower, Kennedy, Stevenson, and Dan Ryan expressways radiated out from the Loop like spokes on a wheel. Daley took steps to replace the landlocked Midway Airport with

O'Hare Airport as the city's main air transport facility. Construction began on an international terminal and a massive parking garage in 1958. More than seventy-two hundred acres were added in 1959, and by 1962 O'Hare's status as one of the busiest airports in the world was secured. All this public spending helped spur private investment. The enormous John Hancock Center (1969) and the First National Bank of Chicago Building (1969) broke ground in the mid-1960s, and several skyscrapers followed, including the CNA Plaza (1972), the Mid-Continental Plaza (1972), the IBM Plaza (1973), the Aon Center (1972), and the tallest building in the world at the time, the Sears Tower (1974).

The national press heaped praise upon the mayor's rebuilding program. The May 1962 issue of *Architectural Forum* devoted its entire issue to Chicago, noting that "the most glamorous structure, the office building, is sprouting again, in the Loop and on its fringes."[39] In an article published on July 2, 1973, *Time* magazine pronounced the 1958 plan a success, but also cautioned that business development alone would not be sufficient: "Chicago's Loop is among the healthiest downtowns in the U.S. At a time when corporations are fleeing other cities for the suburbs, big Chicago firms are not. Even so, the old strategy of preserving and strengthening its economic heart cannot alone save a city. Help is needed from full-time residents who use the city and care for it—especially the middle class. Since 1958, central Chicago has lost 21,000 inhabitants to the suburbs."[40] The mixed message was hard to miss, but local leaders cared to focus on the positives. At about the time that the *Time* article appeared, the mayor and the Chicago Central Area Committee announced a new development plan, *Chicago 21: A Plan for the Central Area Communities.* Its major features included the construction of State Street Mall, a new library, improved mass transit, and a historic preservation plan. Clearly the most innovative aspect of *Chicago 21* was a large residential development program that meant to transform a six-hundred-acre area of abandoned railroad yards south of the Loop, to be called "South Loop New Town." The unveiling of the *Chicago 21* plan met with an enthusiast response from many quarters. The *Chicago Daily News* declared that this "may well be the most far-reaching downtown plan ever for Chicago or any other city in the nation."[41] At the formal public presentation, Mayor Daley explained that it was "one of the great acts in the renaissance of the city."[42]

The *Chicago 21* plan called for a close coordination of public resources and private investment. The plan required the city to finance the purchase of land and provide infrastructure and amenities like streets, sewers, parks, and education services. The city also agreed to provide urban planning expertise to the Chicago 21 Corporation, formed in January 1974 to raise capital, market, and develop the property immediately south of the Loop. The board of directors was composed of leading corporate and civic figures: the chairman and president of the Commonwealth Edison Company, the president of the Continental Illinois National Bank, the vice president for real estate at Sears, Roebuck, and the chairman of Arthur Andersen & Company. The membership list included the president of the Marshall Field Company, a vice president of the National Bank of Chicago, the president of the Standard Oil Company (Indiana), and the chairman of the People's Gas, Light & Coke Company, among other notables.

The members of the Chicago Central Area Community wished, above all, to protect their investments in office construction, and they were also worried that an increasing volume of pedestrian traffic by blacks on downtown streets would push white shoppers out of the Loop. Arthur Rubloff, a prominent real estate developer, told the *Chicago Daily News*: "I'll tell you what's wrong with the Loop. It's people's conception of it. And the conception they have about it is one word—black. B-L-A-C-K. Black. We have a racial problem we haven't been able to solve. The ghetto areas have nothing but rotten slum buildings, nothing at all, and businessmen are afraid to move in, so the blacks come downtown for stores and restaurants."[43] James C. Downs Jr., a real estate executive who headed the board of the Real Estate Research Corporation (and who later served as president of the Chicago Central Area Committee), echoed this view. From his perspective, changing the kind of people who used and lived near the Loop would ensure its economic viability. He pointed to the example of the Marina Towers, an upscale nine-hundred-apartment development that had been constructed in the 1960s on the Chicago River at the northern boundary of the Loop. The architecturally striking, twin cylindrical, sixty-two-story buildings provided occupants with recreational opportunities and amenities within the complex. With direct boating access, the towers' residents also had convenient access to cultural and entertainment venues, restaurants, health clubs, movie theaters, and the other amenities of urban life.

The Marina Towers footprint on the Chicago River marked the physical boundary of the north Loop. From Downs's perspective, it was now essential to protect the Loop's southern boundary. The "Black Belt" and several public housing projects occupied a stretch of land only a few blocks from the Loop along south State Street. According to Downs, "While Chicago's Loop is still strong and continues to grow as a center of office employment, danger signs are appearing. Most Loop streets are deserted after 6 p.m., and there is growing fear of walking them at night. . . . It is, therefore, only on the southern flank where the Loop needs protection."[44] Plans for a middle-class town house development provoked determined opposition from African American leaders. They charged that the project was only "the first step in the whitening of the Loop."[45] A report by David Emmons, released on behalf of the Citizens Information Service of Illinois, reached a similar conclusion: that the South Loop development was aimed at keeping blacks away from the city's center by erecting physical and psychological impediments to their movement.

Of course the plan's proponents put forward a different narrative, claiming that development in the South Loop "offers a source of housing for its employees, retail buyers for its stores, and frequenters for its restaurants and theaters."[46] These lofty goals were greeted with skepticism. Most people doubted that it was possible to reverse the structural changes that had been driving people to the suburbs. The 1973 *Time* magazine story concluded that "the real test, of course, is whether a rebuilt Chicago can lure suburbanites back into town."[47] Downs responded by explaining that "we are shifting to an adult urban society. The birth rate is down, and people are not going to find it very attractive any more to make the commute from the suburbs every day. We've also passed the threshold in the integration battle."[48] Downs's optimistic assessment would prove to be wildly premature.

The first elements of the *Chicago 21* plan began to take shape before Daley's death in office in 1976, and it kept unfolding for years. North of the Loop, the first phase took physical form when Water Tower Place opened on North Michigan Avenue in 1975. Water Tower Place became a national model for living and shopping mixed in a single enclosed space. Its completion firmly established the historic shopping district called the Magnificent Mile as an avenue for upscale entertainment and shopping. The South Loop development began with two major housing projects built for middle-income residents. In 1979 the Dearborn Park development, with a mix of apartments, town houses, and tree-lined

FIGURE 2.2
The Dearborn Park development looking north was the result of multiple construction stages that included high-rise and low-rise projects. Single-family homes (foreground) came in the 1990s. The high rises along the State Street corridor (right) were introduced as part of a planning directive during the 2000s. Courtesy of user Alan Light, Flickr.

walkways and parks, began to take shape on fifty-one acres once occupied by rail yards. Presidential Towers, located on the western edge of the Loop near the expressway, opened in 1985. In 1986 River City, a concrete curvilinear structure containing a skylighted atrium, opened on the south branch of the Chicago River. And in 1988, the second phase of Dearborn Park construction opened (figure 2.2).

The infrastructure and downtown rebuilding projects undertaken under Daley's direction helped Chicago emerge from the worst years of the urban crisis with its status as a vital urban center still functional, if yet shaky. In their biography of the mayor, Adam Cohen and Elizabeth Taylor claim that "Daley may well have saved Chicago":

> He reigned during an era in which suburbanization, crime, and white flight were wreaking havoc on other Midwestern cities. Detroit, Kansas City, Cleveland, and Saint Louis were all prosperous, middle-class cities when Daley took office, and all declined precipitously after World War II. In a twenty-five-year period after the war, Detroit lost one-third of its *Fortune* 500 companies; by the mid-1970s, it had become the nation's murder capital, with twice as many killings per capita as any other large American city. That never became Chicago's fate. In large part due to Daley, the city's downtown business district expanded at the time Detroit's was collapsing, and much of its sprawling white, working-class "Bungalow Belt" remained intact.[49]

The biographers' positive assessments, however, do not change the fact that much remained to be done if Chicago was to fully recover from its postwar malaise.

Daley's successors inherited unresolved problems that threatened to undermine all future revitalization efforts. Aside from the formidable economic challenges that remained, long-festering racial resentments constantly threatened to boil to the surface. A new, younger generation of activists began to point out that the political bargain worked out between Daley and the city's black politicians was costly for blacks. In the estimation of Larry Bennett, a DePaul University political scientist, "As early as the mid-1950s, African Americans had become a principal supplier of the Democratic Party's citywide electoral majorities, but in terms of access to important public offices, patronage, and basic services, the city's black elite and rank and file alike did not receive their 'fair shares.'"[50] Although blacks made up 40 percent of Chicago's population in 1970, they held only 20 percent of the government jobs in the city, and most of those jobs were the least desirable.[51] Another study found that the machine consistently over-rewarded middle-class voters at the expense of loyal working-class voters, with blacks getting the least of all.[52]

African American voters were beginning to display signs of restlessness, and a deep fissure was developing that pitted machine politicians in the black wards against militant activists. In Daley's last two elections, African American turnout fell sharply, a sign that African American voters were deserting the machine.[53] More ominously, there was mounting evidence that Daley, and anyone who succeeded him, would inherent a city rent by rising levels of racial animosity. In the 1972 race for state's attorney of Cook County, highly charged racial issues inflamed African American voters. In the wake of the riots of 1968, the incumbent, Edward V. Hanrahan, had formed special gang units that ran out of his office. On December 1969, officers in one of these units broke into an apartment and killed two Black Panthers and wounded four while they were sleeping in their beds. Blacks loathed Hanrahan, who became so unpopular that the machine dumped him as its candidate for the 1972 election. He decided to contest the Democratic primary anyway. At the ballot box, white ethnic wards delivered huge margins on his behalf, but African American voters "were willing to do the unthinkable, i.e., vote for a Republican nominee."[54] Although Richard J. Daley handily won reelection in 1975, there were gathering signs that the African American electorate was "ripe for revolt."[55] When Daley died a little more than a year later, it was clear that his successor would inherit a volatile political situation.

Chicago's Politics from Daley to Daley

When Richard M. Daley won the 1989 election, some writers referred to a "Daley dynasty," but there were no guarantees that the son would be able to build a political organization as powerful as his father's, or even one that could effectively govern. In his twenty-one years as the city's mayor, Richard J. Daley had presided over the last of the nation's old-style party machines. Although this may give the impression that the political culture and institutions of Chicago tended to produce powerful mayors, the opposite may be closer to the true state of affairs. The elder Daley's overwhelming political authority masked a reality that has not generally been appreciated: in Chicago, with its fifty wards, its racial animosities, and its ethnic multitudes, powerful forces are always working to tear the system apart. His death on December 20, 1976, instantly unleashed those forces.

An entertaining three-ring political circus commenced as soon as news spread that the mayor had died in his doctor's office. In the late afternoon, Wilson Frost, the president pro tempore of the city council, informed reporters that under the city charter he had become the acting mayor. Most of the members of the city council disagreed and promptly retreated behind closed doors to choose the dead mayor's successor. The battle opened fissures within the Democratic organization. Polish leaders on the Northwest side maneuvered to block a take-over by the Irish from the South Side wards. While the behind-the-scenes struggle dragged on, the press and the public fed eagerly on every stray snippet of information and rumor. Finally, the decision reached in the secretive conclave was announced: a reliable but quiet member of the bloc of Democrats who controlled the council, Alderman Michael Bilandic, would serve as acting mayor until a spring election could be held to complete the remaining two years of Daley's term. Bilandic, who came from Daley's Eleventh Ward, was a logical compromise candidate because he was well known as a conciliator among the council members. His selection ensured the autonomy and influence of powerful aldermen.[56]

In his inaugural address of June 22, 1977, Bilandic identified crime, housing decay, economic disinvestment, and problems in the schools as issues that required immediate attention. He expressed optimism about the city's long-term prospects, arguing that "much high-skilled service employment is being retained in the older urban centers" and that "the amenities of urban life are becoming more appealing."[57] In his brief time in office, Bilandic founded ChicagoFest, an annual celebration of food and music. He also pushed a plan to connect paths along the lakefront to create a continuous biking and jogging corridor. These initiatives, as limited as they were, at least demonstrated he was aware that downtown development and quality-of-life issues were important to lakefront liberals and downtown businessmen.

Bilandic's downtown-centric policies did nothing to help blacks, and he offended African American leaders by ignoring their demands for school integration and more responsive housing policies. The 1979 mayoral election revealed a growing chasm separating the machine's faithful followers in the African American establishment from their increasingly restless challengers. A few months before the campaign, African American leaders came together to form a Committee for the Election of a Black Mayor. The work of the committee cast a spotlight on the complicated cross-currents that kept blacks from operating as a bloc. No single candidate representing African Americans emerged from the internal struggle, although the negotiations did set the stage for the election, four years later, of Chicago's first African American mayor, Harold Washington.

Bilandic is remembered in Chicago as an ineffectual blunderer. In the winter of 1979, massive storms piled mountains of snow in the streets, traffic became paralyzed, and fights broke out over parking spots, but the city seemed to do little. Scarcely more than a month after the storm, Bilandic became the first machine-backed candidate since Anton Cermak built the Democratic organization to lose a mayoral election. During the Democratic primary campaign his main opponent, Jane Byrne, framed the blizzard debacle as an example of the incumbent mayor's ineptness and incompetence. Without doubt these attacks increased her vote total, but her success hinged less on this symbolic issue than on her success in appealing to a diverse coalition of ministers, civil rights leaders, and activists on the city's mostly African American South Side and lakefront white liberals, reform politicians, and a cadre of professionals devoted to housing and social welfare issues. Byrne swept into office with 82 percent of the vote in the general election of April 16, 1979. To this day, no other candidate in a mayoral election, including either of the Daleys, has ever won such a high percentage of the vote.

Byrne's abrasive political style and her frequent criticisms of the political machine led her followers to believe she was fully committed to radical change. Her supporters expected her to deliver on that promise, and for a brief time she seemed to be taking the city in a new direction. Among other measures she appointed the first African American to the post of school superintendent and increased expenditures for public housing and crime control. Within a few months, however, her backers grew increasingly restless when Byrne began harping more often about the city's fiscal condition than any other topic. At the beginning of Byrne's mayoralty, Chicago maintained an Aa bond rating, but it was downgraded by Moody's to an A in 1980—mostly, said some critics, because Byrne's oft-repeated public statements that the city's budget was in shambles. Political scientist Esther Fuchs referred to it as a "political strategy of an insecure mayor who wanted to discredit anyone whom she saw as a potential challenger in the 1983 election."[58] Eventually, Moody's investment service downgraded the city's rating to Baa1 in 1984, and it took until October 1987 for Chicago to regain an A bond rating.[59]

For a very long time, Chicago's African American leadership had been accustomed to striking bargains in exchange for political influence, but their disappointment with Byrne prompted them to chart a new path. The prospects for a sea change in the city's politics seemed promising. Several other cities had already elected black mayors, and by the 1980s African Americans made up nearly half of Chicago's population. Several partners of the coalition that had put Byrne in office came together and managed to persuade Harold Washington, a congressman from the South Side's First District, to contest the April 1983 mayoral election. He faced off against two candidates: Byrne and the Cook County state's attorney, Richard M. Daley. In the Democratic primary Washington carried only 36 percent of the vote, but that was enough to beat Byrne, who received 33 percent, and Daley, who garnered 31 percent. Daley had come reasonably close, but all through the campaign his detractors gained traction by calling him a machine puppet who marched in the footsteps of his father.

Harold Washington's Political Legacy

Harold Washington's election ignited a struggle over economic development policy that would be fought all through the 1980s between the remnants of Chicago's machine organization and a diverse coalition of blacks, Hispanics, and white reformers. In

April 1983, two weeks before the mayoral election, the Research and Issues Committee of the Washington campaign released a fifty-two-page document called "the Washington papers." A striking feature of the collection of papers was they did not list economic development as a separate topic among several policy areas. There was a reason for this curious omission. By subsuming economic development under two policy categories, "Jobs for Chicagoans" and "Neighborhoods," the Washington papers defined development as a divisible public good, with specific economic and political benefits.

"Balanced growth" was a central guiding principle of the Washington papers. The idea of balanced growth represented a radical departure from the Chicago tradition of blockbuster downtown projects involving large volumes of money and investor-controlled real estate. Under the machine, virtually all the development money that had not gone downtown had been distributed to neighborhood chambers of commerce, whose members maintained close ties to machine politicians. It may have been called development money, but everyone knew it was patronage. Now the plan was to target money to redevelopment objectives openly, obtained and distributed to neighborhood redevelopment corporations, cooperatives, and private businesses. To build neighborhood institutions, the Department of Planning, through the Neighborhood Planning Service, was empowered to help neighborhood residents participate in drawing up local development plans.

The planning process adopted by Washington's administration injected a novel twist into neighborhood politics that undermined politicians and community leaders aligned with the machine. By encouraging community participation, the process enabled neighborhood organizations and activists to gain a voice in policy decisions. In addition, Washington moved about 15 percent

($13.5 million) of the funds previously held centrally in city hall into neighborhood-based operations. In the past these monies had been used to support the patronage system. Another initiative shifted funding for health care, senior citizen services, and building demolition to the neighborhoods.

Washington also placed a high priority on keeping manufacturing jobs in the city. The planners and development specialists he hired believed that it was possible to persuade industry to stay if enough attention was given to the task. The Center for Urban Economic Development at the University of Illinois at Chicago was founded to assist the work of community-based organizations. The *Chicago Works Together: 1984 Chicago Development Plan*, released in 1984, outlined a strategy for keeping manufacturing jobs and assisting real estate development in various parts of the city. Two reports commissioned by the city called for the utilization of technologies to help the steel, apparel, and printing industries. Finally, the Local Industrial Retention Initiative (LIRI) was formed to support industrial development and community organizations.[60]

The novel aspects of Washington's development policies received the most coverage in the press, but in reality the administration also provided substantial support for development projects in and near the Loop. Forty-three percent of the $163 million budgeted in the 1981–85 Five Year Capital Improvements Program went to downtown redevelopment projects.[61] Washington recognized that downtown business interests were powerful, and he treated them with care. For example, he gave his support to the owners of the White Sox and the Cubs, even when their stadium development plans ran afoul of neighborhood organizations.[62]

The progressive policies being implemented during Washington's administration attracted much attention from academics and policy wonks, but the press was more interested in the high drama that ensued when the city's first black mayor confronted a hostile city council run by a group of entrenched machine politicians. Much was at stake, because Washington was subverting the well-established political processes that were essential to the continued survival of Chicago's Democratic organization.[63] Meetings of the council turned into skirmishes led by a group of twenty-nine white aldermen determined to sabotage the Washington administration at every turn. The "Vrdolyak 29" refused to approve his appointments to city boards and commissions, and instead seeded these nonelected positions with political hacks. The power of the veto was the key resource that made it possible for Washington to govern at all. An alliance of twenty-one African American, Latino, and liberal white aldermen managed, just barely, to deny the Vrdolyak 29 the extra vote they needed to reliably override the mayor's vetoes.

Harold Washington won reelection in April 1987 but died after collapsing of a heart attack in his office the following November. Despite an outpouring of fierce opposition from the African American community, the city council appointed Eugene Sawyer to complete the next two years of Washington's four-year term. Sawyer, an African American, was a soft-spoken alderman who had remained on good terms with his white colleagues throughout the racial wars. As described by a blogger who followed Chicago politics, his selection by the council turned into a riveting theatrical performance: "It was an all night election that had Dick Mell . . . Alderman of the 33rd Ward jump up on the desk at the City Council chambers. That night in the City Council was better than any reality TV, it was Chicago politics. The night ended when in the rather early morning at 4 AM a very tired Eugene Sawyer was elected by the City Council the next Mayor of Chicago, almost passing out and being held up to accept his new position."[64] The new mayor and the cohort of aldermen sneaked out the back door to avoid protesters, and for the next sixteen months the aldermen seized effective control of the city's policy apparatus.

The 1989 election provided further proof, if any was needed, that it would be difficult for any Chicago mayor to assemble a stable and durable political operation. The animosities that separated the multitude of racial, ethnic, and neighborhood interests making up Chicago would be overcome only with great difficulty. Three contenders entered the race: the incumbent, Sawyer; Richard M. Daley, who had lost in 1983; and Timothy Evans, an African American alderman running as the candidate of the recently founded Harold Washington Party. Daley beat Sawyer in the primary and comfortably carried the general election by a margin of 14.3 percentage points, but the racial divide was deep enough to give Evans of the Harold Washington Party 41 percent of the vote total. Although Daley was not an incumbent, his family's name recognition and the city's divisive racial politics secured him overwhelming support among white ethnic working-class voters, who gave him 89 percent of their votes. By contrast, he won only 7 percent of the African American vote.

Richard M. Daley and the New Political Bargain

The circumstances surrounding the younger Daley's first mayoral election victory suggested that it would be hard for him to pursue a downtown-centric policy agenda without provoking the divisions that had brought so much instability in the years since his father's death. The contentious issues in the 1989 campaign did not seem to point the way to a political rapprochement. Daley spoke of the need to make Chicago an international city. The incumbent, Sawyer, had promised to push aggressively on issues of discrimination and continue Washington's efforts to revive the manufacturing sector. As the representative of the Harold Washington Party, Evans presented himself as the candidate who would faithfully complete every item of Washington's unfinished agenda.

After winning this deeply divisive election, Daley managed what no Chicago mayor before him had accomplished: he found a winning formula for economic recovery while also calming Chicago's troubled political scene. The political scientist Larry Bennett has pointed out that except for Harold Washington, every postwar mayor had sought "the transformation of central Chicago into a more formidable corporate management district and upscale residential community."[65] Daley was devoted to these goals too, but he realized that the success of his economic strategy would rest on his ability to bring political stability to the affairs of the city. This may be why he embraced some of the main features of Harold Washington's policies. During the campaign, Daley had criticized Washington's and Sawyer's efforts to support industry within the city, but he later backed the development of two industrial corridors and the creation of dozens of tax increment finance districts that provided financing for neighborhood development. The newly elected mayor's political dexterity opened a space for him to pursue his ambitious goal of revitalizing the lakefront and the downtown core even while preserving the peace. In the next chapter we describe the lakefront complex that was made possible by that unlikely political bargain.

3

Master Builder

When Robert Moses died on July 29, 1981, the obituaries that appeared in the *New York Times* and the *New York Post* referred to him, as people had for years, as New York's "master builder." The placing and length of the *Times* article—on the front page, and five thousand words—attested to Moses's influence in shaping the physical landscape of New York as well as his outsize personality, brutal methods, and skill at accumulating power. In the intervening years, those elements of his character and biography have become the subject of debate, but through it all the physical reminders of his work endure. In the introduction to a 2007 photographic portfolio of his efforts, Hilary Ballon and Kenneth T. Jackson note that for decades "Moses' reputation has been rising, propelled by a fear that New York is no longer capable of executing ambitious projects because of its multi-layered process of citizen and governmental review."[1] The irony is hard to miss, considering that the reforms adopted to curb the abuse of power attributed to Moses now make it difficult to get anything done in New York. Political power can be beneficial, but it is also dangerous, and therein is an inescapable paradox.

Like Moses, Richard M. Daley became a master builder only because he possessed the power, political skills, and resources necessary for accomplishing his aims. It is true that the basic foundation for his infrastructure program was already in place before he became mayor. There was Grant Park, Northerly Island, bicycle and walking paths, and the "open and free" lakefront left by the 1909 *Plan of Chicago*. In addition, his predecessors had already taken steps to build a tourist economy. His father, for example, had built McCormick Place and instituted a hotel tax to finance important public improvements in Grant Park and elsewhere. During her contentious term, Jane Byrne backed arts projects, the performing arts, and festivals (including enthusiastically welcoming "the Blues Brothers" to City Hall). But even when summed together, all the previous initiatives would ultimately be dwarfed by the scale, impact, cost, and coherence of the program undertaken by the second Daley.

Within weeks of his April 1989 inauguration, the new mayor took on the challenge of accumulating the institutional authority to finance and manage an aggressive building program along the lake, and by the time the Illinois legislature ended its session that year, he had persuaded it to replace the Metropolitan Fair and Exposition Authority, which operated McCormick Place, with the vastly expanded Metropolitan Pier and Exposition Authority, which was charged with operating both Navy Pier and the McCormick Place convention center. As a special-purpose authority, McPier, as it came to be called, operated independently of the city, with the mayor and governor each appointing three of the six members of the board and the mayor selecting the board's chair. Daley named his acting chief of staff, John Schmidt, as the first board chair. According to a mayoral adviser, "John is very close to Daley. He has been through every significant political battle Rich has fought since the state's attorney's race. . . . The mayor's office and Rich trust him implicitly."[2] Under Schmidt's guidance, McPier soon turned into a giant umbrella organization that financed and managed many of the largest of Daley's lakefront projects. By 2009, McPier had grown to five hundred administrative staff positions, and it had well more than a billion dollars in bonding authority.[3]

In 1993 the plans for the renovated Navy Pier were unveiled, and in the same year Daley outlined an $800 million development proposal that would have included several gambling boats docked along the Chicago River. In his announcement, Daley responded to critics by declaring, "I have the right, just as any mayor to propose things. [The casino plan is] a win-win situation for everyone in Illinois."[4] The gaming proposal failed to gain approval from the Illinois General Assembly, but the setback was hardly noticed, because so much activity was already taking place along the lakefront. In subsequent years McPier provided the bond funding for the massive Museum Campus project, floated bonds for two expansions of McCormick Place, raised capital for projects connected to the renovation of Soldier Field, and, years later, pledged bond funding for the city's bid for the 2016 Olympics.[5]

At the same time Daley took control of the Chicago Park District, with its thousands of employees, by replacing the majority of the commissioners of the seven-member board that had been appointed a few years earlier under Harold Washington. David Mosena, Daley's choice for chief of staff, focused on department mergers and privatization efforts and served as the city's planning commissioner. In addition, Daley chose thirty-four-year-old Richard Wendy as the new deputy planning commissioner to replace Washington's appointee, Elizabeth Hollander. The park district budget in 1989 was $270 million, extended over seventy-two hundred acres, and during the latter part of the 1980s employed as many as fifty-nine hundred people.[6] The mayor also hired carefully vetted professional staff to run the Department of Planning and the Department of Cultural Affairs. Tax Increment Finance districts provided a funding mechanism for investing in public infrastructure throughout the city, but especially along the lakefront and downtown.[7] By 2009, 152 districts were in place. In addition, Daley tapped into the multimillion-dollar budgetary and bonding authority of the Chicago Park District. Daley controlled the park district through key appointments, and the great majority of these came from his personal and professional circle. In 1994, he identified John W. Rodgers Jr., a top political fund-raiser and one of his longtime supporters, to lead the organization. Over the years, the funding for the park district increased significantly, from $301.3 million in 1995 to $366.5 million a decade later. By the time Daley left office in 2011, the Chicago Park District budget had reached almost $400 million.[8]

With these pieces of the institutional puzzle in place, the mayor was in a position to assert command over a closely coordinated series of lakefront projects. He took care, as well, to provide ample resources for an ever-changing mix of cultural and leisure activities. Early in his first term he restructured the Office of Special Events and the Department of Cultural Affairs. The Office of Special Events organized and administered a growing number of major music festivals, and the Department of Cultural Affairs staged a series of highly popular public art exhibits, such the wildly successful "Cows on Parade." In 1981, the Office of Special Events employed thirteen staff with a budget of $330,383; in his 2005 funding request, the mayor proposed sixty-eight staff and a budget of just over $25 million.[9]

Just before Daley's election to a fourth term, in 1999, a writer for the *Chicago Tribune* proclaimed that the mayor "should be searching for the next Burnham, the next Burnham Plan and the next great blueprint."[10] A formal document of that kind never did emerge during his tenure, but by the end of Daley's last term in office the interlocking nature of the several lakefront projects made it appear that everything had been guided by a master plan. Some writers began to associate his name with Robert Moses. The City of Spectacle built by Daley along the shores of Lake Michigan shows why the comparison is apt.

The Lakefront Transformation

In his 1989 campaign, Daley expressed his desire to turn a deteriorated and mostly abandoned old pier at the mouth of the Chicago River into a major tourist attraction, and once in office he moved quickly to make good on his promise. When the renovated Navy Pier opened in 1995, it was an instant success with the public, if not with architectural critics. A year before the pier opened, Daley announced the Museum Campus project, and by the time it was completed four years later it had created a fifty-seven-acre space at the southeast corner of Grant Park that tied together the Field Museum of Natural History, the Shedd Aquarium, and the Adler Planetarium. Greenways, walkways, bicycle paths, a pedestrian tunnel, and raised terraces composed a lakefront landscape with sweeping views of the downtown skyline.

And the lakefront projects continued one after another, and often at the same time. In 1996, an expansion of McCormick Place nearly doubled its size; another expansion, completed in 2007, ensured that it would remain the biggest convention center in the world. In 2003, a major reconstruction of Soldier Field— the house of the Chicago Bears football team—transformed an aging stadium built in the 1920s into a bold and controversial statement of modernist architecture. It also became the means of completing the Museum Campus by ultimately including, in the same package, funding for a sledding hill, a new park, a pedestrian bridge over Lake Shore Drive, and scores of acres of landscaping throughout the campus.

The Museum Campus, McCormick Place, and Soldier Field projects dramatically reconfigured the lakefront, but Daley aimed to do more, and this time he employed raw power to accomplish it. A peninsula called Northerly Island, which was originally built as part of the 1909 *Plan of Chicago*, was connected to the southern boundary of the Museum Campus, and on many occasions the mayor expressed his dream to turn it into a park and nature preserve. To resolve a long-standing and frustrating struggle with the governor's office and the state legislature over the status of Meigs Field, a small private airport on the peninsula, in March of 2003, Daley sent bulldozers under cover of night to carve Xs into its runways. In the summer of 2015 the huge construction involved in remaking Northerly Island was completed.

Millennium Park, located in the northwest corner of Grant Park, opened in July 2004. It was originally projected to cost $150 million, but it morphed into a $500 million "sculpture garden on steroids."[11] The project survived years of public criticism over rising costs and construction delays in large part because the financing mechanisms required no public input, and the members of Chicago's civic elite worked behind the scenes with an ensemble of international architects and artists recruited by them. The 24.5-acre venue that finally emerged is made up of a montage of extraordinary architecture, landscape design, and interactive spaces for art, music, food, and spectacle.

In 2002, Daley spoke to twelve hundred Convention and Tourism Bureau members attending the fifty-ninth annual meeting of the bureau held at McCormick Place. Daley boasted that "Chicago has undergone an urban renaissance like no other city in America

. . . [and the millions of] out-of-town visitors make the city one of the world's most popular city destinations."[12] At the time the mayor made those remarks, his building program was far from complete, yet everyone could already see that a City of Spectacle was rising on Chicago's lakefront.

Navy Pier

In a 1993 ceremony announcing the final plans for a comprehensive makeover of Navy Pier, the mayor invoked Chicago's storied past as a device for investing the occasion with historic significance:

> More than a century ago, Chicagoans rebuilt this city from ashes and rubble. Faced with disaster, Chicago emerged stronger than ever, thanks to a determined people. Today, the danger is not a great fire, but indifference and conventional thinking in the face of changing times. We either rise to the challenge of these times, or be engulfed—not by flames, but by decay, despair and defeat. . . . If you doubt it, consider the history of the pier on which we stand. Left for years to rust and rot, this great resource is undergoing a stunning rebirth many thought would never come. After a decade of discouragement and delay, a renovation has begun that will transform this pier into yet another jewel on Chicago's shining lakefront. Because we refused to give in, "because we had a dream and saw it through" we will, on this site, leave our children one more lasting asset.[13]

For many years to come, and on many occasions, the mayor would return again and again to a familiar theme: what was happening on the lakefront on his watch was a rebirth and revival, as transformative, he was fond of saying, as anything that had ever happened in Chicago.

The florid rhetoric notwithstanding, just as the mayor observed, Navy Pier had been deteriorating for a long time. The Municipal Pier, renamed Navy Pier in 1927, opened to the public in 1916 at a cost of $4.5 million. The pier was one of several islands and four piers called for in the 1909 *Plan of Chicago*, but only the Municipal Pier and Northerly Island (now part of the Museum Campus) were ever built. The thirty-three-hundred-foot structure mainly housed warehouses that stored cargo offloaded from lake freighters and provided docking facilities for excursion boats that crisscrossed the lake, but the end of the pier also became a favorite gathering spot and location for public events. Only a few blocks from the Loop and easily accessible by streetcar, the pier was a busy place, but with the coming of the Great Depression, the use of the pier fell so sharply that it often appeared to be abandoned. World War II gave it new life when the city leased it to the navy for use as a training center for pilots and military personnel. Thousands of pilots received their flying credentials there.

That period of frenetic activity turned out to be short-lived, and following the war, city officials looked for other ways to make use of the pier. After the navy relocated its facilities elsewhere in 1946, the University of Illinois housed a new Chicago campus in crowded and dilapidated wooden structures on the pier. Until McCormick Place opened its doors in 1956, the pier also became, from time to time, the site of trade shows. When, in 1964, the University of Illinois at Chicago relocated to a newly constructed campus a mile west of the Loop, the pier fell into another period of disuse. From 1978 to 1983 the ChicagoFest celebration brought millions of people to the increasingly crumbling site, but that once-a-year event could not prevent the pier from slipping into decay, especially when ChicagoFest moved to the friendlier and more accessible comforts of Grant Park.[14]

The renovated Navy Pier opened to the public in 1995, at a cost of $200 million (figure 3.1). The reconstruction turned the pier into an urban amusement park that included the Chicago Children's Museum, a thirty-two-hundred-square-foot indoor botanical garden, a fifteen-story Ferris wheel, street entertainment areas with outdoor stages, an IMAX theater, retail concessions, restaurants, food courts, a festival hall, a huge ballroom, a half-mile-long promenade, and docking facilities for tour boats and water taxis. The pier continued to evolve over the years. In 1997, the $27 million, 525-seat Chicago Shakespeare Theater, modeled after London's Swan Theater, opened its doors. An English-style pub, a Teacher's Resource Center, and an English Garden were also added, and in 2000, the Smith Museum of Stained Glass Windows debuted as the first museum of its type in the United States (it closed in 2014 just prior to a major renovation of the pier).[15]

The pier became the city's most popular tourist attraction in the first year after it reopened. Attendance reached 4.5 million people in 1996, exceeded 6 million in 1997, and surpassed 7.7 million people in 1999. More than 9.1 million visitors came to the pier in 2000, but in the wake of the terrorist attacks of September 11, 2001, those numbers fell to 8.4 million in 2002 before rebounding to 8.7 million the next year. In subsequent years attendance has fluctuated, but the pier has remained the single most popular tourist attraction in the city.[16] In 2012 Navy Pier attracted 9.2 million visitors, breaking the previous attendance record established in 2000.[17] Its popularity also helped to ignite a business and housing boom in the adjacent Streeterville neighborhood.[18]

Because a successful pier was so important to the economy of the city, by the turn of the century, city officials and the McPier staff were looking for ways to transform the structure into something less like a family-oriented theme park and more like a multipurpose entertainment venue that might appeal to a more diverse mix of users. In 2005, McPier hired Forrec Ltd., a Toronto-based consulting firm specializing in themed attractions, and Florida-based Baker Leisure Group, to develop a ten-year strategic vision for the pier. The following year McPier officials endorsed the consultants' recommendations for a radical makeover. Among the more dramatic features envisioned by the plan were a monorail system to run the entire length of the pier and a floating hotel, themed as a 1930s Great Lakes steamship, to be moored alongside the pier. A 260-foot Ferris wheel, almost on the scale of the original one built by George Washington Gale Ferris Jr. for the 1893 World's Fair, would have towered over the complex, and like Ferris's, the cars would have been equipped with a food and drink bar. The most controversial part of the proposal called for the development of an eighty-thousand-square-foot, Great Lakes–themed indoor water park. Other additions would have included a recreational area with rides and a new marina with 250 boat slips.[19] Critics were alarmed, calling the plan an "aesthetic planning lapse," a "cheesy makeover," a "shopping mall," and "a bunch of junk thrown together."[20]

The Great Lakes theme park for Navy Pier never materialized, in part because in the wake of the 2008 economic meltdown its $2 billion price tag raised eyebrows. Nevertheless, Mayor Daley doubled down on his efforts to remake the pier. In 2010 McPier hired the Urban Land Institute (ULI) to offer a realistic renovation plan. The ULI's proposal included an expanded Chicago Shakespeare Theater and called for refurbishing the congested retail areas and the tired and overcrowded food courts. In addition, the plan called for the construction of a four-thousand-seat concert venue, an indoor skating rink, and additional green space. In 2010, when McPier officials revealed that an upgrade, based on the ULI proposal, would cost $155 million ($50 million of it in public funds), they predicted that the renovated Navy Pier would attract twelve million visitors annually.[21]

In the summer of 2011, and in anticipation of the hundredth anniversary of the pier in 2016, Navy Pier Inc., a newly chartered not-for-profit organization responsible for the operation and development of the pier, announced the official plan for its revitalization, *The Centennial Vision: Pierscape.* The aim was to create a public space that would rival the design and architectural statement made by Millennium Park. A family pavilion and expansive indoor and outdoor spaces were to be mixed in with entertainment attractions, all of this informed by environmentally sensitive design principles. The plan also called for a five-story, 150- to 225-room boutique hotel on the grounds fronting the pier, which would bring a sort of "resident" population of visitors.[22] Daley left office before the Navy Pier makeover came to fruition, but major elements of the plan went forward after his departure.

It is significant that Daley faced no consequential opposition in his quest to transform Navy Pier. His administration intended to capture Chicago's imagination with a high-profile project right out of the gate that would project the new mayor as a man of action. Most people seemed relieved to see some leadership after the relative inactivity of the Sawyer years. John McCarron, the *Chicago Tribune* urban affairs writer, praised Daley for delivering state legislation that brought $150 million for a Navy Pier makeover.[23] Daley's commitment to Navy Pier was prominently mentioned as a key accomplishment that influenced the *Chicago Tribune* editorial board to endorse him for the 1991 election.[24] The Navy Pier renovation helped him win that election, but with Navy Pier Daley was making a statement about the future, too: Navy Pier, he said, was only one step in a much grander scheme to make "the convention-tourism-service industry economic base for the next century."[25]

McCormick Place

On the occasion of his first full-term inaugural address of May 6, 1991, Mayor Daley expressed his view that a McCormick Place expansion was one of the most important investments the city could undertake, because, he said, "Chicago's prominence as a convention center is vital to the entire state of Illinois. But other cities across the nation have caught on to the benefits of the convention trade, and they are hard on our heels. We must expand McCormick Place or lose our competitive edge in the battle for convention and tourism dollars."[26] Less than a year later, at a gathering of the Municipal Bond Investors Assurance Corporation, the mayor returned to the same theme, and more than ten years later, in his 2003 inaugural address, Daley beat the drum for another expansion when he warned, "And we must continue to enhance the competitive advantage of our tourism and convention industry, which attracts thirty million visitors to Chicago each year, pumping some $8 billion a year into the Chicago economy."[27] Over the years, the mayor provided crucial backing for two major expansions to McCormick Place, the first in the late 1990s, at a cost of $987 million, the second, completed in 2007, at a price tag of $882 million.

As with the Navy Pier project, there was a historical precedent for the mayor's initiative. More than a century before, Chicago boosters used the occasion of the Columbian Exposition to entice professional associations and their members to visit the industries exhibiting at the 1893 World's Fair. The exposition was instrumental in transforming a disorganized collection of traveling trade shows run by amateurs into a professionalized meetings industry. At the fair, the World Parliament of Religions hosted a seventeen-day conference that attracted thousands of participants, and the closing session drew a crowd of seventeen thousand. At the same time the World's Congress Auxiliary conducted 224 meetings, which ranged widely in subject matter, from the promotion of agriculture to the progress of women to the future of trade shows. Printed programs listed 1,283 sessions at which 5,978 speeches were delivered by 4,822 speakers addressing seven hundred thousand conference participants.[28]

Trade publications promoted the fair to their members. Local department stores and consumer groups tied their promotional campaigns to the fair, which meant that images of the fair were ubiquitous throughout the urban landscape, on posters, in window displays, and in advertisements.[29] Companies in Chicago distributed maps as a means of encouraging their employees to visit the fair, and the fair's sponsors used maps to direct fairgoers to particular businesses even when these were located outside the exposition grounds. According to historian and geographer Diane Dillon, "These advertising maps contributed to the fair's atmosphere of commercial competition in multiple ways. The maps typically led visitors not only to the displays of the promoted goods but to those of their rivals as well, as most of the exhibits were grouped by type. The advertisements thus facilitated, perhaps inadvertently, comparison of different brands of beer, biscuits, or reapers."[30]

Thus was born the organized promotion of professional meetings, both in Chicago and elsewhere. In 1907, the Chicago Association of Commerce charged a local business committee with the responsibility of promoting the city and bringing conventions to the downtown. However, without adequate meetings facilities, tourism bureaus could do little more than advertise, and in any case, meetings were normally financed and organized by companies or independent entrepreneurs. To remedy this situation, in 1934 Frederick Henry Prince, then the president of the Union Stock Yards, built the International Amphitheater at Forty-Second and Halsted Streets. The amphitheater became the site of the immensely popular annual International Live Stock Exhibition, and it also hosted other large-scale events, including political conventions. The arena hosted five presidential nominating conventions, including the 1968 Democratic National Convention.

The Chicago Rail Fair of 1948 and 1949 inspired Colonel Robert R. McCormick, an influential civic leader and owner of the *Chicago Tribune*, to launch a civic campaign to build a public exhibition hall. His goal was to develop a structure that would give Chicago national visibility as the host of shows and exhibitions. In 1955, in one of his first actions as mayor, Richard J. Daley persuaded the Illinois state legislature to create the Metropolitan

Fair and Exposition Authority (later MPEA). The authority opened the McCormick Place convention center in 1960 on the lakefront a few blocks south of Grant Park. At a cost of $41.8 million, McCormick Place contained 320,000 square feet, with an exhibit hall, twenty-three meeting rooms, and a five-thousand-seat theater.[31] By contemporary standards it was tiny, but at the time it was one of the nation's largest exhibition halls.

To the surprise of its builders and the public, who thought its steel and concrete materials made it fireproof, McCormick Place burned to the ground in 1967 in a spectacular blaze that set the night sky south of the Loop aglow. Almost immediately, the first Mayor Daley pushed for the construction of a new building. The new McCormick Place was built on the same site, despite widespread popular support for a location away from the prized lakefront. The new building, later called the East Building, contained 522,000 square feet of exhibit space, twenty meeting rooms, five theaters, and seven restaurants. Conventions quickly filled the space; in its first year, the new McCormick Place hosted fifty-one expositions, compared to a previous high of thirty-eight. In 1977, the Illinois legislature approved a special tax on cigarettes to finance an expansion of the facility.[32]

By the late 1980s, members of the MPEA board convinced themselves that McCormick Place needed to be enlarged and upgraded, and in 1990, less than a year after Richard M. Daley's first election, the board retained KPMG Peat Marwick to give it advice about the center's future. In its marketing analysis, KPMG concluded that McCormick Place was too small, mainly because it could not support exhibit space for events that had more than five thousand attendees. The report recommended that McCormick Place be expanded to ensure that Chicago would maintain its status as one of the nation's leading convention cities.[33]

The mayor favored a major expansion, and predictably, he found ready support among the members of McPier's board. In 1996, a $675 million addition called McCormick Place South was completed. More physical changes included a renovated forty-two-hundred-seat Arie Crown Theater and thirty-one hundred more parking spaces, most of them in an enclosed structure. The 840,000 square feet added to the complex brought the total exhibition space to 2.2 million square feet, which made it the largest convention center in the world. The McCormick Place complex now occupied twenty-seven acres, and a web of pedestrian bridges allowed visitors to navigate among the various structures without ever stepping outside. In 1998, the $108 million Hyatt Regency at McCormick Place Hotel opened its doors, which made eight hundred rooms and six hundred parking spaces available right next to the center. To improve access to the downtown, a dedicated express bus lane began operating, making it possible to go from McCormick Place to the Loop in eight minutes, and a 2.5-mile dedicated roadway opened later, in 2003, which ran parallel to the commuter train tracks that connected McCormick Place to the Loop.

Only four years after the 1996 expansion, in 2000, the MPEA commissioned another study to compare McCormick Place with its constantly growing number of rivals, and this time the authority retained PricewaterhouseCoopers to develop a strategic plan. The consultants emphasized that the convention landscape had changed dramatically in the ten years since the previous study was completed. Year by year more cities had entered the field, making the market intensely competitive. The consultants said that if Chicago hoped to retain its position among the top convention cities (at the time, it was ranked second to Las Vegas), the McCormick Place complex would have to be expanded yet again. Unless this occurred, the consultants warned, the city would lose market share and see a projected decline in sales by more than $1.4 billion over the next ten years and generate 20,500 fewer jobs.[34]

In the aftermath of the September 11, 2001 terrorist attacks, the PricewaterhouseCooper prognosis seemed alarming. Prompted by concerns about the economic impact on the state, in October 2002, the Illinois Fiscal and Economic Commission published its own report, which argued that it was essential for the city of Chicago and the state of Illinois to continue to draw tourists.[35] The authors of the commission's report noted that the tourism sector was the third-largest employer in the nation, following only telecommunications and information technology, and that it would continue to be a key growth sector. They also emphasized that the city's closest competitors, Las Vegas and Orlando, had recently undertaken construction projects to increase exhibition space to 2.0 million and 2.1 million square feet, respectively, and that expansion projects were under way in other cities all over the country.

The state commission's report recommended that exhibit space in McCormick Place be increased from its existing 2.2 million to 2.8 million square feet. If this were done, the authors argued, the expansion would bring huge benefits; it would increase local and state tax revenues, they calculated, by $80 million and generate twenty-one hundred additional jobs. The report declared that "although a recession in the economy aggravated by the September 11th, 2001 terrorist attacks put most convention center plans nationwide on hold, the tourism and convention industries have begun to rebound. Convention centers have issued bonds and construction projects have resumed."[36]

The consultant's and the public agency's reports became the basis for a huge, multiyear building project. The McCormick Place West building opened in August 2007 and became fully operational in 2008. A 470,000-square-foot exhibit hall and sixty-one meeting

rooms providing 250,000 square feet of meeting space were aug-
mented by the largest ballroom in Chicago, at 100,000 square feet.
The ballroom could be divided into five smaller rooms. According
to a survey conducted by PricewaterhouseCoopers for the MPEA,
the west expansion would bring $2.7 billion of business activity to
the local economy.[37] Obviously, a payoff like this would be important, given the price tag of the various expansions.

Even after years of multibillion-dollar investments in Mc-
Cormick Place, Chicago has struggled to maintain its place
in the national race for convention business. According to the
Chicago Convention and Tourism Bureau, 95 events attracting
more than 3 million attendees were held in McCormick Place
in 2003. These numbers slipped to 77 events in 2005 and 78
events the following year before rising to 112 in 2007. However,
in those years attendance rose only slightly, from 2.2 million to
2.3 million attendees.[38]

The convention statistic most coveted by city managers appears
in a list published annually by *Tradeshow Week*. In its annual survey, Tradeshow 200, *Tradeshow Week* ranks the top two hundred
cities based on attendance and the net square footage used by exhibitions and meetings. Even though Chicago had been ranked
second behind Las Vegas for many years, its performance in 2005
dropped the city to the third position, behind Orlando. In 2005,
Chicago had one of its weakest years ever in this important cat-
egory; it hosted only twenty Tradeshow 200 shows, with an attendance of 642,412 visitors and a net square footage used of only
6.37 million. Figures since 2000 place this decline in perspective.
That year, Chicago hosted twenty-one shows attended by 960,149
visitors, and utilized a net square footage of about 11 million.[39]

McCormick Place rebounded in 2006 when some of the biggest shows in the country held their conventions in Chicago. These

included the International Manufacturing Technology Show (eighty-five thousand attendees, with an estimated delegate spending of $158.4 million), the NPE—The Plastics Exposition and Conference (eighty-three thousand attendees, with an estimated delegate spending of $154.7 million), and the National Restaurant Association, Hotel-Motel Show (seventy-six thousand attendees, with an estimated delegate spending of $106.2 million).[40] With a total of 785,101 attendees and a net square footage use of 8.76 million, Chicago once again climbed back to second spot in the national rankings.[41] The next year McCormick Place West opened, and within a few months, sixty-six meetings had been reserved, requiring 1.5 million hotel room nights and generating $921 million activity in the local economy. In the summer of 2007, McPier refinanced its debt to lower the interest rate on its loan and extend the amortization period by six years, to 2048. It intended to use the additional funds to expand the Hyatt Regency McCormick Place and build two additional buildings with as many as one thousand meeting rooms.

It is difficult to make strict comparisons to previous years, because reporting data changed in 2007 (attendance at trade shows was separated from attendance at other meetings), but according to the Chicago Convention and Tourism Bureau, total attendance in 2011 was 768,685, a decline of 9.6 percent from 2010; in the same year, trade show attendance fell by 14 percent. Concerned about declining attendance, in 2012 the MPEA ended a protracted seventeen-month negotiation with labor unions, which reduced exhibitors' costs. The MPEA expected to host more conventions, but it was still unclear how much attendance would increase.[42]

Since the 1990s one of the hottest real estate markets in Chicago has been the neighborhood near the Central Station–Museum

Campus south of Grant Park (figure 3.2). McCormick Place has helped accelerate the pace of development, so much so that in 2008 MPEA officials hired a real estate planning consultant group to help it review the rising tide of proposals received from developers who expressed an interest in business initiatives on land owned by McPier on the Near South Side. Estimates from 2008 put the total residential, office, and retail projects in the surrounding area at $4 billion.[43]

The interlocking nature of the institutions and financing involved in the redevelopment planned for the area near McCormick Place shows how tightly such efforts have been coordinated. The Chicago Plan Commission approved the development of a multipurpose arena and the associated zoning guidelines. McPier also approved the purchase of additional land as well as the construction contract for the project. A 10,000 seat, $173 million publicly owned arena for the DePaul University basketball program and a five-hundred-room hotel became key elements of the redevelopment initiative. In addition, a $400 million convention hotel with twelve hundred rooms was planned for construction, paid for by revenue bonds and funds generated by a Tax Increment Finance District. In 2015, a new Green Line Chicago Transit Authority station was opened to improve transportation access to and from the area, and the City Parks Department began spending significant amounts of money on street improvements and landscaping. Although McPier always remained at the center of the action, and it continued to operate as an independent authority, Daley treated it as a key municipal asset, an asset that has now been passed to his successor.[44] Today, the various projects are being closely coordinated by Mayor Rahm Emanuel and city officials as part of an ongoing program to revitalize the South Loop.[45]

The Museum Campus

On July 31, 1998, Mayor Daley presided over the opening-day ceremonies for the Museum Campus. Although the mayor was eager to put his own imprimatur on it, a proposal for a museum campus had been floated years before, in 1985, to make space for a World's Fair that Mayor Harold Washington imagined the city would host in 1992. The new campus would have made it possible to locate the fair on grounds overlapping the site of the 1933 Chicago World's Fair.[46] The 1992 fair was never held, but Daley thought a campus bringing together the museums should still be built. It was a solution to a problem that had brought complaints for years: to visit the different museums people were forced to negotiate their way across Lake Shore Drive, often at risk of life and limb.

The Museum Campus project was one piece of a broader culturally based redevelopment plan for the lakefront that emerged during Daley's administration. As with Navy Pier, mayors before him had conceived of such an ambitious project, but none had been able to bring it about. In 1994, a bond issue to finance the expansion of McCormick Place also made funds available for the relocation of South Lake Shore Drive. At a cost of more than $120 million, the project would be overseen by McPier, but the mayor provided the political leadership.[47] To create a landscaped topography that would knit together the Field Museum of Natural History, the Shedd Aquarium, and the Adler Planetarium, the northbound, five-lane, Lake Shore Drive had to be relocated. The highway reconstruction was completed in 1996. Additional work followed, including tens of acres of greenway, walkways, and bicycle paths, massive landscaping with a series of raised terraces, a connection between Lake Shore Drive and a major east–west boulevard, Roosevelt Road, and sidewalks and pedestrian tunnels

FIGURE 3.3

A new park space emerged in front of the Field Museum following the development of the fifty-seven-acre Museum Campus in 1998. Courtesy of user Rosa Maria Fiuza Sciullo Faria, Shutterstock Images.

underneath Lake Shore Drive. To make all this possible, more than 120,000 cubic yards of earth were moved, and the ground level in front of the Field Museum was lowered by twenty-two feet to create a tiered lawn (figure 3.3).[48]

A few months after the mayor dedicated the Museum Campus, the *Chicago Tribune*'s architectural critic Blair Kamin suggested that with its opening, Daley was completing Daniel Burnham's work. Kamin called it a "heroic urban planning undertaking. . . . The project rids the shoreline of cars and returns it to the people, just as Daniel Burnham envisioned in his 1909 Plan of Chicago" and that "the rerouted Lake Shore Drive decisively demonstrates how Daley is at once removing barriers and building bridges—literally—to the lakefront."[49] Kamin concluded, "What a boon the $110 million relocation project has turned out to be for Daniel Burnham's vision of a waterfront devoted to recreation and culture."[50] The mayor basked in such praise and welcomed such comparisons.

According to Museums in the Park, a coalition of ten museums located on Chicago Park District property, the group of institutions contributed $500 million a year to the local economy.[51] The Museum Campus project brought more people to the museums. In 2000, annual attendance increased by almost 3 percent at the Adler Planetarium, by nearly 10 percent at the Field Museum, and by a little more than 10 percent at the Shedd Aquarium. These gains were especially notable given that other cultural entities in Chicago experienced a decline in attendance during the same period.[52] To accommodate more visitors, in the years after the campus opened, the Adler Planetarium completed a $40 million renovation, the Shedd Aquarium completed a $50 million makeover, and the Field Museum added a more modest $10 million improvement.[53]

These gains have been sustained over time. In 1997, the year before the redesigned campus opened, 3.7 million visitors used the museums, but by 2002 that number neared the 4 million mark. In 2005 the Shedd Aquarium received almost 1.9 million visitors, the Field attracted more than 1.3 million, and the Adler drew about four hundred thousand.[54] The following year, 2006, the Field Museum and the Shedd Aquarium topped the attendance list of all cultural institutions in Chicago.[55] Over the next few years, museum attendance fluctuated, with 2012 statistics showing an upswing of 2.17 million people visiting the Shedd, a 2 percent increase from the previous year.

Equally important, the Museum Campus also became a promenade and outdoor playground for crowds of people flocking to the beaches and marinas and bicycle and walking paths, camera in hand, to take photos of the soaring downtown skyscrapers for the folks back home. These projects, along with annual public art exhibits such as the 2007 *Cool Globes: Hot Ideas for a Cooler Planet*, made the campus into an agora bringing together walkers, bikers, roller skaters, lakeside fishermen, and strolling and picnicking families. All this activity occurred against a background of Lake Michigan, the boat basin of Monroe Harbor, and panoramic views of the Chicago skyline.

Meigs Field and Northerly Island

In 1992, just before the end of his first term, Mayor Daley expressed an interest in closing Meigs Field and replacing it with a public park and nature preserve. For decades, the airport facility on the Northerly Island had primarily been used to provide business leaders and celebrities with easy access to the Loop. According to Daley, the fifty-year airport lease with the Chicago Park District was scheduled to lapse in 1996, and it would not be renewed. Instead, the mayor proposed to replace the airport with a ninety-one-acre park. At a projected cost of $27.2 million, the plan would link the park with the Museum Campus. It would include botanical gardens, playgrounds, wetlands, a nature center, and a sensory garden for the visually or hearing impaired, and would be accessible by ferry and a rubber-wheeled trolley. City projections noted that the "superpark" would generate over $30 million a year in revenues from parking, concessions, souvenirs, and other fees and would draw more than 350,000 visitors annually. This environmentally friendly park would be fully accessible to the disabled, as ramps would extend to the lake, fully accommodating those using strollers and wheelchairs.[56]

The project was near and dear to the mayor's heart. One of the key features of the 1909 *Plan of Chicago* called for a string of barrier islands to be built from Grant Park south to Jackson Park, the site of the World's Fair. Northerly Island (which is actually a peninsula stretching south of what later became the Museum Campus) was the only one ever constructed. Burnham intended that Northerly Island should be open to the public, but in 1948 it became the site of a small airport. This was a peculiar use for the space. Not only did it violate the most sacred principle of the *Plan of Chicago* that the lakefront remain free and clear; it also put a busy flight path less than a mile from the Loop and with a landing approach over the lake right in front of Grant Park and between the planetarium, aquarium, and natural history museum. As long as the airport remained, any comprehensive plan for the lakefront near to the downtown would be marred by a noisy air corridor (figure 3.4).

Daley was not the first mayor to propose new uses for Northerly Island. The idea of establishing a park there dates back to 1973 when it was included in the Chicago Central Area Plan, but Richard J. Daley's death three years later made the issue moot. In 1983, Mayor Washington announced a plan to build a family-oriented "Discovery Park" on the island, but he subsequently gave the matter little attention before he died in office in 1987.[57] In 1992, when the younger Mayor Daley expressed his intention to close Meigs Field so that he could pursue his own plans for the island, it seemed unlikely that this idea would go anywhere. His statement received a hostile response from Republican governor Jim Edgar and Chicago's corporate community. Arguing that closing Meigs would negatively affect the region's transportation system, the State of Illinois filed a lawsuit to take control of the property.

FIGURE 3.4
Burnham Harbor divides Northerly Island to the right from Soldier Field, the
Field Museum, and the Shedd Aquarium to the left. Courtesy of user Richard
Cavalleri, Shutterstock Images.

Threatened with an expensive legal battle between the city and
the state, in 1997 Edgar and Daley reached a compromise. The
agreement allowed for the reopening of the airfield, which had
shut down in the fall of 1996 after its lease had expired. Following
a five-year period of operation for Meigs, the city would be allowed
to proceed with its plans to create a park on Northerly Island. In
a press release issued by the Office of the Mayor, Daley concluded
that "the compromise is good for the long-term future of Chicago.
The original Meigs Field lease on Northerly Island ran for 50 years.
We have to wait another five years to create a family and tourist's
Park on Northerly Island—but it will be worth the wait. From the
very beginning, I have supported negotiation on this issue—but
with one condition. In the end, the best use of Northerly Island

is for it to become a part of our lakefront museum campus."[58] Clearly, the mayor thought the deal he had reached had finally put the issue to rest.

In the late 1990s when the mayor began to push for a massive expansion of O'Hare International Airport, the new Republican governor, George Ryan, seized on it as an opportunity to kill any possibility that Meigs might be closed. The governor immediately announced his opposition to the O'Hare project, but following behind-the-scenes negotiations, in December 2001, Ryan and Daley struck a bargain. In exchange for the governor's endorsement of an O'Hare expansion, Ryan extracted a promise from Daley to keep Meigs open until 2006; however, the practical effect of the agreement would have delayed such an option for twenty years more because it also stipulated that the city would extend the Meigs lease until 2026.

The arrangement between governor and mayor unraveled when the federal legislation needed to finalize the O'Hare expansion failed in Congress, mostly because of opposition from Republican Illinois U.S. senator Peter Fitzgerald. Angered by this turn of events, Daley issued a secret order, and in the very early hours of March 30, 2003, bulldozers carved a pattern of Xs in the center of the runway.[59] Finally, the controversy over Meigs Field had come to an abrupt and dramatic end. The media dubbed Daley the "X" man, and although public criticism was intense, Daley scoffed at the negative publicity. He claimed that he was protecting the city from potential security threats from the airplanes flying so close to the downtown skyscrapers. The mayor had flexed his political muscle, and there was little that anyone could do about it. By exercising raw power, Daley managed to succeed when political negotiation proved inadequate to the task.

In the summer of 2005, the Charter One Pavilion (later the First Merit Bank Pavilion) opened at Northerly Island, a seventy-five-hundred-seat venue offering outdoor concerts and live music. The stage is positioned in such a way that those in attendance enjoy spectacular views of the city's glittering skyline at night,[60] although reviews of the total experience on social media sites carried frequent complaints about acoustics, sight lines, and comfort. Significant improvements were unveiled in 2013, with an upgraded stage and sound system and more seating on a newly constructed lawn. Outside the pavilion, the Chicago Park District converted Northerly Island into a natural prairie landscape crisscrossed with walking and biking paths. It has become a popular site for locals and visitors alike. In 2014 a construction project began on the southern forty acres of the island, financed by a $2.8 million federal grant and $1.5 million contributed to the Chicago Park District from concert organizers. Most of the improvements were completed by the end of the summer in 2015, and the public was finally able to stroll and bike through an undulating landscape that provided camping opportunities, a nature preserve, and bicycle and walking paths.[61]

Soldier Field

Soldier Field, the home of the Chicago Bears football team, is located within the cluster of cultural institutions and park space created by the Museum Campus, the Burnham Harbor boat basin, and Northerly Island. Opened in 1924, Soldier Field has long been sacred ground for Chicago football fans. Owned and operated by the Chicago Park District, the facility was leased to the Bears, who moved to Chicago from Decatur, Illinois, three years before the stadium's opening. But the relationship between the city and the ownership of the team has often been contentious, especially after 1985 when the club won the Super Bowl and began to press for a new stadium.

Conflicts between Daley and the Bears' owners, the McCaskey family, began almost from the day he won his first election. In 1989 John Schmidt, the chair of the McPier board (and a former aide to Richard J. Daley), proposed that a domed stadium for the Chicago Bears be built alongside McCormick Place. McDome, as the project was soon christened, was projected to cost between $450 million and $600 million, but it never materialized. Despite the fact that the idea was supported by Bears president Michael McCaskey and NFL commissioner Paul Tagliabue, Daley expressed the view that a stadium built exclusively for the Bears would not get enough use: "You cannot stand here today and say you can build a new stadium for eight games," he said.[62] In the absence of his support, a funding bill stalled in the state legislature.

McCaskey had been trying to get public backing for a new football stadium since 1986, and now, four years later, he went to the newspapers and criticized Daley for not pushing hard enough to persuade state legislators to pass a funding package. The mayor responded by scolding, "No one in life likes to be threatened. . . . I hope it's not a threat to the people of Chicago. It gets you upset. It's not proper."[63] Behind the scenes, Daley worked hard to keep the Bears. It was imperative to do so, but equally important for Daley was that he establish he was firmly in charge of the municipal ship. An often contentious public battle dragged on for several years. The mayor branded McCaskey as a wealthy son of privilege who was out of touch with the economic realities and fiscal limitations of the city. McCaskey persisted in demanding public funding, and made sure the media knew he was exploring multiple plans to move out of the city to the suburbs or even Indiana. Some of these plans included partnerships with other institutions such as Rush Presbyterian Hospital and Medical Center to finance the construction of an eighty-thousand-seat stadium and medical complex on the Near West Side, or with other teams like the Chicago White Sox to share a multipurpose facility in the South Loop.[64]

Daley, though, had other plans. Because of Soldier Field's lakefront location and its closeness to the Museum Campus, the mayor was firmly committed to keeping the stadium where it was. He viewed sport as a form of culture, and as far as he was concerned, Soldier Field was one of the key elements in his campaign to restore the lakefront.[65] Daley kept explaining to the press and the public how important it was to keep the Bears on the lakefront, and this meant modernizing Soldier Field. The impasse was finally resolved in February 1999 when McCaskey was removed from his post as president and assigned to serve as chairman of the Chicago Bears Board of Directors. Finally, in the summer of 2000, the mayor and Bears management agreed to a plan. It would involve substantial public subsidies, but much of the cost covered parking and landscaping around the stadium and renovations in and around Grant Park.

By the end of the summer of 2000, Bears officials and Mayor Daley had settled their differences, and they jointly began to promote a sweeping plan for a new stadium that also included substantial ancillary redevelopment. In the months leading up to the 2000 presidential election, the mayor quietly worked with the Republican governor, George Ryan, to push a bill through the state legislature authorizing state support; at about the same time, the Illinois Sports Facilities Authority, organized in the 1980s to build Comiskey Park for the Chicago White Sox, approved $399 million in bonds issued for the project. On January 5, 2001, Ryan signed the bill into law.

Critics, who had been distracted by the protracted controversy over the 2000 presidential election, were blindsided by the backroom maneuvering that led to the legislative outcome. Although letters to the editors of local newspapers indicated that there was some public concern, the only organized opposition came from a not-for-profit group, the Friends of the Parks. In a lawsuit to halt construction, Friends of the Parks argued that the land belonged to the people of Chicago and that it should not be used by a professional football team to make a profit. The organization's leaders also protested that ten acres of park space was included in the project. Through the spring and early summer, opponents pressed their case with the Chicago Plan Commission, which possessed the authority to approve or veto any major project, and the board of the Chicago Park District, which ran the stadium. But Daley's appointments were sprinkled liberally throughout both organizations, and the renovation was never in danger. He heaped scorn on the accusation that the renovated stadium contradicted the spirit of the Burnham Plan, scoffing, "Did they talk to him yesterday? Only they talk to Daniel Burnham."[66]

The winning design for the stadium proposed to save the exterior portion of the 1920s-era stadium by inserting a "spaceship"-like structure composed of curving aluminum panels within and soaring above the neoclassical colonnades arrayed along the east and west facades. Architectural critics and the media excoriated the architectural renderings. Critics considered the aluminum-and-glass structure an unalloyed, monstrous design travesty. The editor in chief of *Building Design & Construction*, Robert Cassidy, wrote that "just looking at it makes me sick," and "it's a real effrontery to the public and to our distinctive architecture here."[67] Barry Rozner, editorial writer for the *New York Daily Herald*, wrote that "it remains inexcusable that the Bears and Mayor Daley conspired to desecrate a war memorial by dropping a spaceship inside the colonnades, and then stuck the public with a $430 million bill."[68] On the whole, the public seemed to share these views, although, it should be said, a few prominent architects defended the design.

Despite (or, rather, because of) the furious criticism, demolition of the interior moved at lightning speed. The first steps were taken in the summer of 2001, and as soon as the Bears played their last game of the season, wrecking crews descended en masse. The next season the Bears played at the University of Illinois' Memorial Stadium in Champaign-Urbana, and by the summer of 2003 construction entered its final phase. Soldier Field was only the anchor of a quarter-billion-dollar project that ultimately cost $680 million. The additional money was devoted to a new parking garage, improved access to Grant Park, to the Museum Campus residential neighborhoods on the other side of Lake Shore Drive, and to the nearby Metra mass-transit stations. More than fifteen acres of landscaping were added to create more green space, over thirteen hundred trees of forty-five different species were planted, a sledding hill was configured, and a children's garden was installed for public use.[69] All this development revealed that the Soldier Field renovation had never been the goal in itself; it provided a way to raise revenues for development all along the lakefront, the Museum Campus, and Grant Park. With this purpose in mind, it is easy to see why Daley became so fiercely wedded to the idea of keeping Soldier Field where it was.

The mayor was harshly criticized for dodging an open debate over the public financing of the new stadium because, in fact, the details were worked out behind closed doors among the principal players. The Bears contributed $200 million, and the remaining cost was financed by Chicago's 2 percent hotel-motel tax. Covering the city's share through the existing hotel-motel tax allowed the mayor to boast that the public had not paid anything toward the project. Because new public money was not nominally required to build the stadium, the mayor managed to avoid a referendum and the controversy it would have brought. The Illinois Sports Facilities Authority (ISFA) issued bonds to cover most of the costs.

The reincarnated Soldier Field held its first event on September 17, 2003, scarcely more than a week before the Bears' opener on the twenty-ninth. Fans immediately embraced the new structure, and by the end of the first year the stadium had hosted close to fifty events. The parkland that surrounded the stadium was completed a few months after the stadium's opening, and it quickly became a favored venue for organized events and for walking and biking. Against this background, few noticed when in 2004 the National Park Service recommended that Soldier Field be removed from the National Register of Historic Places. In 2006, the recommendation was approved. Despite the Park Service's view that the new stadium "crossed the line in terms of too much renovation,"[70] the glass-and-aluminum bowl that sits within the old neoclassical form makes a bold modernist statement, though it seems at odds with the mayor's well-known preference for the neoclassical tradition. If the mayor ever had any qualms, he kept them to himself.

Millennium Park

Since its opening on July 16, 2004, Millennium Park has become the leading iconic image for the new Chicago, and a global model for an interactive park that departs radically from the nature-in-the-city urban parks inherited from the nineteenth century. The prairie landscape of the Lurie Gardens and the neoclassical peristyle hark back to a former time, but Frank Gehry's fluted stainless steel sails soaring above the Jay Pritzker Pavilion strike a dramatic counterpoint. The monumental *Cloud Gate* sculpture erected by the Indian artist Anish Kapoor reflects the city's skyline in the changing panorama brought by the day's light and weather. The glass twin-tower Crown Fountain designed by Spanish artist Jaume Plensa, the Harris Theater, an ice rink/outdoor restaurant, and displays of public art complete the mosaic of spaces making up the park. The hundreds of people gathered around and under *Cloud Gate* ("the bean," as park users call it) and the crowds of children playing in the waters of Crown Fountain offer a playful contrast to the formal Beaux-Arts design of Grant Park and the wall of turn-of-the-previous-century buildings across Michigan Avenue. Millennium Park became a must-see tourist attraction as soon as it opened, and it has largely eclipsed the Picasso sculpture as the symbolic representation of Chicago.

Timothy Gilfoyle, the author of a lavishly illustrated history of Millennium Park, has observed that it is "a hybrid, a vivid illustration of the intersecting relationship of art, corporate sponsorship, urban politics, and globalization."[71] It is all of these, but Gilfoyle should have put mayoral leadership at the top of list. By Gilfoyle's own account, Millennium Park would not have happened at all if the idea had not first incubated in the mayor's own fertile imagination. It all started in 1997, in his dentist's chair:

> Every six months, mayor Richard M. Daley visited his dentist, whose office overlooked Grant Park. From there, Chicago's most important elected official regularly peered down upon the unsightly railroad cut between Michigan Avenue and Grant Park, a visual pox on what Daley called "the people's country club"—Chicago's lakefront. Then one day, Daley summoned Edward Bedore, mayoral advisor and the city's former chief financial officer, to his office. "Ed," he said, "this is something I've been wanting to do for a long time. See what can be done." Thus was born Millennium Park.[72]

By sheer coincidence, events conspired to make Daley's idea more than a bright idea conjured up in a dentist chair. Randy Mehrberg, the man in charge of lakefront development for the Chicago Park District, was displeased that a sunken, dusty, and largely abandoned rail yard in the corner of Grant Park and directly across the street from the Loop continued to be used as nothing but free parking for employees of the Illinois Central Railroad. His quiet investigations revealed that although the rail company had used the land for a century and a half, the fact that it was no longer used for railroad purposes meant the company's easement was no longer valid, and therefore the city could assert a legal right to take it over for other uses. It took only months for the city to regain title, a development that created the opening Daley needed.[73]

Initial discussions about what to do with this eyesore revolved around the notion of building an intermodal transportation hub, to be covered by what would be not much more than a manicured green space, at a cost of perhaps $30 million. A transportation hub at this location would help knit together the major facilities scattered along the lakefront by providing a direct connection between the Loop and McCormick Place, Soldier Field, and the Museum Campus. Ed Uhlir, the director of research and planning for the Park District, was the first to suggest that the park could be, in effect, a green roof over several tiers of parking, and that the parking could be the key to financing the entire project.[74]

On March 20, 1998, Daley announced a plan to create a 16.5-acre park within a park at the northwest corner of Grant Park, and in May, in an open letter addressed to the people of Chicago, he described Millennium Park as "an exciting new cultural destination for families and children, and an economic magnet for visitors and conventioneers."[75] More than a year of planning and design work went into the proposal. A key element was the transportation center beneath the park, which would link automobile, bus, and rail routes. An underground pedway system was to be constructed to connect several venues: the nearby Metra station, the Monroe Street Garage a few blocks south, Bicentennial Plaza, the Art Institute, and the Cultural Center across Michigan Avenue. The work on the transportation connections required the pooling of resources from several agencies, but the first proposal for the green roof—the park—was quite modest. Initial projections estimated the total cost at around $150 million; $120 million of this amount was to come from revenue bonds, with corporate sponsors and private donors providing the rest.

The park's design contained several conventional features, including an outdoor performance stage, an indoor theater, a skating rink, gardens, and concession stands. The Grant Park Symphony Orchestra would move to the band shell, and additional music festivals would be held there. It was expected that the twenty-five-hundred-space parking garages would generate enough revenue to pay off the bonds. The project was scheduled for completion in the summer of 2000 as a way to celebrate the new millennium.[76]

A year later the public learned that the plans for Millennium Park were being significantly expanded. Ed Uhlir, now Millennium Park project director, commented that "Grant Park is Chicago's front yard. Sadly this 16-acre corner of the park has been a blight for too long. Millennium Park will remedy that with a plan that brings Chicagoans together on a year-round basis."[77] New additions to the plan included a warming house and a restaurant, an ice skating rink/outdoor café, an enlargement of the indoor theater from five hundred to fifteen hundred seats, a commuter

bicycle center, a glass pavilion, and an improved music pavilion (figure 3.5). The size of the proposed park increased by a third, to 24.6 acres, and because of its constantly evolving nature it was not completed in time to celebrate the new century.

During the years of construction, the park became a public relations headache for the mayor, but he steadfastly defended its increasing cost and scale. A year before its opening, in 2003, the mayor sought to place the project within a historical context by characterizing it as a "civic project [that] marks the new Millennium as no other project ever before undertaken in the history of Chicago."[78] Such rhetoric did not change the facts, however: the park was not only late; it was far more costly than anyone (including the mayor), had foreseen. By May 2004, when it finally opened, its sticker price had soared close to $500 million. Daley repeatedly offered reassurances that taxpayers were not going to pay anything toward the park. The city contributed $270 million, but as in case of Soldier Field, the mayor could, and often did, claim that no tax dollars went to the project. Since parking fees would pay the public share, the debt burden could be covered through revenue bonds.[79] Private donors contributed $200 million, and the names of the biggest donors became attached to all the park's significant elements: Wrigley Square, Bank One Promenade, BP Pedestrian Bridge, McCormick Tribune Plaza, and the Lurie Garden.

According to Gilfoyle, as the design of the park evolved, the mayor, in effect, played the role of a "culture broker" who intervened as chief arbiter among the planners and donors involved in the design.[80] More than any of Daley's projects, the Millennium Park initiative put on full display his ability to recruit prominent civic leaders and corporate sponsors to his cause. John Bryan, former CEO of the Sara Lee Corporation; Cindy Pritzker, a member of the family that founded the Hyatt hotel chain; Ann Lurie, widow of real estate developer Robert Lurie; and many other individual donors and corporations contributed to the completion of the park. To assemble this august group, Daley asked Bryan to lead the Millennium Park fundraising efforts. Bryan was well known and well respected in the philanthropic community, having been referred to as a "one-man fundraising machine." Cindy Pritzker, a member of Chicago's wealthiest family dynasty, called him "quite a salesman."[81] Bryan also proved to be a perfect fit, since he shared the mayor's vision. He once noted that "I always tell people, don't ask me to raise money to fix the roof. It has to be something that's exciting. Like they say, it takes some magic to stir people's blood. You wrap the civic cloak around the problem."[82]

Overall, private donors covered $205 million of the park's $475 million price tag. The largest gifts, those from $3 million to $15 million, granted donors the right to make decisions about design and to select architects, artists, landscape design specialists. Of the seventy-five donors to Millennium Park, seven individuals, foundations, and corporations made multimillion-dollar contributions, including the Pritzker family ($15 million), the Crown and Goodman families ($10 million each), Bank One ($5 million), the William Wrigley Jr. Company Foundation ($5 million), and SBC Ameritech ($3 million). The remaining sixty-eight donors contributed $1 million each.

Because the donors represented an elite group of civic leaders, the mayor was attentive to their wishes. Daley granted the more generous donors wide latitude in designing particular features of the park, a method that brought cost overruns and delays but also attracted more donors and increased contributions. The Crown family reviewed early drafts of the fountain, and the Lurie family was consulted on the final design for the gardens. Planners and donors spent many hours in meetings. As they met with the international assortment of architects, artists, landscape designers, and planners who had been invited to submit their ideas and proposals, ambitions ratcheted ever upward. For instance, the biggest contributors to the band shell, the Pritzker family, considered the internationally acclaimed architect Frank Gehry to be a "must have" choice (figure 3.6). At a dinner hosted by the Pritzkers, Daley told Gehry, "'I know what you're going to build. I can design it myself. It's going to be one of these.' Daley raised his hand in the shape of a C. 'Why do I need such a fancy architect to build one of these?'"[83] After several meetings with Gehry, the mayor relented, even though he still did not like key aspects of Gehry's proposal, especially his design for a serpentine bridge. There can be little

FIGURE 3.6

The Jay Pritzker Pavilion in Millennium Park draws thousands for concerts during the summer months. The signature trellis designed by Frank Gehry has become an iconic representation of the new Chicago. Courtesy of user Julien Hautcoeur, Shutterstock Images.

doubt that Daley would have had the final say, if he so wished, but there is also little doubt that donors expected to have their voices heard. This was not a case of Meigs Field, where raw power might win the day. The evolving design of Millennium Park presented, at all times, an occasion for amicable negotiation between the mayor and the city's civic elite.

The complicated process guaranteed that the park's design would be a constant work in progress. Gehry's original proposal called for a music pavilion estimated at $17.8 million, but the actual cost ended up at $50 million. Initial estimates for Gehry's bridge were put at about $8 million, but it cost $13 million by the time it was completed.[84] Similarly, *Cloud Gate*, which was thought to involve an investment of approximately $5 million, ultimately cost $21 million because of the daunting technical difficulties of building the first structure of its kind. Millennium Park and its cost never ceased being a moving target until it opened—and even after.

When the plywood barriers were removed from the perimeter surrounding the construction area in the summer of 2004 it was immediately apparent to everyone that no city had ever built anything quite like Millennium Park. The vaulting stainless steel panels framing the Jay Pritzker Pavilion gave way to a trellis of giant tubes holding a network of speakers; anyone sitting on the ample lawn could hear a pin drop on the stage. Gehry clad his serpentine bridge, the first bridge he had ever built, in panels of stainless steel. Anish Kapoor's 110-ton *Cloud Gate* sculpture seemed to combine serious and playful intent. For years Kapoor's artistic statement had been expressed through oval-shaped balls and curved surfaces, but he had never attempted anything like the scale of *Cloud Gate*. Constructed from apparently seamless, highly polished, reflective steel panels, "the bean" instantly became a shape known around the world.

The Crown Fountain, located in the southwest corner of the park, draws crowds all through the warm months (figure 3.7). Designed by Spanish artist Jaume Plensa, the two fifty-foot glass-block fountains stand at opposite ends of a shallow water-covered plaza. Computer diodes embedded in the glass project the facial images of Chicago residents; the optical display, in effect, is a modernist answer to gargoyles. When the mouths of the faces open, water pours from a pipe into the reflecting pools, dousing the crowds of children waiting to get soaked.

A few steps away, people may stop by a formal restaurant, the Park Café, or have drinks at the outdoor bar-café (in the winter, the same space is an ice-skating rink). Or they may choose to take a brief stroll to the natural prairie landscape of the Lurie Garden,

FIGURE 3.7
Crown Fountain at Millennium Park. Courtesy of user Christian De Araujo, Shutterstock Images.

some of them stopping to dangle their toes in the stream coursing through. Nearby, a pedestrian bridge rises to meet the Modern Wing of the Chicago Art Institute; both were designed by acclaimed architect Renzo Piano. From the top of the museum's pedestrian bridge the entire park spreads out below, bringing into perspective the startling contrast between this twenty-first-century version of a city park and the historic skyline that hovers over it.

Millennium Park has had a tremendous impact on Chicago's cultural image and economy. In the first year after the park opened, more than 1.5 million people came. The numbers climbed to 3 million people by 2006, and to 3.5 million in 2007.[85] According to the study conducted for the planning department, visitors to the park were expected to spend, on the average, $300 per day, and overnight domestic visitors about $150 a day. In 2009, attendance surpassed the 4 million mark.[86] An economic impact study commissioned by the Chicago Department of Planning estimated that Millennium Park would generate $1.4 billion in revenues in the city over the next ten years.[87]

A "Millennium effect" has spread to surrounding areas. Of the more than ten thousand residential units that were scheduled to be constructed nearby by 2015, 25 percent of them were attributed to the presence of the park. In 2005, consultants claimed that the park leveraged a 3 to 5 percent increase in housing values and a tripling in per square foot residential sales.[88] These estimates, of course, did not anticipate the crash in the national housing market that came three years later.

Despite its manifest popularity and economic impact, Millennium Park has had its detractors. The park helped spark an unparalleled high-rise residential explosion in Streeterville, located just north of the Chicago River. In 2005, local residents organized the Streeterville Organization for Active Residents (SOAR), which opposed what it called the Manhattanization of the neighborhood brought on by the construction of several high-rise condominium towers. According to the local alderman, "We've been struggling to negotiate with developers, on a volunteer basis, to reduce the size and alter the projects."[89]

Other critics harped on the theme that Millennium Park was a perfect example of misplaced priorities. A letter to the editor of the *Chicago Tribune* posed (and answered) this question: "Let me get this straight: Millennium Park cost $475 million for 24.5 acres of park with a giant, shiny bean in the middle. Do you think the city could have spent the money a little better—maybe for the crumbling schools or the crumbling streets? What a waste of money."[90] The people splashing in the waters of the Crown Fountain, however, paid no mind to such criticisms. They were just having fun.

The Lakefront Renaissance

Today, Chicago's standing as a global city relies, in equal measure, on a concentration of financial, corporate, and high-end service-sector activities taking place in a forest of architecturally significant high-rise buildings, and a tourist economy that draws fifty million visitors annually from around the world. In 2012, total spending for travel to Chicago amounted to more than $12.76 billion, generated $805.6 million in local tax revenue, and created more than 132,000 jobs.[91] If the City of Spectacle that visitors inhabit did not exist, Chicago's economy would be in shambles and not only because a lot of out-of-town tourists would be missing. According to study conducted in 2004, 39 percent of the visitors to Navy Pier came from the city of Chicago and 32 percent from the suburbs.[92] In Chicago, sooner or later, almost everyone, including the locals, becomes a tourist.

Much of the physical infrastructure that made Chicago's cultural and economic transformation possible was built on Richard M. Daley's watch. Robert Moses was called a master builder, and it may be appropriate to consider the second Daley one as well. Moses was also called, famously, a power broker. This may be said of Daley, too. During his time in office he became, arguably, the most powerful mayor of any American city, and in the next chapter we describe how he managed to pull off this equally challenging task.

4

Power Broker

Robert Caro titled his eleven-hundred-page book about Robert Moses *The Power Broker*. He employed that phrase not only as an acknowledgment of Moses's consummate political skills, but also as a denigration and damnation of Moses's authoritarian style. Caro weaves in exhaustive detail a story describing how Moses accumulated bureaucratic posts until his reach extended over a vast region stretching over at least two states and a multitude of local jurisdictions. Caro's verdict is that his "love of power" turned into a "lust for power."[1] In a similar vein, Richard M. Daley, too, was often accused of wielding autocratic authority. John Kass, a columnist for the *Chicago Tribune*, took to calling him Lord Mayor Shortshanks of Daleyland. Evidently, though, Kass's opinion was not shared by a majority of voters, who returned him to office term after term.

Daley won all his bids for reelection by huge margins. Electronic media, big money, and corporate support were key elements in this remarkable record. Media-based campaigns required massive resources, and these came primarily from the sectors making up the new global economy—corporate heads, lawyers, bankers and financial consultants, insurance companies, advertising and public relations firms, lobbyists, insurance agencies, and the many players in the convention, tourism, and entertainment industry. This was the civic coalition that provided critical financial and political support for Daley's legacy projects—a program that also bought and secured the loyalty of affluent voters and the professional class.

Daley also attended to the task of building a political base that reached far beyond the downtown interests and the civic elite. The lessons from 1983 and 1989 were clear: big money could do many things, but it could not bring an end to the bitter political divisions that had gripped the city since the death of Daley's father. Once in office, Daley carefully attended to the symbolic aspects of identity politics, distributed funds throughout the city for economic development and environmental initiatives, and spent money on addressing neighborhood concerns. By these means he succeeded in defusing a contentious political struggle that had become a staple of Chicago's politics since the racial turmoil of the 1960s, and this freed him to focus much of his considerable energy on his downtown projects.

Daley succeeded in bringing enormous political authority into the mayor's office, but his image as a nearly unchallengeable power broker began to fray in his last two terms. Daley's leadership style seemed to become more erratic and less disciplined over time, with his increasing irritability and annoyance at criticism frequently on public display. In 2002, when the *Economist* referred to him as "King Richard,"[2] the label seemed mostly affectionate; but it took on a different meaning by the end of his fifth term, after the city's bid was rejected by the Olympic Committee in its first round of voting, in October 2009, and in the wake of the Great Recession, which savaged the city's budget. These events marked a sort of beginning of the end for a mayor who had become accustomed to getting almost everything he wanted. When he announced in

2011 that he would not run again, it seemed like a propitious time to make an exit.

The Electoral Juggernaut: Money, Media, and the Civic Coalition

Long before the younger Richard M. Daley won his first mayoral election, the rules of the political game in Chicago had begun to change. It would not have been possible for Richard M. Daley to resurrect a disciplined party machine that much resembled his father's. The chronic infighting that erupted in the years after the senior Daley's abrupt departure reaffirmed the impression that his style of politics had become divisive and dysfunctional. The son was well aware of the negative side of his father's legacy. In his first inaugural address, the new mayor took pains to assure his audience that "you don't hand down policies from generation to generation."[3] A few weeks later he declared, "The city is different now. Politics is different. . . . You're dealing with bureaucrats. You're really the CEO of a large corporation. For all these years, you've had those independents drumming it into the voters' heads, 'You can't vote a straight ticket.' That had an effect. Then there was the Shakman decision [ending most patronage]. And television changed the political equation dramatically."[4] With these comments, Daley was signaling his understanding that the political landscape had changed and that his political style would need to reflect that fact.

Daley's words about the importance of television were prescient, but nothing about his prior history suggested that he was at all suited for the media age. Like his father, he struggled in public settings and in front of a microphone, and was prone to tangling his words in a way that sometimes generated laughter. Once referring to his support of the death penalty, Daley said, "I am pro-death."

On another occasion, responding to criticism that he had not been campaigning hard enough for a candidate he had previously endorsed, he noted, "What do you want me to do? Take my pants off?"[5] Fortunately for Daley, media-based politics brought with it an army of media consultants, professionals working in public relations firms, and advisers working in a beefed-up mayor's press office, all eager to massage the mayor's words and public persona. Earl Bush, who had been, many years before, Richard J. Daley's press secretary, had famously requested at a media conference, "Don't write what he says, write what he means."[6] The coterie of professionals surrounding the younger Daley worked hard to make such advice unnecessary.

In 1989 Daley's campaign hired Bush to assist the candidate with his public appearances. The positive press the new mayor received following the election indicated that his media consultants had done an admirable coaching job. Joel Kaplan, City Hall writer for the *Chicago Tribune*, and Thomas Hardy, the newspaper's political writer, expressed surprise when assessing Daley's first one hundred days in office. They noted that "upon assuming the mayoralty April 24 . . . Rich Daley was transformed. He began to speak clearly, if not elegantly, and was often funny, even quotable. It became clear that he relishes his new job and enjoys it in his own low-key, hands-on fashion. . . . His repartee with reporters and general aw-shucks demeanor has resulted in an unprecedented amount of good press for the new mayor. The credit for this is attributed to Daley's own personality and a staff that carefully packages his daily pronouncements."[7] And in this way did Richard M. Daley became, arguably, the first of the nation's big-city mayors to come into office through a marriage of corporate money and media, a political style that today characterizes the American political system from top to bottom.

Although the Daley name worked against Richard M. in some quarters, for corporate donors and labor unions it still held considerable cachet. Irving J. Rein, a communications consultant to the future mayor from 1981 to 1989, noted that "in Chicago, the name Daley stood for job expansion, new building projects, and excellent maintenance of infrastructure. The Daleys' reputation for delivering on their promises engendered the trust of Chicago's big money."[8] In his campaigns, the younger Daley relied upon direct mail and television ads crafted by skilled political consultants, and this kind of campaigning cost a lot of money. For the 1989 campaign, he raised $7 million, most of it from city contractors, labor unions, and the firms of the new service or global economy. In that campaign the financial services industry contributed roughly 10 percent, and the legal community produced 5.5 percent of his campaign receipts. Roughly 4 percent of his campaign contributions came from the tourist-related sector, including a $10,000 gift from the owner of the Chicago Blackhawks hockey team, and another $10,000 from a livery firm from Frankfort, Illinois (which offers carriage rides in tourist areas of the city). The union representing hotel employees also contributed $30,000 to the candidate's war chest. By contrast, government officials produced only 1.6 percent of Daley's financial support, which was even less than they had given in Mayor Harold Washington's final race for office in 1987.[9]

A shared vision resulted in a mutually supportive alliance that lasted through all of Daley's years in office. Daley needed to raise money from private contributors for his campaigns, but it was clear that even larger volumes of private capital would be required to fund his ambitious lakefront projects. On the other side of the equation, the members of the civic coalition that helped put him in office stood to reap big rewards if Daley were successful. In a feature story published in the *Chicago Reader*, a local journalist, David Moberg, described how a well-organized political operation seemed to be emerging from this alliance: "[This is] not a machine of pinky rings and tavern owners, but one of alligator briefcases and law-firm partners. In some cases, especially in the big law firms, there may be a hope of a quid pro quo attached to these big donations; compared with the past, however, the payoffs for most of the political contributions are likely to be less direct, but more lucrative."[10] Daley used whatever patronage remained from the Democratic organization and grafted onto that an operation that distributed benefits from contracts, property transactions, professional services, and public money to his allies in business and high-level professions. As two scholars who studied this arrangement observed, "There are still patronage jobs given to precinct workers and contracts to contributing businessmen just like under the Richard J. Daley machine. But now there are the amenities like flowers in the Parkway, wrought iron fences, Millennium Park, and most important, a tax structure favorable to the new global economy."[11]

Daley took care to nurture the city hall–corporate connection. In 2000, Daley persuaded corporate leaders to merge two civic organizations, World Business Chicago and the Chicago Partnership for Economic Development. The Civic Committee of the Commercial Club of Chicago had founded World Business Chicago only two years before, with the stated goal of increasing international business investment in the Chicago metropolitan region. Daley had created the Chicago Partnership for Economic Development in 1999 with the aim of promoting business growth in the city; funded by the city and the private sector, this group intended to help Chicago position itself as an influential player in a highly competitive global economy. Bringing these two entities together under the World Business Chicago label institutionalized the increasingly close relationship that Daley had been forging through the 1990s with key leaders in the corporate community.

The new organization was cochaired by the mayor and Michael O'Halleran, then president and CEO of Aon Corporation. At the press conference announcing their collaboration, both men enthusiastically described the benefits to come from their partnership. Daley noted that "World Business Chicago is now in the best position to reach out to international businesses looking for a North American home. And by home, I mean anywhere in this region. We are one region, and one economy. We go forward together, or we will be left behind together. If a business doesn't want to locate in Chicago, so be it, it's the company's choice. I would much rather that they move to Palatine or Markham than to Atlanta."[12] O'Halleran agreed, noting that "under the leadership of Mayor Daley, the new organization will maneuver the Chicago region into the prominent position on the world map of great cities that was first defined generations ago in the Burnham Plan."[13] Bringing Burnham's name into the conversation squared the circle by connecting politics with noble ideals (figure 4.1).

World Business Chicago culminated a decade's worth of collaborative efforts. J. Paul Beitler, president of the Miglin Beitler Management Corporation and the Beitler Company, had supported Daley's first successful mayoral bid in 1989. A big downtown developer and a Republican who lived in one of the wealthiest North Shore suburbs, Winnetka, Beitler maintained a laser focus on the Loop and its immediate environs. Uninterested in the neighborhoods, which he seemed to consider irrelevant, Beitler enthusiastically supported Daley's big projects; above all, he wanted a downtown boom to take off.

FIGURE 4.1

Mayor Daley opens *Revealing Chicago: An Aerial Portrait by Terry Evans,* June 9, 2005, at Millennium Park. Commissioned by Openlands Project and Chicago Metropolis 2020, the exhibit featured more than eighty oversize photos and was displayed from June 10 to October 10, 2005. Courtesy of user thetodd, Flickr.

The motive for Beitler's interest in Daley's success was shared by other North Shore suburban business leaders who headed up firms located in or near the Loop. For entrepreneurs like Beitler, the mayor's leadership nurtured a stable investment environment. Campaign contributions gave them an avenue for exercising political influence. Beitler put it succinctly when he said:

> We are not out to buy a piece of Chicago. We already own a substantial piece of Chicago. The property that we own pays more property taxes as a single building than most communities. The unfortunate thing is since we don't live in the city, we don't have

any right to vote and participate in the decision-making process. Most of those who gave do not live in the city. The only way we can make our voices heard is to support financially the best candidate who will do the best job for creating a city environment that will be fertile ground for development and business.[14]

Clearly, corporate leaders regarded use of their financial support for the mayor not only as a substitute for votes at the ballot box but, of greater consequence, as a way of inserting themselves into the city's policy process.

An analysis of contributions to Daley from August 25, 1999, to February 19, 2007, reveals that corporations or individuals headquartered or residing in the near north lakefront, the Loop, Lincoln Park, and suburban Winnetka gave more than $8 million to his reelection efforts. During this period, the top five individuals who made the highest contributions included self-identified Republicans or active supporters of Republican election races. Bruce Rauner, Fred Krehbiel, Richard Driehaus, Sam Zell, and Patrick Ryan all looked past party identification; much more important to them was that they shared the mayor's global Chicago vision. In 2010, Rauner, chairman of GTCR, a venture capital and private equity firm and Daley's largest single contributor, was appointed by the mayor as chairman of the influential Chicago Convention and Tourism Bureau. In 2014 he emerged as the Republican front-runner in the Illinois governor's race. He went on to beat Democratic governor Pat Quinn and was elected the forty-second governor of the state of Illinois.

Others supporters included Republican Ronald Gidwitz and James McHugh. Gidwitz had once led as CEO of Helene Curtis, and ran as a candidate for governor in 2006. His wife, Christina Gidwitz, was the daughter of James Kemper, the founder of Kemper insurance. Gidwitz had long served on a number of civic, cultural, and education boards. He provided vocal backing for Daley's privatization efforts. McHugh led an influential construction company that had benefited from its relationship with the city for many decades. In 1989 he gave $27,000 to Daley's mayoral campaign. All through Daley's tenure McHugh's company was awarded city projects along the lakefront.

For developers, the mayor's policies came at a crucial time. During the years of the Washington administration, McHugh's company had come under financial pressure because developers were expected to make contributions to a low-income housing trust fund. Daley went to some lengths to revise those policies. He opposed an ordinance that required projects with ten or more units to allocate at least 25 percent of the units for moderate-income families. Under pressure to meet goals for housing set-asides, the mayor eventually approved a less restrictive version of the ordinance; apparently he thought fewer requirements would encourage private developers to invest in the city.[15]

The mayor's close attention to their needs played well with the business community. A survey of CEOs conducted in April 1998 revealed that 72 percent gave Daley good or excellent ratings for his efforts to advance economic growth and support policies that were advantageous to business. Only 24 percent gave the mayor fair or poor marks. In the same survey, Republican Jim Edgar received 64 percent favorable and 33 percent unfavorable ratings. Dennis Whetstone, president and CEO of the Illinois Chamber, once noted, "Rich Daley can work with anybody. The thing that's remarkable for me is . . . I have yet to find a CEO who is really a Rich Daley basher."[16]

Daley's initiatives also brought him favor with the professionals working in the global economy and with middle-class homeowners and gentrifiers. As one political observer noted, "We have a growing black middle class in Chicago, and they approve [of] what Daley is doing. Property values are property values. People with investments want stability."[17] Wealthy and middle-class homeowners liked what his programs did for neighborhoods and for property values. Professionals living downtown were dazzled by new amenities and the city's policies to promote culture. Like Daley's alliance with the business leadership, this bargain, too, was beneficial to all parties.

In 2011, in a retrospective interview about his time in office, Daley spoke fondly of the public-private civic alliance that had given him the capacity to translate his lakefront vision into a reality. He once noted that "business has been the backbone of everything I do: education, public housing, jobs, economic development, charities, and foundations. I don't care who they support politically, business leaders have been, and need to continue to be, in the forefront."[18] At a speech given at suburban Wheaton College, he declared that "I believe the success of Chicago has been [because of] public-private partnerships."[19] In 2012, at the annual Aspen Ideas Festival, hosted by the Aspen Institute, he reflected that "the most interesting thing is the public-private partnership. . . . You take Millennium Park, school reform in Chicago. It isn't the government it's the business community and not-for-profits working with the city in order to basically improve the quality of life. . . . So everybody is talking about public-private partnerships in America. They should go right to Chicago and talk to all the business people—many of whom are here, and they will tell you about public-private partnership; every museum, every university, every hospital, public-private partnerships."[20] The speech revealed much about Daley's approach to power. Many people thought that he governed from the top down, just as his father had, but the people admitted to Daley's inner circle had a completely different understanding.

The "People's Mayor"

In an April 4, 1989, special election, Richard M. Daley defeated the incumbent, Eugene Sawyer, to become Chicago's mayor. Selected as an interim mayor by the city council a few weeks after Harold Washington's death, Sawyer had been in the office for about eighteen months, until the special election was held to complete Washington's four-year term. Daley was acutely aware that he would have to build a base of support for the next regular election, which was just two years away, and he appreciated that by defeating an African American candidate he risked a significant political hazard. Immediately, he praised the late Mayor Washington and gave assurances that Washington's legacy would be protected. "[Washington] opened city government to many citizens who felt excluded and ignored. As long as I'm mayor, those doors will remain open to all our citizens."[21] In his inaugural address he told his audience that he intended to govern inclusively. One could hear the speechwriter's craft at work in the mayor's soaring rhetoric: "Like an orchestra, a city is made up of many sounds, the voices of people and communities, speaking out for their concerns and their fair share. Each of these voices has a place. . . . The mayor's job is to act as the conductor, blending the sounds so that no voice is drowned out and city policies serve the common interest of the Chicago community. Today, I've been handed the conductor's baton. And to the people of Chicago, wherever you live, let me assure you that your voices will be heard."[22] Barely more than a year later he told a reporter for the *Chicago Tribune*, "Now you [have to] ask [people] what they think."[23] The title of the *Tribune*'s story, "Nation's Mayors Find a New Daley and a New Era," demonstrated that Daley's attempt to cast himself as a

FIGURE 4.2

Mayor Richard M. Daley at the annual Von Steuben German parade in Chicago on September 12, 2009. Daley reached out to the city's racial and ethnic groups during his tenure to develop the electoral support that kept him in office for more than two decades. Courtesy of user TheeErin, Flickr.

democrat with a small "d" was working, with both the press and the public (figure 4.2).

The newly elected mayor and his political team immediately set about constructing an electoral coalition diverse enough to keep him in office. In his father's day, ethnic voters descended from a mixture of Poles, Irish, Italians, Eastern Europeans, and Jews were the main components of the machine; in addition, in exchange for patronage and payoffs, a few powerful black politicians delivered the African American vote. The younger Daley realized that he would govern under a very different set of circumstances. The influential African American publication *Jet* magazine noted that in an interview after his victory, "Daley sought to assure Blacks that there would be no personnel bloodbath in City Hall."[24] Two weeks later, at his swearing-in, Daley called for a permanent end to the "Council Wars." Daley mollified some critics when he admitted to *Jet* that "Harold Washington was a tough act to follow. He gave a sense of belonging to many who felt disenfranchised by their own government. And whatever your politics, you had to appreciate his strength, leadership and commitment to our city."[25] Praise like that brought much goodwill from African American political leaders who remained skeptical about the new mayor and his intentions.

Daley quickly moved a diverse array of community leaders into city government. Eleven of the twenty-one members of his first cabinet were from the African American, Hispanic, or Asian communities. Even though Chicago was less than half a decade past the council wars, no one publicly complained about the ethnic makeup of the mayor's cabinet. All but the most obtuse members of Chicago's political establishment understood the new political realities. Aldermen who for years had resisted Harold Washington's policy proposals approved a program to promote minority supervisors in the police department. Daley also persuaded them to pass a minority set-aside ordinance, which required that 25 percent of city contracts be given to minority-owned businesses, and 5 percent to businesses owned by women.

Daley reached out to Latinos, too. In the 1980s Latinos were emerging as a powerful electoral force, and Daley intended to garner their support. Congressman Luis Gutiérrez was one of the first Latino leaders to endorse the mayor, and over the years the two politicians formed a symbiotic relationship. In the 1990s the mayor appointed several Latino leaders to important positions, including Daniel Alvarez Sr. as commissioner of the city's Department of Human Services, Raymond Orozco as the city's fire commissioner, Benjamin Reyes as general services commissioner, and Mary Gonzalez-Koenig as the executive director of the Mayor's Office of

Employment and Training. He also appointed Miriam Santos, an up-and-coming Puerto Rican Hispanic, as the city treasurer.

The mayor also recruited Latinos to fill vacant aldermanic posts. In 1993, Daley appointed Ricardo Muñoz as alderman of the Twenty-Second Ward, and in 1996 he chose Danny Solis as alderman of the Twenty-Fifth Ward. Solis emerged as one of staunchest supporters of the mayor and his agenda. Daley's connections with the Latino community paid electoral dividends all through the 1990s; for instance, in 1996 Daley carried more than 90 percent of the vote in the heavily Hispanic Twelfth Ward, which included the predominantly Mexican neighborhood Little Village. In 2007 a leading Latino activist, Juan Andrade, president of the United States Hispanic Leadership Institute, enthused, "It was incredible. It was just incredible. We just went,— My God, this guy's really a breath of fresh air. He's nothing like his father."[26]

Years earlier than most of his peers in other cities, Daley realized that the gay and lesbian community was becoming an important inner-city voting bloc. In June 1989, on the occasion of the twentieth anniversary of the city's Gay and Lesbian Pride Parade, he became the first mayor to lead the parade,[27] and made annual appearances every year after. Long before it had become a hot-button issue nationally, he pushed for giving homosexual partners of city workers the same benefit plans that married couples received. In the mid-1990s he persuaded the aldermen to pass the Domestic Partners Ordinance, which provided health and bereavement plans to gay couples. When the opportunity emerged in 2002, Daley appointed Tom Tunney (Forty-Fourth Ward) as the first openly gay member of the city council. These actions ensured that gays would become a reliable core constituency throughout his mayoral tenure.

Daley's success in defusing the divisive politics that had long bedeviled Chicago was a notable and unexpected achievement, although, as may be expected, he continued to have his share of detractors. Alderman Robert Shaw, for instance, once expressed his disapproval of Daley when he observed, "Whatever suit he's got on that day, he just pulls his plan out of his vest pocket. We need to talk about more than an abandoned building that needs to be razed. We need to talk about bringing the whole neighborhood together, about curtailing some of the criminal activity." Lu Palmer, a highly vocal political activist, called Daley "public enemy No. 1" of the black community and joked that "I've got these 'Dump Daley' buttons. I can't hold on to them. I'll leave here with a 'Dump Daley' button on, and I can't wear it all day. Someone will want it."[28] Maybe the African Americans Palmer was talking about were taking the buttons as souvenirs, because the opposition always came up short on Election Day, when it counted most.

In April 1999, when he ran for his fourth term, Daley received 68.9 percent of the vote, despite a high-profile challenge from a longtime African American congressman, Bobby Rush. Even Rev. Jesse Jackson Sr., at a time when his son was being mentioned as a potential mayoral candidate, acknowledged that Daley "has certainly reached out—you see him frequenting the black community, the Latino community. [He has a] quiet, coalition-building style. He's responsive when he's called. We have disagreements about things structural, not things personal or petty. He's a problem solver as opposed to an antagonistic fighter."[29] Clearly, Daley had managed to disarm even some of his staunchest critics.

The electoral juggernaut Daley constructed put him effectively beyond challenge at the ballot box. Six years after his first election, Daley managed to win 21.6 percent of the African American vote (compared to only 9 percent when he first ran in 1989). During the 1995 election he won more than a fifth of the vote in nineteen predominantly African American wards in the south and west sides of the city. In the seven majority Latino wards, Daley received 80.6 percent of the vote that year.[30] Daley's dominance twelve years later (in the 2007 election) was based on a strong showing not only in the minority wards, but nearly everywhere else in the city, too. His overwhelming electoral support extended from the Bungalow Belt of the white, working-class residents of the Southwest and Northwest neighborhoods, the white lakefront liberals, and to the solidly Hispanic and African American neighborhoods. He found even stronger support in gentrified and wealthy neighborhoods located in and well beyond the downtown. With his base of support this broad, no challenger stood a chance.

Frustrated Visionary and Autocrat

The mayoral election held in February 2003 posed no threat to Daley. His main opponent, Rev. Paul Jakes Jr., was not exactly a heavyweight capable of galvanizing the African American community. Daley comfortably won with 78 percent of the vote. Margins like this could not be explained solely by the sophistication and resources of Daley's well-oiled reelection machine. The constant praise Daley received in and beyond the city had already elevated him to urban superhero status. Like his father, he had become so synonymous with Chicago that the city and his persona could hardly be distinguished. Chicago's turn to culture, entertainment, and urban amenities received constant national and international attention, with Daley invariably placed at the center of the action. For instance, a story in *USA Today*, published just before the unveiling of Millennium Park, noted that "when Millennium Park is dedicated this weekend, the ceremony will celebrate a landmark civic achievement and a 15-year quest by Mayor Richard Daley to 'green' this industrial metropolis."[31]

In the spring of 2007, Daley swept into his sixth term in office with more than 71 percent of the vote. He faced only nominal opposition—two largely unknown African American candidates, Cook County circuit clerk Dorothy Brown and former Harold Washington aide Doc Walls. Daley was beyond effective challenge at the polls, even though he had been dogged for years by a series of corruption scandals, including a highly publicized federal investigation of illegal hiring practices, and bribes paid by trucking companies for city contracts.

Despite the mayor's long string of successes, as time passed his governing style began to generate some uneasiness. In the run-up to the 2003 election, Daley had pushed through the renovation of Soldier Field by working behind the scenes and pointedly avoiding public debate. And just a few weeks later, on the night of April 1, he stepped outside the arena of democratic engagement entirely by sending bulldozers in the dark of night to carve Xs into the Meigs Field runways. The mayor invoked Daniel Burnham's name on behalf of his vision to turn Northerly Island into a public park, but the methods he used made some people think the mayor's high-minded rhetoric sounded a bit self-serving.

The Meigs Field episode signaled a decisive shift toward a more authoritarian style, and it surfaced more and more when he was dealing with political opposition and the press. The incident provoked expressions of alarm. In the estimation of the editorial writers of the *Chicago Tribune*, "The unilateral strike was a tactic practiced for more than 20 years by his father, Mayor Richard J. Daley, another Chicago mayor with a huge political following and a legendary arsenal of power who wielded his unchallenged authority in dozens of instances that changed the face of Chicago forever. . . . As Daley the Second undoubtedly learned at his father's kitchen table, when 8 out of 10 voters give you their approval, sometimes you just ignore the critics, do what you want and let history be the judge."[32] A poll conducted by the *Tribune* indicated that 65 percent of Illinois voters disapproved the mayor's decision to close the airport,[33] and a *Daily Southtown* article referred to Daley as "the prince of Chicago."[34] Meigs Field even received national attention; Republican senator James Inhofe of Oklahoma, for instance, described the closing as an "act of arrogant recklessness."[35] A National Public Radio story about the incident noted that this "unilateral decision brings to mind how his father, Richard J. Daley, long wielded power here."[36] The mayor might have wanted the public to think of Burnham, but, in this instance, for most people his father came to mind.

Not everyone, though, saw the mayor's covert strike in a negative light. For several years the Canadian city of Toronto had been embroiled in a frustratingly slow process of redeveloping its waterfront. In a series of newspaper articles, the Toronto media criticized their mayor for inadequate leadership and held Daley up as an example he should emulate. The *Globe and Mail* noted that

> Mr. Daley is famous for having transformed his city's waterfront into a showpiece, with beautiful parks and brilliant cultural facilities. . . . Does anybody remember what Mr. Daley did about Meigs Field, his own version of our island airport, after he got tired of trying to persuade various entrenched agencies and interests to close it down so that he could make another waterfront park? He dispatched a platoon of city bulldozers that broke through its fences in the dead of the night and plowed its single runway back into dirt. . . . So hey, Mr. Daley. Tell our guy about that. Tell him to buck up. Tell him that nobody is going to do anything for him unless he makes them do it. Tell him that it's good to have an accomplishment or two to boast about at re-election time.[37]

In Chicago, too, there were people willing to excuse Daley's methods if they approved of the results. Governor Rod Blagojevich's spokeswoman commented that "this is a landing strip smack dab in the middle of downtown Chicago. The governor thinks closing Meigs Field is a good idea."[38] The Millennium Park project brought a similar public reaction. The project took more than two years longer than originally projected, and stories of cost overruns, construction delays, and questionable contract practices became a staple of local press coverage. In the end, however, even opponents like Patricia Nolan of the Neighborhood Capital Budget Group, who had referred to the park as a boondoggle, conceded that "it's a monumental architectural achievement. . . . Nobody can argue with how it turned out."[39] Obviously, the Meigs episode could be interpreted in a variety of ways, and in the end it probably redounded to Daley's benefit.

Daley telegraphed a growing impatience with political opposition and criticism, and frequently put his ill temper on display in press conferences and exchanges with reporters. No doubt his sour mood was related, to some degree, to the city's deteriorating fiscal condition. Increasingly, Daley turned to the sale, leasing, or contracting out of public assets to raise the revenues needed to plug budget shortfalls. In 2005, the city consummated a deal to lease the Chicago Skyway (an elevated toll road connecting commuters to Indiana and I-80) to a group of investors for $1.83 billion, and in 2006 the privatization of four downtown parking garages yielded $563 million. Daley also explored the possibility of privatizing McCormick Place and Midway Airport. In 2008, he rammed a highly controversial seventy-five-year deal that surrendered downtown parking fees to a Morgan Stanley firm for $1.16 billion. As with previous deals, the city used the proceeds to cover budget gaps and short-term expenses. This strategy moved fiscal problems to future budgets and allowed the mayor to avoid increasing taxes or implementing service cuts on his watch.

In 2008 Daley found himself in the middle of an acrimonious controversy when he decided to back a plan by the board of the Chicago Children's Museum to move this popular institution from Navy Pier to the Daley Bicentennial Plaza in the northeast corner of Grant Park. The proposal included plans for a $100 million structure, and because it would be built on park land, most of the cost would be picked up by bonds issued by the Chicago Park District. Many people thought the arrangement was a bit incestuous, because the initiative was led by members of the Pritzker family, who enjoyed particularly close relationships with the mayor; billionaire Jean Pritzker was chair of the board of directors of the museum, and her cousin, Penny Pritzker, was a business entrepreneur and formidable political fund-raiser who served as the national finance chair of President Obama's 2008 campaign. (A couple of years later, in 2010, Daley appointed Bryan Traubert, Pritzker's husband, as Chicago Park District board president.)

The New Eastside Association of Residents (NEAR), which represented the affluent population living in the wall of high-rises on Randolph Street along the park's northern border, loudly opposed the project, and they were soon joined by an assortment of other influential players, including Preservation Chicago, Friends of Downtown, Landmarks Illinois, the Committee to Keep Lincoln Park Public, Friends of the Parks, and Save Grant Park. The Randolph Street residents were partly motivated by NIMBYism concerns about crowding, but what truly brought this diverse array of groups together was the idea that a new building in the park would violate court rulings going back more than a century based on the principle that the park must be preserved from development.

Daley was practically apoplectic that anyone would stand in the way of something he considered so obviously beneficial. When Brendan Reilly, the newly elected alderman of the Forty-Second Ward (which encompassed the area north of park), announced his opposition, Daley went for the jugular. A reporter for the *Chicago Reader* website summarized Daley's reaction:

> Witness how Daley reacted to rookie alderman Brendan Reilly (42nd), who after weeks of community meetings decided to go with the majority of his constituents and oppose the mayor's plans to move the Chicago Children's Museum to Grant Park. Daley laced into Reilly, albeit screwing up his name. He was so riled he misquoted Reilly in his efforts to tarnish him. Reilly and his constituents, he insisted, were child-hating bigots whose opposition imperiled the future of the entire city. His face got red. His hair fell across his forehead. He snarled. He sneered. He threatened.[40]

The episode made it appear, to some, that Daley was beginning to lose control of his own behavior.

The city council approved the plans for the Chicago Children's Museum in June 2008, but the 33–16 vote showed that an unprecedented number of aldermen refused to back the mayor's proposal. The council's approval followed an equally unusual split 6–3 vote by the city's zoning commission. Despite these actions, ultimately the Children's Museum did not move. Court challenges did not stop the project, but fund-raising for the project lagged because of a struggling economy and a divided city leadership. The increasingly bleak fiscal condition of the city and the arrival of a new mayor who was not interested in pursuing the plan finally sunk it for good. The Children's Museum episode marked the first time in all his years in office that Daley could not automatically count on the backing of the city council and his civic alliance. In the end he

FIGURE 4.3

The Olympic rings at the McCormick Tribune Plaza, Millennium Park, November 25, 2008. Chicago's business and civic elites supported Mayor Daley's election campaign bids since they viewed his ambitious lakefront redevelopment program as a prerequisite to the city's quest for global status. Courtesy of user Mike Warot, Flickr.

succeeded in gaining enough political support, but it turned out to be a pyrrhic victory won by a wounded warrior.

Daley's pursuit of the summer 2016 Olympics and Paralympic Games demonstrated that right to the end of his last term in office he was still capable of mobilizing powerful constituencies for big undertakings—indeed, the Olympic bid was the most audacious initiative he had ever undertaken (figure 4.3). The civic elite would be required to raise billions of dollars, and the city would have to find financing for several big infrastructure projects and be willing to devote extraordinary levels of public services to a single event. As with the Children's Museum, Daley proceeded without much deliberation and public debate. In September 2007, Chicago became one of seven cities to formally submit a bid to host the 2016 Games. A Chicago 2008 Bid Review Task Force dating back to the mid-1990s had concluded that "it is simply not good business risk" to invest $15 million on a 2008 bid,[41] and it recommended that the city wait and consider a 2012 Olympic bid. But Daley had never given up on the idea of hosting the Olympics.

Like the 1893 Columbian Exposition and the 1933 Century of Progress, the Olympics would last only a brief season, but Daley promised big payoffs, and he became fond of comparing the Olympic bid to those two events. In a press conference he waxed on about the transformative effects he expected to see: "Cities always have to change. If you don't change you live in the past, and if you live in the past, you have no future. When the Olympics leave, what do you have? You have housing, you have parks, you have improvements in schools, you have improvements in public transportation."[42] Daley argued that the infrastructure investments would help transform large swaths of the South Side, renovate an aging city transportation system, and bring improvements to streets, the lakefront, and urban amenities. The mayor promised that market-rate housing would be sold off after the Games, and that more than 20 percent of the residential housing built for the Olympics would be reserved for low- and moderate-income families. According to the plans, the Olympic stadium would be turned into a ten-thousand-seat community amphitheater for concerts and other performances.

A truly extraordinary infrastructure program would have been required to host the Olympics. Daley promised that construction and the Games themselves would add almost $7 billion to the local economy. But the cost of obtaining those benefits would be enormous. The mayor proposed a $500 million Olympic Stadium on the South Side, as well as a $1 billion Olympic Village to be constructed a few blocks south of McCormick Place. The estimated price tag of under $5 billion was, though, far below what recent Olympic Games had cost. The 2004 Games in Athens cost at least $12 billion; the 2008 Games in Beijing officially neared $44 billion (but probably cost at least $50 billion), and the 2012 Games in London cost $14 billion.

To mobilize the $25 million needed to make a bid, the mayor reached out to corporate leaders and philanthropists. Patrick Ryan, founder and former CEO of Aon Corporation, led the fund-raising effort. Fund-raisers held in March 2007 yielded $9.4 million, with $12 million more collected in July 2008 and an additional $5 million in August 2009. These and an assortment of other funds and pledges totaling $70 million supported the domestic and international phases of the bid.[43] The mayor guaranteed that, if needed, the city would commit $500 million to ensure the smooth functioning of the Games. In spite of a rising volume of public opposition, Daley persuaded the city council to back his commitment, which it did with a 49–0 vote. The city also assumed full financial responsibility for the proposed $4.8 billion operating budget at a time when the city's fiscal condition was rapidly deteriorating.[44]

Daley often expressed his conviction that the Olympics would be a pivotal moment in Chicago's quest to become a leading global city. "You don't realize the importance, the global importance that Chicago will receive," he proclaimed. "If you get this, it's a major coup for the whole marketing strategy of Chicago."[45] On September 21, 2009, just days before the winning city was to be announced in Copenhagen, Daley held a press conference at Navy Pier to discuss Chicago's Olympic aspirations. Appearing with Governor Pat Quinn, Daley claimed that "without the spending boost from tourism, unemployment in metropolitan Chicago would have surpassed 15% last year. Tourism goes a long way just in putting people to work."[46] Quinn was equally enthusiastic, if rather more vague: "Tourism is a key part of our economy in this growing world. . . . This is a very important part of our 21st century economy." A lot was being promised, and considering the resources the Games would require, it had to be.

The Olympics bid brought into full view the mayor's increasingly autocratic style and dismissive rejection of dissent. In an interview with a reporter for the *Chicago Sun-Times* he said of his critics, "You're against it. You were against Millennium Park. . . . You were against Soldiers Field. You were against Meigs Field. What else were you against? You're against a lot. . . . But, in the next five years, six years, tell me one [other] thing that can bring jobs and economic opportunities and, besides that, guarantee an investment by the federal government [of] billions of dollars in infrastructure. If you have something better, I'd love to see it."[47] The reporters, perplexed by this outburst, busily took notes for the next day's papers.

The announcement of the Olympic Committee's vote in Copenhagen on October 2, 2009, had all the hallmarks of a reality TV show, with a global simulcast playing upon the faces of the expectant crowds gathered in four different cities. Daley and his entourage, which included President Obama and First Lady Michelle Obama, White House senior adviser Valerie Jarrett, Governor Quinn, Oprah Winfrey, retired NBA player Dikembe Mutombo, and Olympians Jackie Joyner-Kersee and Mike Conley Sr., gathered in anticipation of the announcement. When Chicago was rejected on the giant outdoor screen in the first round, it drew a gasp from a crowd gathered in the plaza surrounding the Picasso statue in front of City Hall. It was a bitter pill for the mayor to swallow. The next day, when Daley arrived in Chicago, he displayed an uncharacteristic air of disappointment and defeat. Even before

the Olympic fiasco, his approval rating had fallen to 35 percent—
mostly as a result of the parking meter lease—and now it seemed
obvious that he had pursued the Olympic bid even though it carried a multitude of financial risks and potential cost overruns.
Alderman Joe Moore (Forty-Ninth Ward) noted that Daley came
back to a ballooning deficit and an "angry and cynical electorate."
He added, "I've always admired the mayor's ability to think big and
do big things, but I do take issue with the mayor's penchant for
secrecy, and I think that harmed him locally in terms of the bid."[48]
Indeed, the wounds went deep enough to make Daley consider
leaving city hall altogether.

Facing increasing fiscal pressure, rising disapproval from a un-
settled public, growing media criticism, and an increasingly res-
tive city council, Daley decided not to seek reelection for a seventh
term. By the time he left office, his governing style had become a
familiar echo from Chicago's political past. At the beginning of his
classic collection of essays, *Boss*, Mike Royko observed that the father, Richard J. Daley, had come to be a defining figure in Chicago's
history: "If a man ever reflected a city, it was Richard J. Daley and
Chicago. In some ways, he was this town at its best—strong, hard
driving, working feverishly, pushing, building, driven by ambitions so big they seemed Texas-boastful. In other ways, he was this
city at its worst—arrogant, crude, conniving, ruthless, suspicious,
intolerant. He wasn't graceful, suave, witty, or smooth. But then
this is not Paris or San Francisco. He was raucous, sentimental,
hot-tempered, practical, devious, big, and powerful. This is, after
all, Chicago."[49] United States congressman Luis Gutiérrez, who had
provided crucial support in every one of Richard M. Daley's election bids, once noted "Mayor Daley cringes when you call him a
boss, but that, in fact, is what he's become."[50] It may not be where
he started, but perhaps too many years with too little political

opposition had tempted him into thinking he should have his way every time, or his critics be damned.

The Temptations of Power

For nearly all of his five and a half terms in office, Richard M. Daley governed without effective opposition. His reelection campaigns were financed by corporate and private donors who shared, and benefited from, his vision of Chicago as a twenty-first-century global city. It was hard for Daley's opponents to get traction. The only notable group to put forth a challenge was the Neighborhood Capital Budget Group, which represented a collection (rather than a coalition) of more than two hundred community organizations. Its executive director, Jacqueline Leavy, maintained that the mayor's programs neglected the communities not located near the lakefront; "there is," she said, "an increasing preoccupation with the cosmetic. Neighborhood areas continue to struggle, industry continues to leave for the suburbs and public transportation continues to decline."[51] Most local and virtually all national media, though, constantly praised Daley as the architect of a transformed city that had gone beyond the urban crisis and its industrial past. He accumulated enough power to realize an evolving and increasingly optimistic vision of what the city could become; and as Daley himself was fond of noting, his critics were not able to offer a compelling vision of their own.

Despite the high level of support he commanded in his years as mayor, Daley's legacy appears today to be in tatters. His lakefront transformation attracted so much attention during his tenure that it was sometimes difficult to see beyond it, but by the time he left office, the other side of the ledger was coming into full view. When he handed off to Rahm Emanuel in 2011, he left the city in a fragile fiscal state, and the lingering effects of the economic downturn came together with stories of crime, trouble in the schools, and a range of other social problems. After 2010, gang violence put Chicago on the map almost as much as did its great architecture and cultural scene. This is a surprisingly ambiguous legacy for a mayor who accomplished so much. In the next chapter, we explain how this came to be.

5

Richard M. Daley's Ambiguous Legacy

It may seem unlikely in hindsight, but the broad support that Richard M. Daley enjoyed during his time in office can be explained in part by the early reputation he established as a reformer and manager. A few weeks after entering City Hall, he decommissioned the $50,000 stretch limo Eugene Sawyer had used and put it up for sale, and called for revisiting hiring practices to ensure that qualifications, not political connections and clout, would determine future city employment. Against union objections he privatized a wide range of city services. In an op-ed piece published in the *New York Times* just weeks after his full-term reelection in 1991, Daley conveyed his support for privatization by noting that "we've introduced privatization in city government, and the innovation hasn't been nearly as distasteful as many predicted. In this union town, there were plenty of skeptics. But privatization has worked—with bumps. . . . City government should stick to basic services it provides very well and buy others. It matters little to the tax-paying public, which expects good service, who renders it."[1] In an op-ed that appeared in *Business Forum*, Daley declared that "privatization was one of the first tools I used to reinvent Chicago's government. Privatization . . . recasts government as more of an overseer than a provider—the guardian of the public well-being instead of the source. Fulfilling this new, more sophisticated role requires new skills of government employees. They have to sit down with private-sector professionals and set performance standards. They must be more analytical."[2] This message played well with the national press. *U.S. News & World Report*, for instance, put him in company with Republican Richard Riordan of Los Angeles and Democratic mayor Ed Rendell of Philadelphia as three mayors who have been "privatizing services and slashing budgets."[3]

Just a few weeks before the April 1991 election, a *Newsweek* article profiled the city's recently awakened devotion to efficiency and professionalism:

> Chicago is dishing out contracts for city services as disparate as sewer cleaning and addiction treatment. In several cases, services have improved while costs declined. Private towing companies have hauled away 50,000 abandoned cars with far more efficiency than city crews ever displayed. Net savings: $2.5 million a year. Private custodial companies have replaced 156 city janitors; the hallways are tidier and the city has saved $900,000 a year. Since December, three nonprofit medical clinics have been helping a city clinic reduce from 125 to 60 the number of days a pregnant woman must wait to see a doctor.[4]

Striking a similar tone, a few days before the election, a *Chicago Tribune* editorial praised the mayor by noting that his administration "cleaned up and modernized the city's revenue collection procedures, got tough—finally—with illegally parked cars and contracted with private firms to perform a variety of services at a savings to taxpayers. . . . In one area the Daley administration deserves special praise. It has begun to resolve one of Chicago's most vexing problems, the thousands of abandoned buildings and empty lots that blight so many city neighborhoods."[5] Based on this record, the *Tribune* concluded that Daley "has earned the chance to guide Chicago for the next four years."[6]

Perhaps because of Chicago's long history of political corruption, Daley's image as a reformer had great appeal to groups all across the political spectrum. In all his reelection victories, huge voting majorities were delivered from the Bungalow Belt of the white, working-class residents of the Southwest and Northwest neighborhoods, the white lakefront liberals, the solidly Hispanic and African American neighborhoods. He found even stronger support in gentrified and wealthy neighborhoods located in and well beyond the downtown. Every member of this broad constituency had other reasons to vote for him, but the mayor's image as a reformer and efficient administrator put the finishing touch on the sale.

Daley was a popular mayor over a very long period, but in his last term his public standing began to seriously sag. In 2010, just a few months before he announced he would not run for a sixth term, a *Chicago Tribune* poll showed that his job approval rating had dropped to an all-time-low of just 37 percent. Almost half the voters, 47 percent, disapproved, while only 31 percent expressed support for his reelection.[7]

Several things converged to tarnish the mayor's image. His reputation took a hit after the city's failed bid for the 2016 Olympic Games, but by then a growing sense that he had lost his touch was already gaining momentum. In his last two terms the list of controversies and policy failures began to grow: there was a fight with some of his own supporters over siting of the Children's Museum; bitter battles over his attempts to reform the schools and public housing; a constantly unfolding series of scandals; a fiasco over a scheme to privatize parking; a looming crisis in municipal finances. Notably, Daley's image continued to tarnish after he left office. In 2013, the former mayor's brother Bill Daley, formerly a U.S. secretary of commerce under President Clinton and White House chief of staff for President Obama, explored a run for governor of Illinois. He quickly discovered that the family name had become a liability. A poll of likely Illinois voters conducted in June 2013 showed that 40 percent were less likely to vote for Bill Daley because his brother had served as mayor of Chicago, while only 8 percent said they were more likely to vote for him because of that relationship (32 percent declared it to be irrelevant).[8]

Two competing versions of Daley's accomplishments emerged during the years he served as the city's mayor. The story line that prevailed through much of his tenure portrayed him as a brilliant leader who put Chicago on the path of economic recovery and international stature. In his last two terms, however, an opposing narrative began to gain traction with the press and in the public's imagination. Daley was criticized for his failure to solve pressing problems involving the schools, crime, public housing, and the city's fiscal health. More than any other issue, though, a constant round of stories about political corruption dogged Daley, year in and year out. Even today, echoes of those episodes occasionally make the news, like reruns of an old television program.

A Pattern of Corruption

In 1989 Daley entered city hall under a cloud of suspicion that he would resurrect his father's style of politics. For a time he managed to disarm skeptics by pursuing a politics of inclusion and reform, but by the time he left office more than two decades later an unceasing drumbeat of corruption scandals had changed those early impressions (figure 5.1). Some of the most lurid stories emerged as a natural consequence of a bargain that Daley struck with the aldermen

Mayor Richard M. Daley at a press conference, May 22, 2010. Often animated and passionate, Daley developed a reputation over the years as a leader who deeply cared about Chicago. Courtesy of user Chris Eaves, Flickr.

on the city council. To buy the aldermen's loyal support, he allowed them the authority to operate their wards virtually as independent fiefdoms, and for many of them, the temptation to use their prerogatives for personal financial gain proved too strong to resist. According to political scientist Dick Simpson, between 1989 and 2011, twelve aldermen were convicted, and one was indicted but died before going to trial. Bribery, extortion, conspiracy to defraud, and tax fraud were the most common charges brought by state and federal prosecutors.[9]

The cases of Arenda Troutman of the Twentieth Ward and Isaac Carothers of the Twenty-Ninth provide typical examples of the type of corruption that aldermen were prone to. In 2007, an FBI investigation revealed that Troutman had accepted a bribe in return for preferential treatment for a real estate developer who

sought a zoning change for a property within her ward. Troutman was convicted and served four years in state prison, in the
process becoming the first woman alderman in the city's history
to be found guilty of corruption. Carothers followed in his father's
footsteps when he faced wire and mail fraud charges in 2007 for
accepting $11,000 in campaign contributions from a real estate
developer who was seeking zoning changes. (Carothers's father,
William, also an alderman, had been convicted of conspiracy and
extortion in 1983.) Following a plea deal, Isaac Carothers served
a twenty-eight-month prison term. As Simpson observed, "There
are patterns to these crimes. . . . The bribe-payers either assumed
or were told that payment was necessary to receive zoning changes,
building permits or similar city or state action."[10]

In the Daley years, reports of cronyism and scandals became a reliable staple for local reporters on the lookout for a story, but no other
news item proved to be as juicy or more enduring than the hired truck
scandal, which broke in 2004. An FBI investigation revealed that the
city had spent $40 million a year for the use of privately owned trucks
that sat idle. The companies providing the trucks maintained close
connections with public officials in and beyond city government,
and some of them even had ties to organized crime figures. Daley's
brother John sold insurance to some of the trucking businesses, and
several of them made contributions of $100,000 or more to the may-
or's campaigns. Bribes were paid to officials who gave out the trucking
contracts. In the end, the trucking scandal resulted in forty-nine con-
victions; thirty-one of them involved city employees. Through it all, in
statements repeated month after month, Daley denied any knowledge
of a huge operation that involved his closest aide, Robert Sorich, and
which had been taking place right under his nose.[11]

The FBI investigation brought to light a widespread pattern
of questionable hiring practices in city hall. Federal prosecutors

charged that Sorich, who was Daley's patronage chief, regularly distributed city contracts to well-connected companies and individuals. After weeks of well-publicized testimony, a judge sentenced Sorich to a forty-six-month prison term. Sorich's trial provided evidence that patronage and fixed contracts were deeply embedded practices within city government and that they probably reached beyond what prosecutors had uncovered. A report prepared by Dick Simpson and his collaborator, Thomas Gradel, estimated that corruption cost the taxpayers in Chicago, Cook County, and Illinois approximately $500 million a year. Their research uncovered numerous instances of corruption in the Department of Fleet Management, the Fire Department, the City Treasurer's Office, the Chicago Park District, the Building and Zoning Department, O'Hare Airport, McCormick Place, and the Department of Procurement Services. The authors concluded that "throughout the agencies examined in this report, we see patterns of bribery, patronage, contract rigging, conflict of interest, nepotism / family ties, clout, and theft. These problems are not confined to one specific agency but occur in many government offices."[12]

The same media outlets that had effusively praised Daley in past years now began to adopt a different tone. In 2010, writers for the *New Yorker* reviewed Daley's record on corruption and concluded, "Like his father, Daley has not been accused of personally profiting from the city, but he has done little more than take pro-forma steps to stop others from doing so. His efforts to reduce the kind of quasi-legalized bribery known as pay-to-play have been half-hearted."[13] In 2012, a headline in the *Christian Science Monitor* read, "Chicago Area Called Most Corrupt in US,"[14] and the city's alleged culture of corruption became a theme of the Republican Party's presidential campaign of that year.

Reports of corruption continued to surface in the years after Daley left office. At the end of 2013, a lawsuit charged that the former mayor's administration had negotiated a sweetheart lease agreement with the Park Grill, the popular restaurant located on the grounds of Millennium Park. Among other provisions, the arrangement provided free natural gas, water, and garbage collection to the restaurant at an annual cost to the city of $5 million. In the summer of 2014, lawyers for the former mayor argued that he could not testify in court because of a medical condition. Even if he had done so, however, it is doubtful he would have provided much information. During depositions for the case, Daley answered "I don't recall" 139 times.[15] This performance prompted the local media to respond with headlines such as "Daley: A Falling Star in Chicago"[16] and "Millennium Park Built 'the Chicago Way.'"[17]

A few months later, in the fall of 2014, a vehicle scam came to light that, once again, traced its origins to the Daley years. An indictment of Chicago taxi operator Alexander Igolnikov alleged that more than 180 taxis in use from 2000 to 2010 had been involved in accidents, but that members of the administration and even the mayor's son, Patrick Daley, had intervened to return them to the streets of Chicago as taxis with clean titles. Mayor Daley had tried to end the controversy before completing his last term by seeking a $1 million settlement.[18]

Despite numerous indictments and successful prosecutions of members of his administration, Daley was never implicated directly in any of the federal corruption probes. He made it a habit to adamantly deny any wrongdoing, but over time the press and the public became increasingly skeptical. Nevertheless, the culture of corruption that flourished in and around City Hall eventually convinced a great many people familiar with his father's political style that the apple had not fallen far from the tree.

Police Brutality and Corruption

The newspaper headlines that tied Daley to corruption during and after his days in city hall frequently shared front-page space with riveting accounts of police brutality that had occurred as early as the 1980s, when Daley served as the Cook County state's attorney. In 2006 a series of lawsuits revealed that between 1981 and 1989, police commander John Burge and other officers tortured more than fifty men to secure confessions.[19] The shocking details turned the Burge story into a favorite go-to item for local newspapers and broke into the national news as well. Critics charged that when Daley served as state's attorney he had turned a blind eye to the abuses. It was a story line that just would not go away, and every time an account of a new Burge atrocity hit the front page, the accusation was aired anew. By the end of Daley's last term, the city had paid $19.8 million in settlements to Burge's victims, and more continued to surface, leading to estimates that the city might eventually pay more than $120 million before the Burge saga finally comes to an end.[20] Burge was eventually sentenced to four and a half years in federal prison but continues to receive his state pension, which also has been a subject of furious controversy.[21]

The Burge scandal yielded up a treasure trove of lurid tales, and it soon became clear that a pattern of corruption and misconduct was deeply embedded within the Chicago Police Department. As mayor, Daley was obliged to spend millions of dollars in city money to defend officers who had systematically engaged in torturing African Americans and employed humiliating, derogatory, and racially charged tactics to secure confessions. These forced confessions had been used to convict dozens of defendants, and even put some of them on death row.[22] Almost three hundred police officers were found guilty between 1960 and 2012, with more than one hundred of those cases occurring after 2000. Officers were convicted of drug dealing, destroying evidence, theft, gang and organized crime activity, and even murder. Between 2000 and 2012, forty-seven law enforcement officers were convicted of gang activity, collusion with gangs, and drug dealing. These are remarkable numbers, especially since a code of silence within the police department made it very difficult to investigate cases of abuse.

In those instances when Daley's office and police officials tried to address the problem of police corruption, they found it next to impossible to change the culture of silence that impeded anticorruption oversight.[23] Because the police department was charged with investigating abuse cases within its own ranks, few officers were ever found guilty of committing offenses. A 2007 study revealed that between 2002 and 2004, 10,149 complaints of police brutality, ranging from excessive force and illegal searches to racial and sexual abuse, were submitted by citizens. Between 2001 and 2006, 2,451 police officers were named in four to ten complaints each, and 662 Chicago police officers had more than ten complaints filed against them. However, an examination of "sustained rates" (the cases when there was a finding of sufficient evidence of abuse to justify an action against an officer) showed that the proportion of sustained brutality complaints per year rapidly fell from 4.8 percent in 1999 to 2.3 in 2002, and to 0.5 percent by 2004.[24] Only 15 percent of the internal investigations led to an interview with the accused officer, and only nineteen cases resulted in suspensions of one week or more. In the end, 75 percent of repeat offenders were never disciplined.[25] Statistics such as these made it appear that, in reality, the police department allowed citizens to file complaints merely as a public relations exercise.

The public probably had less interest in statistics like these than in the news accounts that connected the dots between police misconduct and Daley's name. One of the more damning tales emerged in December 2012, when a judge with ties to the mayor was assigned to preside over the trial of Daley's nephew Richard Vanecko, who was charged with knocking down and killing a young man in an altercation outside a bar.[26] Stories surfaced revealing that investigating officers had misrepresented and covered up evidence because of Vanecko's family connections. Vanecko's trial played out in the press for weeks, and he was ultimately found guilty of involuntary manslaughter and served a sixty-day jail sentence.[27]

The impression that all was not well on Daley's watch was reinforced by local and national news coverage of gang violence. A report by the Federal Bureau of Investigation revealed that in 2009, 458 homicides took place in Chicago, but in the same year New York, which was three times larger, recorded just 471. In 2010, the level of gang violence in Chicago became so serious that state representatives called on Illinois governor Pat Quinn to dispatch the National Guard. Daley rejected this idea and argued that curbing gang violence required special training not available to the National Guard. Instead, the mayor reiterated his frequently repeated demand that the legislature enact tougher gun-control restrictions. Year by year the problem only grew worse, and by the time Daley left office in 2012, 500 murders were committed within the Chicago city limits; in the same year, New York City registered 431 murders. According to Chicago Police Department estimates, 80 percent of those incidents were gang related.[28] It had become painfully obvious that, for all the political authority at his command, this was a problem the mayor did not know how to solve.

A few years later, in 2015, the case of Laquan McDonald made national news, revealing the extraordinary level of corruption and brutality within the Chicago Police Department. From a close distance, a police officer fired sixteen shots and killed the seventeen-year-old McDonald who was walking away down the middle of the street. In an apparent cover-up, it took more than thirteen months for the video of the incident to be released. Mayor Emanuel fired Chicago police chief Garry McCarthy a few days later, citing the presence of "systematic challenges that will require sustained reforms."[29]

An April 21, 2016, press conference revealed, however, that it was unclear how much reform Emanuel was prepared to press for. A week earlier, a devastating task force report detailing years of systematic racism in the Chicago police department found that "people of color-particularly African Americans-have had disproportionately negative experiences with the police over an extended period of time [through] the use of force, foot and traffic stops and bias in the police oversight system itself."[30] In response, Emanuel pledged that he would implement some of the group's suggestions, but would not say if he was willing to dismantle the widely distrusted Independent Police Review Authority, which had been covering up police misbehavior for years. The task force recommended the creation of a new civilian agency, but Emanuel demurred on this and on another recommendation, which called for the city to create an inspector general for public safety. A yet-to-be-released Justice Department report was expected to urge still more reforms.[31]

The Public Housing Controversies

Daley's reputation as an effective problem-solver also came into question in policy areas he declared to be among his highest priorities. During his years in office, Daley fought an often bitterly contested campaign to tear down the massive high-rise public housing projects located just north and south of the Loop. The issue was of great importance to Daley and to property developers, because these aging eyesores potentially undermined not only the Loop's revival, but also made it more difficult to lure middle-class professionals and homeowners back to the city. Housing advocates, while not necessarily defending the projects, were concerned that any attempts to dismantle them would displace the residents who lived there. Sometimes pitched battles were fought, but Daley's influence with the Chicago Housing Authority (CHA) consistently carried the day, and within a few years the CHA had torn down virtually all the high-rise projects in Chicago. Town houses and residential tower developments quickly sprang up, and nearby streets became jammed with coffeehouses, restaurants, and boutiques. Many of the mayor's supporters considered the reclaiming of these areas to be among Daley's most important achievements, but the controversies never died down, and for a large community of housing and social-justice advocates, Daley's name became associated with indifference to Chicago's deeply seated racial and social problems.

Chicago's public housing programs date back to 1937, when the city formed the CHA in order to become eligible to receive grants from the nation's first federally funded public housing program. The public housing supply increased during World War II, when thousands of units were constructed to house war workers, but the high-rise projects constructed after Congress approved the 1949 Housing Act dwarfed all previous efforts. Vast, imposing, sprawling complexes sprouted up, mostly in the near south, near west, and near north sides of the city. The Frances Cabrini Homes (1942), ABLA (1940s and 1950s), the State Street Corridor that included Stateway Gardens (1955), and the Robert Taylor Homes (1962) became some of the nation's largest, and most notorious, public housing developments.

The history of the Cabrini-Green project north of Chicago's Loop tells a typical tale about how public housing became an example of failed social policy. All the occupants of the first units that went up during the war, which were built as two-story brick row houses, were white, but in 1958 most of these units were razed to make space for fifteen high-rise buildings, and another eight high-rises were constructed in 1962. These nineteen-story rectangular monstrosities loomed over the surrounding neighborhoods, and by then virtually all the tenants were black. Like several other public housing complexes in the city, these concentrated clusters of cement silos guaranteed that blacks would be more marginalized and isolated than ever before.

The construction of the freeway system in the postwar years also contributed to a pattern of rigid segregation. When, for instance, the Dan Ryan Expressway opened in 1962, the fourteen-lane corridor divided the African American population of the Douglas neighborhood on the Near South Side from the predominantly European-descent residents of the Bridgeport neighborhood to the west. The white flight of the postwar era left blacks utterly cut off from suburbanites or from surrounding neighborhoods, living in public housing projects within segregated neighborhoods. The deleterious effects associated with such extreme isolation are illustrated by conditions in the Robert Taylor Homes.[32] In 1980, though the official population of the Taylor homes reached twenty thousand, an estimated additional six thousand unregistered adults lived there. All registered residents that year were African Americans, and 70 percent of the occupants were minors. Almost 95 percent of the families with children were headed by women, and approximately half the adult residents were unemployed. Astonishingly, although less than 1 percent of the city's population lived in the Robert Taylor Homes, its residents committed 11 percent of the city's murders, 9 percent of the rapes, and 10 percent of the aggravated assaults.[33] By the 1970s, if not before, Chicago's public housing had become national signifiers for the problems of racial division and inner-city decay.

By the time Richard M. Daley became mayor, the failure of public housing policy in Chicago and elsewhere had become accepted as established fact. In the 1990s the federal Department of Housing and Urban Development (HUD) mostly abandoned traditional public housing by turning to subsidies for developments constructed through public-private partnerships. The mayor quickly jumped on board, and in May 1995, the federal government, with Daley's approval, took over the administration of the Chicago Housing Authority, and immediately ousted the long-serving CHA chairman, Vincent Lane. At the time of the takeover, CHA operated forty thousand housing units with eighty-six thousand residents in seventeen developments.[34]

HUD administrators pushed for the demolition of high-rise buildings, and Mayor Daley enthusiastically supported the cause. The idea was that displaced public housing tenants would use housing vouchers to move elsewhere or move into the new mixed-use units alongside middle-and upper-income residents. The reality, though, was that a great many tenants were put on waiting lists, with thirty thousand families in search of replacement housing. At the same time, more than thirteen thousand units were unoccupied because they needed significant repairs. Tensions between HUD administrators and CHA staff reached an all-time high when city officials revealed to the local press that hundreds of air conditioner units were piled high in storage. At that point Daley declared he would take control of the situation by reforming the CHA.

In 1999, the city announced the ambitious Chicago Plan for Transformation, which called for the demolition of the Robert Taylor Homes, Cabrini-Green, Stateway Gardens, and the Henry Horner Homes. Even mid-rise structures were to be leveled, and those remaining would be comprehensively rehabbed. The plan indicated that this demolition would be immediately followed by an aggressive rebuilding program aimed at producing mixed-used housing projects designed to accommodate both low-income and middle-income residents. As critics predicted, however, the Chicago Plan for Transformation ultimately fell far short of its goals. Community leaders had suspected from the beginning that the program was merely a land grab granting developers in rapidly gentrifying neighborhoods access to sites near the Loop, and as time went by they felt their suspicions were confirmed.[35] For Daley, the destruction of high-rise eyesores was something else entirely, "a rebuilding of a society" and the end of a "legacy of slime."[36]

The CHA proceeded to tear down the public housing projects Daley's father had built only a generation before (figure 5.2). Some people praised the mayor for designing a national model that might be emulated by other cities, and Daley saw it in those terms, too, but the results proved to be far more complicated and uneven. The question of whether mixed-income communities could succeed when market forces collide with the promise of affordable housing remained unresolved. In 2004 *the Christian Science Monitor* published a story on the Chicago Plan of Transformation that posed some key questions: "If mixed-income communities are the goal, how do you balance the needs of the market-rate tenants while still serving the public-housing population? Do strict requirements cater to middle-class anxieties without looking at the realities of people's lives? Assuming some demands are necessary, just how much is reasonable to ask?"[37] Chicago had undertaken an

Figure 5.2
Demolition of a public housing building at the Cabrini-Green public housing development. Courtesy of user Henryk Sadura, Shutterstock Images.

experiment that affected thousands of people, but no one seemed to have an answer to these important questions.

Debates about this social experiment erupted among housing specialists and community organizations. Hundreds of publications and reports poured forth. Political scientist Larry Bennett represented a broad consensus among skeptics when he wrote, "One of the promises of mixed-income neighborhood development has been that it would spark entrepreneurial and job opportunities for the less prosperous local residents. At this time, Chicago's new neighborhoods are not being built in a manner that will enable them to deliver on this expectation."[38] An evaluation of CHA's Plan for Transformation published ten years after its inception concluded that "most early scholarship showed mixed results at best" and that "the highly varied process led to early gains for some groups, losses for others, and unknown outcomes for most of the original population." Finally, the authors of the study concluded, "relocation did not help most residents improve their employment situation or incomes.... Those that moved into Chicago neighborhoods using housing vouchers most often relocated to neighborhoods with high poverty and deep racial segregation."[39] Overall, it seemed, the demolition of public housing had made many things worse, not better, for some of the city's most disadvantaged residents.

A study by the Urban Institute followed the experiences of the CHA families to determine if relocation had increased social mobility and improved housing opportunities for low-income families. The report found that the Housing Choice Voucher program had spawned a growing bureaucracy, but with all its resources it had not prevented people from being disconnected from their communities or improved access to critical support services. The report cautioned that "without sustained funding and attention, the CHA and its counterparts risk sliding back into the kinds of disinvestment and neglect that created distressed housing and neighborhoods in the first place."[40]

One of the most significant outcomes concerning the public housing policies of the Daley years was the repurposing of valuable land in rapidly gentrifying neighborhoods close to the Loop. Unmoved by the chorus of criticism, Daley declared before leaving office that "from [São Paolo] all the way to Paris—guess what they're talking about? High rise public housings and how many socioeconomic problems they have in these with gangs, guns and drugs; destruction of their family. So again transformation for CHA has been working and we've been very proud of that, which is important."[41] It is certain, however, that many people did not share the mayor's rosy take on the situation.

The Mixed Results of Daley's Educational Reforms

In 1995 Mayor Daley persuaded the Illinois state legislature to give him control of the Chicago Public Schools (CPS) so that he could reform an ossified bureaucracy and improve teaching performance. In the national press Daley's move was hailed as a bold experiment, and within a few years the mayor received copious praise for his educational reform efforts. In 1999 he was named the recipient of the Education Excellence Award of the National Conference for Community and Justice, and in 2000 the National Association of State Boards of Education identified him as the "Policy Leader of the Year." As time passed, however, a less favorable, or at least more ambiguous, picture emerged, and by the time he left office criticisms were pouring in from many quarters.

Daley's first appointee to lead the CPS, Paul Vallas, launched an aggressive effort to measure teacher and administrator performance through the application of quantitative metrics. Low-performing schools faced closure; at the same time, in 1997 the CPS invited applications for charter school proposals, and several were approved.[42] After Vallas left to lead the School District of Philadelphia in 2001, the mayor appointed Arne Duncan (who later became the secretary of education in the Obama administration) to head the CPS. Duncan accelerated the effort to close poor-performing schools and added more than seventy charter schools. The "No Child Left Behind" federal legislation that followed in 2002 fit Chicago's model perfectly and gave added momentum to the Daley administration's efforts to restructure the city's public schools.[43] In 2004 Daley and Duncan bundled their reform strategy into the Renaissance 2010 program, which called for closing more underachieving schools and replacing them with charter schools with their own independent administrators, better-qualified teachers, innovative instructional methods, updated curricula, and improved physical surroundings. By 2011, about one hundred charter schools had replaced eighty neighborhood schools.

Business leaders enthusiastically embraced Daley's educational policy agenda. Private firms stood to benefit from the contracts awarded to operate the schools; at the same time, the same companies could pursue funding opportunities through nonprofit organizations. As a bonus, privatization allowed them to alter the long-standing employment practices that protected administrators and teachers. Predictably, such changes provoked strong pushback. Controversies erupted not only because of opposition from the Chicago Teachers Union, but also because Renaissance 2010 undermined funding for public schools in marginal neighborhoods. Some supporters of reform began to wonder if the results justified the stormy controversies. A January 2010 report by the *Chicago Tribune* led with the headline "Daley School Plan Fails to Make the Grade." The newspaper's investigation showed that the scores from the Renaissance 2010 elementary schools were "nearly identical to the city average," and the scores of the restructured high schools were "below the already abysmal city average."[44] Even worse, said the report, Renaissance 2010 might have created more problems than it solved by clustering students from the poorest families in the weakest schools and increasing youth violence and gang activity in non-charter schools.[45]

A 2011 study by a research collaborative at the University of Chicago, the Consortium on School Research, concluded that over the previous twenty years there had not been a significant improvement in reading among elementary school students. Such a statistic, though, masked a troubling and even less reassuring trend: despite the overall gains, racial disparities had increased.[46] Critics pointed out that Renaissance 2010 reduced opportunities for the majority of African American and Latino students because the college-prep programs of charter schools became increasingly differentiated from a skills-based curriculum in the remaining schools, and research revealed that standardized testing reinforced differences in learning culture, curriculum development, and related instructional practices.[47]

Many people interpreted such findings as evidence that Daley's reforms had failed; but the mayor was using his own yardstick. Although Daley was generally reluctant to admit as much, it was clear that he regarded his educational policies as a central component of his strategy to revitalize Chicago by luring back the middle class. During his welcoming remarks at the 2009 National Chinese Language conference, for instance, Daley remarked that

> in 1995, I was the only mayor in the country that took full responsibility of our public schools. If you are going to make a great city, you have to educate people. . . . We want to give opportunities to create a middle class. That is the only way cities will exist. Otherwise people move out. The rich move out, and then eventually the middle class will move out in order to get a good quality education closer to a rich community.[48]

By the time Daley left City Hall, neighborhoods in many parts of the city had gentrified, and there can be little doubt that his educational program had supported the process.

The distribution of school funding revealed the close connection between educational policy and the mayor's urban development priorities. A large portion of revenues from Tax Increment Finance (TIF) districts was used to fund the rehabilitation and construction of new public schools rather than paying for street repairs and job training in some of the most challenged neighborhoods across the city. An analysis of TIF funds earmarked for education concluded that "neighborhood open enrollment schools compose 69 percent of the CPS . . . but only receive 48 percent of TIF revenues."[49] Though Daley often claimed otherwise, more investment in charter schools translated into less investment in the city's open-enrollment neighborhood schools.

Perhaps because the school reforms were tilted so heavily in favor of high achievers and middle-class students, even after two decades of reform, Chicago's public school system was still in disarray, with a $720 million deficit in 2011 and a 55.8 percent graduation rate.[50] And there were significant political costs as well. Daley's aggressive reform efforts provoked a permanent rift with the Chicago Teachers Union, and soon after he left office tensions came to a head. Following failed contract talks in the fall of 2012, for the first time in twenty-five years the teachers went on strike, an action that brought a very public and acrimonious conflict between the union and Daley's successor, Rahm Emanuel.

Emanuel carried Daley's educational priorities forward. Under his leadership the city expanded the number of International Baccalaureate programs and selective-enrollment high schools. The completion of the $115 million addition to Jones College Prep in Printers Row in 2013 was fully paid by TIF development funds. In 2014, an announcement called for a $17 million annex to Walter Payton College Prep in Old Town. Also to be paid for by TIF funds, the new structure would house additional classroom and lab space. Finally, a new selective-enrollment high school was slated to go up on the Near North Side near the Cabrini-Green public housing site, an area that has experienced rapid gentrification. As during the Daley years, a chorus of voices criticized these plans, calling instead for construction and updating of neighborhood high schools in the most socially and economically distressed parts of the city.

A Fiscal Mess

When Rahm Emanuel entered the mayor's office on May 16, 2011, Chicago was deeply mired in a fiscal mess that had been growing worse for many years. The Great Recession of 2008–9 caused fiscal problems for cities all across the country, but a structural deficit had begun to pinch Chicago's budget years before. One of the issues that had become increasingly intractable was an unfunded pension liability, which reached more than $19 billion by the end of 2012. For years the city had not been contributing fully to its four public employee funds (firefighters, police, municipal, and laborers), yet reallocating the money elsewhere had still not enabled the city to avoid deficits. To avoid cuts in core services like health, police, and public safety, Daley had, year by year, relied on borrowing to balance the annual budget. He strongly opposed raising local taxes because, many people suspected, such a move might have posed a threat to his reelection prospects (figure 5.3).

Between 2005 and 2009 the city's tax revenues increased by 6.5 percent; at the same time, expenditures rose by 17.3 percent. As a consequence, by the 2009 fiscal year, revenues from taxes and fees accounted for about $3.1 billion of a $5.3 billion budget. From 2000 to 2012, proceeds from $9.8 billion in bonds were distributed to meet short-term expenses, most of which were allocated to equipment, legal fees, judgments and settlements, and bond refinancing.[51]

In addition to borrowing, Daley balanced the budget by using funds from the long-term leasing of the city's parking meters and money from the Chicago Skyway. In exchange for a ninety-nine-year lease agreement for the Skyway toll road, an international group of investors agreed pay the city a lump-sum payment of $1.83 billion. Views differ about the wisdom of the toll-road deal,

Figure 5.3
Some neighborhoods, like Chicago's West Side, have been subject to chronic disinvestment. Their residents have not benefited from the restructuring and massive lakefront investments. Courtesy of user Nitram242, Flickr.

but the city's decision to privatize parking meters fueled controversy and resentment that endures to this day. In 2008, the city negotiated a $1.16 billion parking meter lease with Deeside Investments, a subsidiary of Morgan Stanley. This raised hackles because the company has a close financial connection to the Abu Dhabi Investment Authority, an entity formed to invest on behalf of the Emirate of Abu Dhabi. Chicago Parking Meters LLC, a company created to manage the meters, subsequently has had numerous run-ins with the city and has been a constant source of complaint for commuters.[52] When the parking meter deal was signed, Daley said it would provide a cushion that would last for many years, but he balanced his final fiscal 2010 budget by spending all but $76 million of the money derived from the meter sale.[53]

Daley also resorted to a variety of suspect gimmicks to pay for the construction and maintenance of his legacy projects in Grant Park and along the lake. For example, from 2004 to 2011 the mayor borrowed about $30 million to pay for the annual $6.1 million cost of operating Millennium Park (the interest cost of this loan to the taxpayers exceeded $3.5 million). When questioned about the arrangement in 2013, he sidestepped the issue with a rhetorical statement that "Chicago now has world-class stature, the foundation on which new opportunities are built."[54] In addition, but less noted at the time, the city borrowed more than $37 million in tax-exempt bonds to fund various maintenance costs, including urban beautification. About $7 million of that went for landscaping of street medians.[55]

In a 2011 report titled "Financial Challenges for the New Mayor of Chicago," the Civic Federation took note of the city's structural debt, growing annual budget deficits, and increasing reliance on nonrecurring revenues to manage budget shortfalls. In its executive summary, the report's authors argued that

> the City of Chicago has a structural deficit, a condition character-
> ized by annual expenditure increases that consistently exceed recur-
> ring revenue increases during normal economic times. Over the past
> ten fiscal years, the City has had significant budget deficits. . . . [The
> city] closed annual deficits with temporary spending reductions and
> non-recurring revenues, including over $1 billion in proceeds from
> the long-term leases of the Skyway and parking meters. . . . The new
> mayor of Chicago will need to make difficult choices to close the im-
> mediate budget gap of at least $500 million and set the City on a path
> to long-term fiscal stability.[56]

Other people noticed the mounting problems, too. In the summer of 2013, Moody's Investor Service downgraded Chicago's general obligation bond rating three levels, from Aa3 to A3, and graded the future outlook as "negative." Moody's gave special attention to the pension liabilities, public safety concerns (crime rate), and the persistent failure of the city to effectively address its underlying fiscal problems. Even before the downgrade, Chicago's credit rating was one spot below that of New York and Los Angeles. The Moody's decision not only pushed the city far below those peer cities, but also positioned it lower than Milwaukee and Cleveland. Of the twenty-nine government rating reviews conducted by Moody's, Chicago and Cincinnati were the only two to be downgraded. Cincinnati dropped by only one notch from Aa1 to Aa2, a rating still four spots above Chicago's.[57] In March 2014, Moody's downgraded Chicago's credit rating to Baa1,[58] and in May 2015, once again, to junk bond status.[59]

Chicago residents are increasingly concerned about the direction of the city and unhappy with its leadership, and much of this dissatisfaction can be traced back to the Daley years. A poll by the *Chicago Sun-Times* in May 2014 surveyed 511 registered voters and found that 51 percent of respondents felt that Mayor Emanuel is not doing a better job than his predecessor. For 25 percent, his performance is "about the same" as that of Daley's.[60] A *Tribune* poll published in August 2014 asked eight hundred voters to compare Daley to current mayor Emanuel. The findings supported Emanuel's frequently stated position that the city's fiscal problems started before he became mayor. A majority of the survey respondents agreed. When asked to identify who was responsible for the city's current financial condition, 54 percent of respondents identified Daley, and 21 percent named Emanuel, but this was not necessarily comforting news for the new mayor. Only 17 percent said that Chicago was better off since Emanuel became mayor, with 49 percent indicting "about the same" and 32 percent "not better off."[61]

The Legacy Projects

It is startling to realize how far and how fast Daley's star has fallen since the days when he was hailed as one of America's greatest public leaders. If it survives the other aspects of his record, his most enduring positive legacy will be connected to the many projects of his lakefront program and his efforts to beautify neighborhoods throughout the city and encourage arts and culture. Daley's success at building a tourist economy established a foundation upon which his successor is building. In a 2014 press release titled "Mayor Emanuel Outlines Vision for Continued Expansion and Growth of Tourism in Chicago," the Emanuel administration announced a goal of attracting fifty-five million tourists by 2020, an increase of five million visitors over 2014. Emanuel asserted that "since taking office, I have been focused on tourism as a key driver of our economy" and that "now is the time for us to continue that growth, including focusing on iconic events and opportunities that will place Chicago at the center of the global conversation."[62]

Emanuel is accurate in his assessment that in building an economy of this kind, the city was following a path dictated by the logic and opportunities connected to the global economy. Averaging 4.4 percent growth per year, travel and tourism will support 297 million jobs worldwide and possess 10.5 percent of the global GDP by 2018. It is projected that in 2018, 1 out of 10.8 jobs globally will be tied to this sector.[63] Public and private capital investment in these sectors is expected to reach as high as $3.15 trillion globally by 2018—double the investments made in 2012.

World-class museums, restaurants, hotels, shopping opportunities, recreational options, and cultural and sporting events have brought people from all over the world to Chicago, not only as visitors, but also as permanent residents. Urban amenities have played a key role in attracting businesses and corporate headquarters. In late 2013, Archer Daniels Midland (ADM) announced that it would move its international offices to Chicago. It is hard to imagine that the move was not prompted in large measure by the cultural and lifestyle advantages of Chicago compared to ADM's previous headquarters city, Decatur, Illinois. Similarly, in September 2015, Motorola Solutions announced that it will relocate its corporate headquarters and eight hundred jobs to Chicago from suburban Schaumburg.

When Emanuel entered City Hall as the fifty-fifth mayor of Chicago in 2011, his inauguration speech contained this retrospective assessment:

> A generation ago, people were writing Chicago off as a dying city. They said our downtown was failing, our neighborhoods were unlivable, our schools were the worst in the nation, and our politics had become so divisive we were referred to as Beirut on the Lake. . . .
>
> . . . Chicago is a different city today than the one Mayor Daley inherited, thanks to all he did. This magnificent place [Millennium Park] where we gather today is a living symbol of that transformation.
>
> Back then, this was an abandoned rail yard. A generation later, what was once a nagging urban eyesore is now a world-class urban park. Through Mayor Daley's vision, determination and leadership, this place, like our city, was reborn.[64]

A year later, Emanuel announced a $7 billion regional infrastructural development trust dubbed "Building a New Chicago," which focused on investments in energy and public utilities, transportation, and education. The new mayor also embarked on a number of ambitious lakefront projects; most of them had their origins in the Daley years. These included the Chicago Riverwalk, scheduled for completion in 2016 (figure 5.4); the Maggie Daley Park at the north

FIGURE 5.4

The Chicago Riverwalk, along Wacker Drive. This project received extensive attention during the Richard M. Daley administration, and Mayor Rahm Emanuel continued its expansion following his election. Courtesy of user Lissandra Melo, Shutterstock Images.

end of Grant Park, which opened in December 2014 (figure 5.5); a Navy Pier renovation; a DePaul basketball arena and associated development near McCormick Place; and the completion of a Northerly Island park and nature preserve.

In October 2012 Emanuel announced a $100 million concept plan to transform six blocks of the Riverwalk. When completed, this project will result in a 1.25-mile walking corridor along the banks of the river. The Emanuel development would extend from west of Michigan Avenue to Lake Street and include walking and jogging paths, commercial development, and six themed areas for outdoor activities. The Riverwalk will permit boat docking, kayaking, and include open-air performance stages and even classroom

Maggie Daley Park, April 10, 2015. The new park adjacent to the Millennium Park was the result of an extensive conversion of more than twenty acres that once occupied the Daley Bicentennial Plaza on the north part of Grant Park. Courtesy of user f11photo, Shutterstock Images.

settings for instruction on ecology. The high-profile project, which is funded through public-private partnerships and a $98.6 million federal loan, will become, in Emanuel's words, the "next recreational frontier."[65]

Daley had introduced a similar plan as far back as 1990 and announced expanded versions in 1995 and in 1997. In 2009, an elaborate concept titled "Chicago Riverwalk: Main Branch Framework Plan" was released by the Chicago Department of Zoning and Planning and the Chicago Department of Transportation. Over the years, Daley referred to the river as the "second lakefront" and the Riverwalk as his $50 million, San Antonio–like project; as in that city, the plan included gathering areas, restaurants, retail space, and docking zones. Although the Daley plan did not fully materialize, a three-block-long section called the Wacker Drive Riverwalk was completed, plus a stretch from Lake Shore Drive to Michigan Avenue.[66]

When the massive construction of the Northerly Island park and nature preserve was completed in September 2015, it was one of the signature legacies from the Daley years. As the speakers at the opening ceremonies pointed out, the construction of the reserve would not have been possible if Daley had not forced the closing of Meigs Field, the airport that once occupied the site.

Prior to this, the most recent reminder of the mayor's work is the park that opened in December 2014 in his wife's honor, the Maggie Daley Park. Late in 2011, just months after Daley left office, civic leaders took up the idea of giving a face lift to the Richard J. Daley Bicentennial Plaza. The plaza, which first opened in the late 1970s, was located on the other side of Columbus Drive from Millennium Park, at the end of Frank Gehry's serpentine bridge. As soon as Millennium Park opened, millions of visitors were drawn to the new park's mosaic of interactive attractions; by comparison, the formal spaces and lawns of Daley Plaza, just to the east, seemed tired and uninspiring. For this reason Gehry's masterpiece was often referred to as the "bridge to nowhere." In August 2012, Emanuel announced that a new twenty-acre park would go up on the Daley Plaza site, to be named after Maggie Daley, the much-beloved first lady who had died of breast cancer a few months before. Mayor Daley had long before identified this area as a high priority for redevelopment. In 2008, he had backed the relocation of the Children's Museum at Navy Pier to the Daley Bicentennial Plaza but had run into a firestorm of opposition. Daley was bitterly disappointed that his plans failed to come to fruition. Like Emanuel, Daley was motivated by the need not only to make use of the space in a more effective way, but also to attend to the realities of a failing infrastructure. As the *Chicago Tribune* reported, "The reconstruction of Daley Bicentennial Plaza is necessary because the waterproofing membrane that protects the parking garage beneath it is falling apart and will have to be removed to prevent water from seeping into the garage."[67] Had Daley won a sixth term, it is certain he would have found a way to renovate the site.

In May 2013, Emanuel announced that an entertainment district would be built adjacent to McCormick Place, as part of a broad strategy to draw tourists and revitalize neighborhoods on the Near South Side. The idea was not new; indeed, Daley had begun development of the area years before when he backed two expansions of the convention center complex, the Museum Park project, and the renovation of Soldier Field. In 2003 the Central Area Plan prepared by the Chicago Plan Commission outlined a Cermak Road Corridor, which was intended to be a residential and high-density mixed-use corridor linking Chinatown and the largely Mexican American Pilsen neighborhood on the western end to McCormick Place and the lakefront. Planners, and the mayor, were especially interested in developing the historic Motor Row and Prairie Avenue neighborhoods near to the convention center.[68] Today, the Emanuel administration is aggressively pursuing development in this same area.

The completion and further elaboration of Daley's tourism strategy will give Emanuel much to brag about. Despite the city's fiscal problems, Emanuel has benefited from the job gains directly linked to the strength of the downtown and the tourist economy.[69] Emanuel's toughest challenges are the same ones that tripped up Daley when he sat in the mayor's chair. As one former aide to Emanuel noted, "There are two Chicagos. Until we are one, Chicago is not back."[70] Emanuel has attributed his sagging popularity to the nagging social problems that continue to trouble the city, and American cities everywhere. Daley did not solve these problems; but does that mean his mayoral service should be regarded as a failure? Did he, in the end, build a city of bread and circuses that entertains tourists and middle-class residents at the expense of everyone else? We will take up that admittedly difficult question in the next, and concluding, chapter.

Epilogue

A CITY OF BREAD AND CIRCUSES?

On August 26, 1976, when Quincy Market opened in downtown Boston, it is doubtful that anyone could have foreseen how much this one festive event would become a catalyst for an urban transformation that would soon sweep across the nation and change the economy and culture of nearly every city in America. Located as it was in the center of a tattered downtown, Quincy Market represented a roll of the dice, for both Boston and the developer, James Rouse. But on the very first day a crowd of more than one hundred thousand people showed up, and in its second year it drew twelve million visitors—more than Disneyland that year. The media hailed Quincy Market's extraordinary success as a sort of miracle, a sign that after decades of urban decline an urban renaissance was at hand.

What started as a mall in downtown Boston quickly morphed into a standard template for downtown revitalization copied by cities all over the country: typically, a "tourist bubble" emerged composed of a redeveloped waterfront, a festival shopping mall, at least one luxury hotel (preferably one with a multistory atrium), a new sports stadium (domed, if possible), a new convention center, all integrated into plazas and streetscapes.[1] An adoring national media singled out Baltimore's Mayor William Donald Schaefer and his massive project, the Harborplace development, for special attention. Completed in 1980, Harborplace succeeded beyond anyone's expectations. It attracted eighteen million people the first year, and between 1980 and 1986 the number of visitors tripled and a surge of private investment spilled over into nearby residential neighborhoods. To raise the public and private capital needed for an undertaking of this scale, nearly three dozen special authorities were incorporated to take expenditures and borrowing off the city's ledgers. This method of financing became a standard model copied by other cities.

Despite the positive press, critics did not share the widespread enthusiasm for this mode of urban development. Writing about Baltimore's Inner Harbor development, a leading urban scholar, David Harvey, proposed that the reconstruction of Baltimore's harbor as a tourist site was little more than a smokescreen hiding the festering problems in the neighborhoods of the surrounding city: "Like the city fair, the Inner Harbor functions as a sophisticated mask. It invites us to participate in a spectacle, to enjoy a festive circus that celebrates the coming together of people and commodities. Like any mask, it can beguile and distract in engaging ways, but at some point we want to know what lies behind it. If the mask cracks or is violently torn off, the terrible face of Baltimore's impoverishment may appear."[2] Just as Harvey intimated, the drumbeat of good news about Baltimore's revival overlooked the conditions in its deteriorating neighborhoods. The renovation of the harbor did not change the fact that the city's population continued to decline, schools remained segregated, and poverty and unemployment grew worse. Kurt Schmoke, Baltimore's first African American mayor, who succeeded Schaefer in 1987, observed, "If you were visiting Baltimore today after a 20-year absence, you would find us much prettier and much poorer."[3]

Urban scholars joined in a rising chorus of criticism aimed at the newly minted formula for downtown revival. In his best-selling book, *City of Quartz*, Mike Davis drew a causal connection between inequality and Los Angeles's cultural resurgence: "The current Culture boom, and its attendant celebrity-intellectual influx . . . must be seen as an epiphenomenon of the larger social polarization that has revitalized Downtown and enriched the Westside at the expense of vast debilitated tracts of the inner city."[4] In a similar vein, the political scientist Peter Eisenger criticized the misplaced priorities that he thought defined what he called "the politics of bread and circuses": "The amount of fiscal and political resources and the level of energy that local elites must devote to the realization of large entertainment projects are so great that more mundane urban problems and needs must often be subordinated or ignored. In pursuing big entertainment projects, local elites create a hierarchy of interests in which the concerns of visitors to cities—including commuters, day-trippers, tourists, and business travelers—take precedence over those people who reside in the city."[5] As seen through this lens, the revitalization taking place in the inner cities made things worse, not better, for the vast majority of the people living within them.

Critics of Richard M. Daley's lakefront complex have lodged similar complaints. In a letter to the editor of the *Chicago Tribune*, a subscriber seemed to speak for many when she wrote bitterly about Chicago as a place where

> we have philanthropists who donate tens of thousands of dollars to house whales. We have corporate leaders who will mortgage the farm to finance Navy Pier and legislators who will mortgage their souls to support fleets of gambling boats, and we have city officials

who plan to spend millions of dollars re-creating parks where beautiful parks already exist. In the City of Chicago, we house our fish better than we house our people. We seem to choose profits and egos again and again over the real needs of the citizens, such as good and safe housing, quality education and equal opportunity to use that education. The money we plan for the aesthetics of Lake Shore Drive should be used to improve the quality of life for the poor by buying books before roses, building houses before aquariums or training people before seals.[6]

In a similar vein, a citizen who wrote a letter to the editor of the *Chicago Sun-Times* posed a long string of rhetorical questions: "If Chicago is so financially strapped, why doesn't Mayor Daley stop planting, removing and replanting unnecessary flower pots? Why do we need the old-time street lights? Why is he planting trees 5 feet apart on the side streets? Do we really need that many trees? Most of all, why do we need Millennium Park? Grant Park is just fine. How many millions over budget is this park costing us so far? . . . Let's get our priorities in order!"[7] It seems clear that even while the press and much of the public celebrated Daley's beautification efforts, some critics regarded them as a pernicious form of blight.

In this epilogue we offer a rejoinder to such a dismal interpretation of a city's life and purpose. In our view, the urban experience would be a grim and stifling if it were to be defined solely by the things that people do when they are engaged in work and the preoccupations of everyday life. What the critics of tourism, recreation, and urbane culture fail to offer is a positive vision that defines urban life expansively—one that embraces both "bread," which is to say prosperity, and "circuses," a term that signifies spectacle, play, and a sense of shared experience in the urban community. A great city must offer both.

The White City and Its Detractors

Contemporary complaints about the style of redevelopment taking place in Chicago and elsewhere faithfully echo sentiments that were expressed more than a century ago. In the 1890s it was understood by everyone that the White City was an island of utopian dreams amid a Chicago beset with staggering social problems. The phrase "black city" sprang forth almost immediately, making its appearance, for example, in Henry Blake Fuller's 1895 novel, *With the Procession*: "[It was] the universal expectation that the spirit of the White City was but just transferred to the body of the great Black City close at hand, over which it was to hover as an enlightenment-through which it might permeate as an informing force."[8] Others, however, were convinced that the White City had stood less as "an informing force" than as a monument to wealth, greed, and avarice. Depending upon one's perspective, it could be either or both; but if the White City was to act as an informing force, the task of making it so would be daunting indeed.

The inspiring architecture and landscapes of the White City and, a few blocks away, the escapism on offer at Jackson Park and Washington Park were accompanied by the painful reality that a serious national recession was claiming its victims disproportionately among the poor. Just a month after the closing of the White City and the attractions on the Midway, Ray Stannard Baker wrote in the *American Chronicle*, "What a human downfall after the magnificence and prodigality of the World's Fair. . . . Heights of splendor, pride, exaltation, in one month: depths of wretchedness, suffering, hunger, cold, in the next."[9] In 1900, Chicago novelist Robert Herrick, in *The Web of Life*, noted the same juxtaposition: "The poor had come lean and hungry out of the terrible winter that followed the World's Fair. In that beautiful enterprise the prodigal city had put forth her utmost strength, and, having shown the world the supreme flower of her energy, had collapsed."[10]

Three years before the fair, in 1890, Jacob Riis published his enormously influential *How the Other Half Lives*, which chronicled, in mesmerizing photographs and angry text, the abysmal living conditions of immigrants in New York City. Had he lived in Chicago, he would certainly have found ample material for a virtually identical book. The census of 1870 found that an astounding 87 percent of the city's population were first- or second-generation immigrants, and the proportion dropped only modestly, to 78 percent, by the time the century came to a close.[11] Nearly all the recently arrived immigrants lived in densely packed neighborhoods of appalling squalor.

The May 1892 issue of *Scribner's Magazine* featured a photo essay on Chicago's immigrants. In it, Joseph Kirkland detailed everyday life as a result of his visits to notorious districts like the Dive, the Levee, the Bad Lands, the Dismal Swamp, and Little Hell. The "prevalent dirt and flagrant vice in Chicago exceeded anything in London," he wrote, and, he added, "It is hard to imagine just how filthy, how squalid, how noisome, how abhorrent it all is. Walking along between inhabited houses and the brick abutments of the raised way is like walking between the walls of a sewer—like it to every sense— sight, smell, hearing, and feeling." And more: "When the back streets of Chicago are undergoing their spring cleaning, the mass of mud collected for removal in this quarter is incredible. The piles along the street-side are as high as they can be made to stand erect, and as close together as they can be."[12] Conditions like these created fertile ground for social and political conflict.

Chicago was engulfed in labor strife for nearly a decade following the Haymarket riots of 1886, and when the World's Fair opened, memories of the recent Haymarket trials were still fresh.

The dangers such clashes posed to the city's economic health were much on the mind of the fair's sponsors, who enthusiastically seized the opportunity to showcase industrial progress and divert attention from the city's troubles, if only for a few celebratory months. For fairgoers, the magic of marketing transformed the Union Stock Yards from a stinking eyesore to a tourist attraction featuring the Yards as one of the industries that "make Chicago the metropolis of the West," something "unlike anything to be seen elsewhere the wide world over."[13] The Pullman Company distributed pamphlets lauding George Pullman's company town as a progressive social experiment, a "radiant little island in the midst of the great tumultuous sea of Chicago's population."[14]

The Pullman experiment's moment in the sun lasted scarcely longer than the fair. Within months, Eugene Debs, leader of the American Railway Union of the American Federation of Labor, led a strike of four thousand Pullman employees at the South Side paradise "of pure air and perfect sanitary conditions" that promised to elevate workers "to a higher plane of wholesome living."[15] In July 1894, a general strike against the Pullman Company mushroomed into a nationwide revolt involving one hundred thousand railroad employees, who showed their solidarity with the workers at Pullman by refusing to handle Pullman cars.[16] Federal troops were dispatched to Chicago, but their presence led to full-scale rioting. On July 5, 1894, the spiritual connection between the World's Fair and Pullman's company town became material reality when an angry mob protesting wage reductions imposed by Pullman moved through the South Side, entered Jackson Park, and burned down seven buildings left over from the fair.[17]

To many, it must have seemed like a karmic turn of fate that some of Burnham's buildings were burned to the ground in a labor riot. Burnham meant for his White City to symbolize civic order, harmony, and beauty as a means of uplifting the human condition. When the mob of workers torched his precious monuments to progress, it could be taken as a confirmation that Burnham's utopian city upon a hill stood not as a shining example but, instead, as an unbearable affront to the poverty-ridden masses living outside its gates.

The Assault on Burnham's Legacy

The White City inspired Burnham to found the City Beautiful movement, and across the country architects, sculptors, landscape designers, and civic leaders joined the cause. As Burnham conceived it, the City Beautiful represented much more than a prescription for well-proportioned landscapes and buildings in a park. What truly energized him and his followers was an ideology built on the premise that a transformation of the physical environment would by some alchemical means also solve the terrible social problems of the industrial city. In 1910, George B. Ford pointed to the critically important role of design and planning by declaring, "What American cities most need and should strive to attain is a healthful, orderly, and symmetrical development along sane and progressive lines."[18] Four years before, an editorial published in the *Municipal Journal and Engineer* noted, "American cities are earnestly striving after the beautiful, the artistic, and the attractive. Everywhere evidences of this can be seen, in public parks, in civic centers, in improvement societies."[19] The City Beautiful was a cause readily embraced, because a reform designed to fit the tastes and comforts of well-heeled and middle-class urban dwellers could, at the same time and seamlessly, be offered up as a remedy all the ills of industrial life.

Critics began excoriating Burnham and the fair even before it closed. Leon Trotsky described the Columbian Exposition as an exercise in capitalist excess: "The Chicago exhibition, like all exhibitions, is a striking example of imprudence and hypocrisy: everything is done for profit and amusement—from boredom—but noble aims of the people are ascribed to it. Orgies are better."[20] Edward Bellamy, author of the utopian novel *Looking Backward* (1888), a book that predicted the shape of the world in the year 2000, argued that the "underlying motive of the whole exhibition, under a sham pretense of patriotism, is business, advertising with a view to individual money-making."[21]

Throughout the twentieth century, urban historians and planners savaged both the esthetic and social ideals of Burnham and his followers. Louis Sullivan, writing in 1924, thought that "the virus of the World's Fair, after a period of incubation in the architectural profession and in the population at large, especially the influential, began to show unmistakable signs of the nature of the contagion. There came a violent outbreak of the Classic and the Renaissance in the East, which slowly spread westward, contaminating all that it touched . . . the selling campaign of the bogus antique."[22] Sullivan's views about Burnham's aesthetic failings were echoed in the years to come by a great many planners. In his magnum opus *The City in History*, Lewis Mumford dismissed the several city plans drawn up by Burnham as false and misleading exercises in baroque planning, with "the typically baroque failing: no concern for the neighborhood as an integral unit, no regard for family housing, no sufficient conception of the ordering of business and industry themselves a necessary part of any larger achievement of urban order." The audacious scope of Burnham's plans reflected, he said, "an innocence of, if not a contempt for, practical needs."[23] For Sullivan, Mumford, and many to follow, Burnham's claim to a grand vision was understood to be nothing more than an arrogant detachment from the world and its problems.

Writing in 1991, the historian William Cronon argued that Burnham's ennobling ideal actually had the opposite effect from what he had intended; rather than serving as an inspiring example, the human idealism and beauty projected by the World's Fair made the poverty, vice, and criminality outside the fair's gates all the more obvious. While "rural Wisconsin had no wealth to match Potter Palmer's [mansion] . . . it also had no poverty to match the slum neighborhoods that encircled Chicago. The journey to the Columbian Exposition gave one a glimpse of those neighborhoods, and the juxtaposition of the two made one wonder about the city's contrasts all the more."[24] For the tourists to the White City, this environment was "hollow glitter," causing anxiety, and even fear.[25] Jane Jacobs echoed this sentiment. In her classic work, *The Death and Life of Great American Cities*, Jacobs pilloried Burnham for building "one heavy, grandiose monument after another arrayed in the [Columbian] exposition garden, like frosted pastries on a tray"; taken together, these buildings added up to "an orgiastic assemblage of the rich and monumental."[26]

What irritated Burnham's critics most of all was his claim that grand architecture and great plans could also have beneficial social effects. In his magisterial work, *Cities in Civilization*, the British scholar Peter Hall asserted that the City Beautiful was "quintessentially American, both in its underlying assumption that what was good for business was good for the region, and also in its confident belief that a private group of people could bring it all about." Hall firmly rejected the notion that the planners had any social aims at all, except to secure a space for the middle class: "The City Beautiful movement was a city designed by and for the bourgeoisie, a city fit for new money to live in and conspicuously consume in; it deliberately rejected any social agenda."[27]

Like many of Burnham's critics, Jacobs wasted few words in expressing her damning judgments, devoting just half a dozen paragraphs to the cause; likewise, Hall allocated scarcely more than two pages to the same task. Mumford, in his thousand-page classic, found a way to dismiss Burnham in a couple of lines. But while some critics may have wished to banish Burnham's name from the historical record, others thought he deserved to be remembered for his numerous sins. In his book *The City as Theme Park*, the urban geographer Michael Sorkin suggested that the White City of 1893 provided the original template for "the physical formula of the theme park, the abstraction of good behavior from the total life of the city."[28] Numerous scholars have registered their views that Burnham's influence can be found in the Disneyfication of urban landscapes (figure E.1). According to the urban historian Eric Avila, Walt Disney built Disneyland as an explicit antidote to "a turbulent sea of social, economic, and cultural upheaval" to be found outside the park. The sociologist Leonard Alvarez went further, proposing that all spaces devoted to tourism and urban amenities should be interpreted a confirming evidence that the urban environment had not itself been made more pleasant, livable, and equitable: the "quality-of-life district," he argues, should be understood as "a different kind of industry location, where visitors' tastes valorize place-based amenities against a backdrop of industrialization and urban sprawl."[29] And thus, just as in Burnham's time, critics of late twentieth-century urbanism believed that those spaces devoted to the playful aspects of urban culture had the effect of bringing the less favored areas of the city into sharp relief.

FIGURE E.1

The *Cloud Gate* sculpture at Millennium Park, affectionately referred to as "the bean," has emerged as an iconic representation of the city and the Disneyfication of urban space. Photo taken June 25, 2011. Courtesy of user Lissandra Melo, Shutterstock Images.

If Burnham has a lot to answer for because he built the original template, it follows that Richard M. Daley would be held accountable for constructing a latter-day version. Burnham claimed that the White City and the City Beautiful and the 1909 *Plan of Chicago* offered an uplifting vision of what the city might become; almost a century later, Daley cited the Burnham legacy as the inspiration for his lakefront complex. Janet Abu-Lughod, the late urban scholar who wrote copiously about Chicago, also discerned an intimate connection between the two eras. The *Plan of Chicago*, she wrote, created a "'dual city' of façade and backstage," a geographic division between the lakefront and the rest of the city that "served to insulate them [the commercial elite] from the masses."[30] She considered Daley's lakefront program to be the latest phase in a century-long project to create privileged spaces for Chicago's elite: "Daley's success in getting wealthy Chicagoans to fund the new and impressive Millennium Park at the lake front recapitulates and expands the Burnham Plan that was used almost a century ago to separate the classes."[31] In Abu-Lughod's view, we come full circle: the ghosts of Chicago's past not only continue to haunt the present, but they have returned to wreak their havoc anew.

The Return of the "Bread and Circuses" Debate

The critics of Burnham's White City and of Daley's City of Spectacle steadfastly argued that the material welfare of urban residents (the "bread") trumped all other goals of urban life, and that resources devoted to any other purpose—the "circuses"— should be understood as a diversion from more pressing matters. Claims by the earlier generation of reformers that they were motivated by a desire to improve the lives of all urban dwellers were greeted with derision; likewise, a century later critics have heaped scorn upon civic leaders who promote publicly subsidized redevelopment schemes as expressions of the public interest. In the late twentieth century, just as in Burnham's time, there was ample reason for skepticism.

In recent decades the debates about public priorities have been reawakened because huge public investments have been poured into a constantly changing bundle of infrastructure and amenities to support tourism, entertainment, and urban culture. Convention centers and sports stadiums are only two of the more expensive items on a long list that generally includes festival malls, entertainment complexes, convention hotels, performing arts venues, cultural districts, and an ever-expanding list of urban amenities.

Almost every day, in a city somewhere in the United States, public officials breathlessly announce a big-ticket project meant to burnish the city's image and grow the local economy. With so many claimants on the public purse, who is minding the store to ensure that public dollars are wisely spent?

The insider-game politics that drives major urban development projects puts into doubt any notion that local political and civic elites can be trusted to act as reliable guardians of the public purse. Civic leaders feel compelled to defend their development proposals by advancing a version of cost-benefit analysis that generally includes some combination of economic data and less quantifiable assertions about the value of a project to their city's image or standing among its peers, and they possess the resources to hire consulting firms to produce a supporting analysis. Because an array of consultants and industry specialists stand ready to provide the relevant financial, public relations, marketing, and expertise to all cities, a predictable process of persuasion is replicated over and over and from place to place.[32] Engineering and architectural services are offered by a handful of firms. Public relations companies with international reach are hired to manage promotional campaigns. Firms specializing in accounting and public finance prepare the principal financial justifications.[33] At the heart of these reports are data and information gathered from industry associations that share an interest in expanding their influence. Bond-rating agencies rely on the same sources of data and on consulting reports produced by the same firms that offer advice to cities. It is a tightly organized and remarkably closed community.

Producing evidence to convince the local citizenry that a project is a good bargain may be a political necessity for politicians and their backers, but in reality a strict cost-benefit calculation is largely irrelevant to local boosters. They are instead driven by a standard narrative of urban decline and growth that ties public investment to the overall well-being of the city. As the urban scholar David Harvey has observed, "the grim history of deindustrialization and restructuring . . . left most major cities in the advanced capitalist world with few options except to compete with each other."[34] This competition has imposed a relentless logic that requires urban leaders to project to potential investors a commitment to transformation and positive change. For this reason, major urban projects carry great symbolic value that cannot be translated into dollars. Mark Douglas Lowes explains Vancouver's attempt in the 1990s to host an annual Indycar race by observing, "Economic growth is the ultimate objective, but major league franchises and international events are also widely understood as badges of a city's stature, a symbolic sign of 'arrival' from which other forms of growth will presumably follow."[35]

Civic leaders share a belief that there is no alternative but to compete, and this conviction explains why they often display what appears to be a cavalier attitude toward taxpayers' money. Public officials and local boosters do not, on the whole, much care if individual projects pay for themselves. Based on a study of ten cities, two urban researchers concluded that development projects have "little [to] do with the . . . profitability . . . of a project" and far more to do with the vision officials share about the overall direction a city is taking.[36] If new projects fail to pay for themselves, they can be, and often are, justified as loss leaders that bring other investments in to the local community.[37]

In recent decades a countless number of projects have been built as a result of this loss-leader logic. Since the early 1980s, for example, hundreds of cities have built new convention centers or expanded their existing facilities. From 2000 to 2005 public capital spending on convention centers doubled, to $2.4 billion annually, and the pace of construction has continued to accelerate year by year.[38] The frantic pace of construction proceeded despite the fact that market shares for most cities were falling in direct proportion to the proliferation of facilities available to convention planners.[39] Rather than acting as a deterrent, this circumstance spurred cities to double-down. In a typical case, in the first decade of the twenty-first century officials of Chicago's McCormick Place undertook huge and costly expansions despite (or, rather, because of) a steady decline in convention business. In 2007 a nearly billion-dollar bond supported the construction of the giant McCormick Place Convention Center West, which added 2.6 million square feet of space and guaranteed that McCormick would continue to be the nation's largest convention facility. To try to generate enough business to fill its vast interior, McCormick officials have, in recent years, offered major rebates and reduced the costs paid by exhibitors. These measures slowed the decline, but barely.[40]

Convention centers are not sexy, and they often fly under the radar, but in recent years sports facilities have received a great deal of public attention. In little more than a decade, from 1990 to 2002, new sports facilities were completed in the downtowns of thirty North American cities.[41] From 2000 to 2006, public funds supplied 54 percent of the construction cost for new Major League Baseball stadiums and 55 percent of the costs for football stadiums.[42] What galls so many people is that these subsidies amount to a transfer of public resources to the pocketbooks of wealthy team owners (and players). Professional sports is a big business. Between 2010 and 2011, the value of Major League Baseball teams increased 7 percent and reached an average high of $523 million per team. The New York Yankees topped the list at $1.7 billion.[43] The Yankees opened their season in 2009 in a new stadium that cost $1.5 billion to build, while just a few miles away in New Jersey, the NFL Jets and the Giants moved into one costing $1.6 billion.[44] Fans of the Mets, the Yankees, the Giants, and the Jets expressed outrage at the escalating price of tickets. At the three stadiums in New York, ticket prices doubled or more. Season tickets for the best seats that had cost $1,000 each in the old Yankee Stadium jumped to $2,500 when the new stadium opened in 2009.[45] In August 2008, the Giants announced that they would charge from $1,000 to $20,000 for personal seat licenses (PSL), which entitled only the holders to buy season tickets. "Here I am, buying a stadium for John Mara," a Giants ticket holder complained. "This is a greedy ploy with the only benefits going to them."[46]

In January 2015, the Atlanta Falcons announced a PSL plan with club seats ranging from $10,000 to $45,000.[47] The next month, in February 2015, officials in the state of Missouri and the city of St. Louis announced an ambitious plan to build a new $985 million riverfront stadium (which soon rose above the $1 billion mark) for the NFL Rams, a move, they hoped, that would keep the team from moving to Los Angeles. More than $350 million in state and local funds would be required to supplement private dollars to complete the facility. In announcing the project, Missouri governor Jay Nixon noted that "this is a historic opportunity to bring hundreds of millions of dollars in private investment to this area, build an iconic stadium that will stand the test of time, and transform these deserted streets into a thriving destination for residents, workers, tourists and football fans."[48] Because the deal would commit the city to a payment to the team's owner of $6 million each year plus, a sum equivalent to two-thirds of the taxes generated by the stadium, a large segment of the public and several members of the city's board of aldermen were not persuaded, and for months the controversy raged. The St. Louis Chamber of Commerce weighed in by hiring the accounting firm PricewaterhouseCoopers to show that the stadium would bring huge benefits to the city and region and to St. Louis's image. The report was released in late November 2015, just in time for a decisive decision by the St. Louis Board of Aldermen to support the project. The consultants estimated that the stadium would bring $1.8 billion into the local economy in just three years; in addition, they wrote, keeping the Rams would enhance the "community brand, media exposure, quality of life and central city development."[49] Such a refrain would have sounded very familiar to anyone paying attention to stadium controversies in other cities. In January of 2016, to the surprise of St. Louis officials and fans, the NFL owners, calling the St. Louis plan "unworkable," voted 30–2 to allow the Rams to move to Los Angeles for the 2016 season. Jim Woodcock, spokesman for the St. Louis stadium task force, noted that "the decision by the NFL concludes a flawed process that ends with the unthinkable result of St. Louis losing the Rams.[50]

Whatever consultants may claim otherwise, it is not plausible that every convention center or stadium project is worth the public investment in every city. A transparent democratic process requiring public hearings, the release of consultants' reports, and voter referendums, if required, would all help shed light on this question, but perhaps not as much as critics might hope. It is undoubtedly true, as the consultants and their clients assert, that image and standing are important, and that their value is impossible to precisely calculate. There was a time when most academic studies were uniformly skeptical, but in recent years the conversation has shifted from a focus on public costs to the impact major projects may have on the future development of the city. Sports economist Andrew Zimbalist, who has devoted years of research to this issue, has pointed out that "cities spend millions of dollars to support a variety of cultural activities that are not expected to have positive economic effects, such as subsidizing a local symphony or maintaining a public park. Sports teams can have a powerful cultural or social impact on a community. If that effect is valued by the local residents, then they may well decide that some public dollars are appropriate."[51] The economist Roger Noel has concluded that "a well-managed arena can be occupied 250–300 nights a year. And they can break even. And indeed, I don't think there are very many cities out there who regret having built an arena."[52]

A great many people may disagree with this view, but even when they do it is safe to say that ambiguity rules the day, in large part because sports teams have long been central to the civic and cultural life, and even the identity, of American cities. Oddly, the assumption that a team expresses a city's essence, spirit, and sense of community has not been much eroded since teams, owners, and their players became highly mobile. Local boosters regard professional sports teams as a signifier of "big league" status for a city, and many urban residents do too. As a consequence, sports teams carry a substantial emotional charge, so their worth is rarely, if ever, calculated in straightforward economic terms. It may pain critics to admit it, but many urban residents—perhaps most—want circuses as well as bread.

Two Eras of Urban Transformation

When public leaders and civic boosters announce grand schemes to promote the local economy, a healthy skepticism is well advised, and details matter. A series of really dumb decisions can compromise the health and well-being of local residents, but the fate of cities and the people who live in them depend, at least as much, on circumstances and structural forces beyond the control of any single community. At least twice in this nation's history there have been periods when urban leaders faced a stark choice: either pursue an aggressive strategy to transform the local economy and physical environment, or run the risk of abject failure. These two eras bookended the twentieth century, and the second of them has not yet run its course.

By the late nineteenth century it had become obvious that something had to be done to address the sordid and chaotic conditions of the industrial cities. A sense of urgency was provoked, in equal measure, by the dissatisfactions of the upper and middle classes with the conditions they encountered, and also by a realization that the problems in the immigrant wards threatened the health and welfare of urban dwellers of every social class. In this understanding they were correct: all members of the urban community shared an interest in improving urban services and changing the physical environment of cities, and for this reason the rising popular discontent of urban elites and a rising middle class demanded improved urban services and infrastructure. Systems of separate sanitary and storm sewers were completed in most cities late in the nineteenth century, and by then most of the cities were expanding their public health efforts. By using the latest science of bacteriology, health inspectors examined children in schools, checked buildings for ventilation and faulty plumbing, and inspected food and milk.[53] Such public health measures, when combined with the completion of integrated sewer systems and installation of new water filtration technology, dramatically reduced typhoid mortality rates.[54] Overall death rates fell sharply in the big urban areas, by 20 percent or more in New York, Chicago, Cleveland, Buffalo, and other urban centers in the 1890s,[55] and just as abruptly again after the turn of the century.[56]

Reformers also aimed to change the physical environment, and in doing so they brought the twentieth-century metropolis into being. Improvements begun in the late nineteenth century ushered in a golden age of American city-building. The massive investment in physical infrastructure placed city governments at the cutting edge of technology, resulting in such engineering marvels as the Brooklyn Bridge and New York's Croton aqueduct system, with its thousands of miles of pipes and reservoirs. The Parks Movement and the City Beautiful Movement swept the nation, resulting in urban amenities such as recreational areas with parks, ponds, formal gardens, bandstands, ball fields, broad tree-lined avenues, and ornate public buildings. Urban residents came to expect a level of municipal services that would have been inconceivable in an earlier time. The squalor of the nineteenth-century industrial city began to yield to the relative safety, cleanliness, and health of the twentieth-century metropolis. Obviously, urban elites and middle-class residents benefited disproportionately from these efforts, but the building regulations and public health measures also sponsored by reformers improved conditions in the slums as well.

The second great period of urban transformation was provoked by the national urban crisis that unfolded in the years following World War II, when suburbanization and deindustrialization devastated central-city economies and older urban regions. By the late 1970s the process of decline seemed to have become so irreversible that the members of a national commission appointed by President Jimmy Carter issued a report darkly suggesting that the problems of the older cities had become so intractable that they threatened the economic health of the nation. According to the commission's report, "Ultimately, the federal government's concern for national economic vitality should take precedence over the competition for advantage among communities and regions.

To attempt to restrict or reverse the processes of change—for whatever noble intentions—is to deny the benefits that the future may hold for us as a nation."[57] Before long the Reagan administration followed that advice and cut most urban programs, leaving cities to fend for themselves. A generation of mayors accepted the new reality, and largely through their efforts and with the application of huge public resources, downtown business and entertainment/tourist districts became popular destinations for tourists and local (mostly middle-class) residents alike, and the money they infused into local economies was absolutely essential to the cities' escape from the gloomy forecasts issued only a few years before. The economic restructuring that made this historic turnaround possible contained many interlocking components, but tourism, entertainment, and culture were central ingredients to the mix.

Over the years, critics have indulged in a great deal of finger-wagging at virtually every scheme to promote economic growth, with a special enmity reserved for tourism and its related sectors. Many of the academics and activists who fall into this camp reject the notion that the pursuit of growth and jobs should ever be the primary goal guiding urban policy. In their sweeping study of post-millennium projects in New York, the urban scholars David Halle and Elizabeth Tiso encountered this attitude often; they quote, for example, one analysis of the projects undertaken during Mayor Michael Bloomberg's tenure in which the author argue that New York City should provide "a comfortable life to those not wealthy, well credentialed, and ambitious," that it should be "a city that honored and cared for longtime residents and the neighborhoods they created."[58] Halle and Tiso respond that this hortatory declaration "seems unreasonable" because "we do not see how these worthy goals (e.g., 'a comfortable life for those not wealthy') can be sustained without jobs and growth that also protects and even expands the tax base that supports services."[59] In this assessment, Halle and Tiso signal their disagreement with an entire generation of urban scholarship.

No one should suppose that economic growth, physical revitalization, or the social values that define urban culture automatically remedy inequality and its many ills. Urban success in the present era has brought many problems, and one of them is that it comes at the expense of a great many people who cannot share in its benefits. Urban failure, though, does not work as an antidote to this disease. A visit to Detroit or Gary shows that the results of disinvestment are catastrophic, and it benefits no one at all. Cities that have succeeded have become not only economically viable; they also offer an unprecedented quality of life for many—perhaps most—of their urban residents (figure E.2).

Today, the effort to restructure the economies of American cities has been largely accomplished, and in any case, the period when urban leaders could afford to fixate on economic development to the exclusion of other priorities has ended. The events of August 2014, when disorders broke out in Ferguson, Missouri, may have signaled that a new imperative, social justice, now commands a high priority on America's urban agenda. Ferguson may or may not turn out to be a tipping point, but urban leaders are now forced to deal with mounting concerns about the systematic inequality and racial injustice embedded within American society. Such issues as mass incarceration, police misbehavior, and the humiliations and injustices of everyday life are keenly felt by African Americans, but they tap into grievances shared by a great many people across the racial and even the partisan divide. In the United States, a yawning chasm, exacerbated in recent years, divides rich from poor, black from white, and the very wealthy from everyone else. As recounted

FIGURE E.2

New residential neighborhoods, like this one in the South Loop, emerged around the downtown area following the development of an amenities infrastructure during the Richard M. Daley years. Courtesy of user Mark Baldwin, Shutterstock Images.

by the writer Matt Taibbi, these inequalities are implicated in race relations, the American system of justice, the electoral system, and everyday economics.[60]

The popular discontent has been seized on by politicians at all levels. In 2013, a Democrat, Bill de Blasio, won the mayoral race in New York City by running a populist campaign that took aim at the policies of his Republican business-oriented predecessor, Michael Bloomberg. Likewise, in the winter and early spring of 2015, Chicago's mayoral race featured a campaign by the incumbent, Rahm Emanuel, which touted his policies to fund universal preschool and community college tuition. In the months leading up to the election, the city council approved a ten-dollar minimum wage ordinance and legislation requiring developers to set aside a portion of units in new projects for affordable housing. In the presidential campaign of 2015–16, the candidacy of Bernie Sanders struck a chord, and it forced Hillary Clinton to the left. It may be said that de Blasio, Emanuel, and the contenders for the Democratic nomination were products of their time, as Richard M. Daley was of his.

Richard M. Daley: A Final Word

Robert Caro, in his monumental study of Robert Moses, wrote, "It is impossible to say that New York would have been a better city if Robert Moses had never lived. It is possible to say only that it would have been a different city."[61] As the years passed, Caro grew increasingly certain that Moses had made New York worse. Since he left office Richard M. Daley's legacy has come into question, but we believe criticisms as harsh as those once aimed at Moses would not be justified. At the time he served as mayor, it was transcendently important that Chicago restructure its economy and remake its physical and cultural environment. Daley's leadership was instrumental in bringing Chicago into the global era, and his lakefront program brought about a remarkable economic and cultural transformation that will affect the city for decades to come.

Although it is tempting to rely on hindsight to evaluate Daley's actions and policies, such an exercise obscures more than it reveals. As we have earlier noted, we believe that Daley was both visionary and a product of his times. It should be kept in mind that he served as mayor in a period when all cities were in the midst of a historic economic transformation. The basic outlines of the strategy Daley pursued to restructure Chicago's economy looked very similar to the approach taken in many other urban centers, but what he accomplished in Chicago carried Daley's unique imprimatur. Daley imagined that the city he wanted to build was a natural expression of the Burnham legacy and Chicago's history, and because he spent more years in office and exercised more political authority than most of his peers, he was able to see his vision through.

As his detractors were always eager to point out, Daley was less successful in other areas. It may have been necessary for Daley to assemble a "new machine" to give him the power he sought, but the process of building it ensnared him in a train of corruption scandals that constantly dogged him throughout his mayoral years. In addition, Daley failed to understand how important the problem of police misbehavior was for many Chicago residents, and as a consequence, he handed this festering issue on to his successor. He handed off other serious problems, too. Daley was an exceedingly ambitious mayor who tried to tackle almost every policy issue the city faced, no matter how intractable. His strategies to reform education and public housing helped make Chicago more appealing to middle-class gentrifiers, but that made things worse for many of the city's residents and also stirred political conflicts that endure to the present day. In the spring of 2016 Mayor Emanuel's hard-line management approach in dealing with Chicago Public Schools and the teacher's union served as continuing reminders that Daley's school reforms had fallen short.

Chicago's chronic fiscal crisis is an issue that continues to adversely affect Daley's post-mayoral public image. Even after all these years, the sale of the city's parking meters still irks not only his critics but also everyone else, and from time to time media stories about Chicago's ongoing fiscal crisis continue to refer to it as an example of bad fiscal policy. What gets lost in such stories is that Daley's success in orchestrating a downtown building boom undoubtedly saved the city from becoming a true economic basket case. His rebuilding program set the stage for Emanuel to announce in 2016 a new program that would shift money charged to downtown developers to projects undertaken in the city's economically depressed areas. Estimated between $40 million to $50 million in the next three to four years, these resources are expected to generate needed economic development in the neighborhoods.[62]

Assessing Daley's legacy may seem to require us to weigh his success in remaking Chicago against his policy failures, but we believe that is a fool's errand and unnecessary. It is sufficient, in our view, simply to acknowledge that the remaking Chicago lakefront and economy under his leadership should be regarded as a significant achievement. During his mayoral years Daley was hailed as one of the greatest mayors in America, a verdict that reflected, above all, admiration for his lakefront projects. We confess that when we, this book's authors, stroll along the lakefront with friends or out-of-town visitors, their comments, and ours, about Chicago do not sound much different from the praise that was lavished on Daley's lakefront program when he was in the midst of implementing it. The City of Spectacle remade Chicago, and this is Richard M. Daley's enduring and positive legacy.

Notes

Introduction

1. Richard Lloyd, *Neo-Bohemia: Art and Commerce in the Postindustrial City* (New York: Routledge, 2006), 126.

2. Nancy Gibbs, "The 5 Best Big-City Mayors," *Time*, April 25, 2005, 17.

3. Jim Kirk, Dan Mihalopoulos, Sarah Karp, Mick Dumke, Don Terry, and David Greising, "The Daley Legacy, Inescapable," *New York Times*, September 12, 2010, 35A.

4. Susan Saulny, "Urban Development: Chicago Is Mayor Daley's Kind of Town," *New York Times*, September 12, 2010, 3.

5. Dan Mihalopoulos and Katherine Skiba, "Daley Rallies Support for Olympic Bid ahead of Copenhagen Trip: Mayor Declines to Address Possible Developer Conflict," *Chicago Tribune*, September 27, 2009.

6. John W. Mashek with Mary Galligan, "Chicago's Bare-Knuckle Race for Mayor," *U.S. News & World Report*, February 21, 1983.

7. "Tigerman Urges Architects to Consider Doing Good and Building Green," *Architectural Record*, February 1, 2007, http://archrecord.construction.com/news/daily/archives/070201tigerman.asp.

8. Richard M. Daley, speech to Chicago Greening Convention, March 8, 2002.

9. Blair Kamin, "City Has a Field Day Planting Trees—with Mixed Results for the Museum," *Chicago Tribune*, July 8, 1999.

10. John McCarron, "Daley as Visionary: One Man's Grand Plan for Chicago," op-ed, *Chicago Tribune*, April 14, 2002.

11. Blair Kamin, "How 2 Strongmen Got Things Done," *Chicago Tribune*, March 11, 2007.

12. Robert Caro, *The Power Broker: Robert Moses and the Fall of New York* (New York: Vintage Books, 1975).

13. Kara Younkain, Carlos Carrion, and Jack Lu, "Robert Moses—Master Builder," paper for course CE 5212/PA 5232: Transportation Policy, Planning, and

Deployment, MURP Program, University of Minnesota, http://nexus.umn.edu/courses/cases/ce5212/f2009/cs3/cs3.pdf.

14. Todd Berkun, "Robert Moses Re-reevaluated," LI & NY Places That Are No More, http://placesnomore.wordpress.com/2011/01/21/rmoses1/.

15. Thomas Hardy, "Daleyland vs. Illinois: Bordering on Delusion," op-ed, *Chicago Tribune*, December 8, 1996.

16. McCarron, "Daley as Visionary."

17. Dick Simpson, *Rogues, Rebels, and Rubber Stamps: The Politics of the Chicago City Council, 1863 to the Present* (Boulder, CO: Westview, 2001), 6.

18. Quoted in Alex Keefe, "Pregnancy Tests? Pigeon Poo? What Chicago Aldermen Actually Do," WBEZ 91.5, June 11, 2013, http://www.wbez.org/series/curious-city/pregnancy-tests-pigeon-poo-what-chicago-aldermen-really-do-107648.

19. Dick Simpson, quoted ibid.

20. Quoted in Kim Phillips-Fein, "The Still-Industrial City: Why Cities Shouldn't Just Let Manufacturing Go," *American Prospect*, November 30, 2002, 28.

1. The Founding City

1. See the discussion in John Hannigan, *Fantasy City: Pleasure and Profit in the Postmodern Metropolis* (New York: Routledge, 1998), 25–28.

2. Michael Steiner, "Parables of Stone and Steel: Architectural Images of Progress and Nostalgia at the Columbian Exposition and Disneyland," *American Studies* 42, no. 1 (2001): 56. Walt Disney was born in Chicago in 1901; his father, a carpenter, had helped in construction of the Columbian Exposition of 1893.

3. Quoted in Jon Teaford, *The Rough Road to Renaissance: Urban Revitalization in America, 1940–1985* (Baltimore: Johns Hopkins University Press, 1990), 253.

4. Quoted ibid.

5. "Messiah mayors" is Jon Teaford's felicitous term; see ibid.

6. Alexander Ganz, "Where Has the Urban Crisis Gone? How Boston and Other Large Cities Have Stemmed Economic Decline," *Urban Affairs Quarterly* 20 (June 1985): 449–68; Mark Gottdiener, "Whatever Happened to the Urban Crisis?," *Urban Affairs Quarterly* 20 (June 1985): 421–27, and Eric Monkonen, "What Urban Crisis? A Historian's Point of View," *Urban Affairs Quarterly* 20 (June 1985): 429–47.

7. Quoted in Arnold Lewis, *An Early Encounter with Tomorrow* (Urbana: University of Illinois Press, 1997), 17.

8. Rudyard Kipling, *American Notes* (Boston: Brown and Co., 1899, new ed.), 99.

9. Robert W. Rydell, *All the World's a Fair: Visions of Empire at American International Expositions, 1876–1916* (Chicago: University of Chicago Press, 1984), 38–71.

10. John R. Davis, "The Great Exhibition," *British Heritage*, June/July 2001, 15, and Paul Young, "Economy, Empire, Extermination: The Christmas Pudding, the Crystal Palace and the Narrative of Capitalist Progress," *Literature and History* 14, no. 1 (April 2005): 14–30.

11. Richard Nicolai, *Centennial Philadelphia* (Bryn Mawr, PA: Bryn Mawr Press, 1976), 13.

12. Janet Abu-Lughod, *New York, Chicago, Los Angeles: America's Global Cities* (Minneapolis: University of Minnesota Press, 1989), 101.

13. Samuel P. Hays, *The Response to Industrialism, 1885–1914* (Chicago: University of Chicago Press, 1957), 73.

14. Michael Steiner. "Parables of Stone and Steel: Architectural Images of Progress and Nostalgia at the Columbian Exposition and Disneyland," *American Studies* 42, no. 1 (2001): 49. Bloom later served six terms in the U.S. House of Representatives.

15. Hubert Howe Bancroft, *The Book of the Fair* (Chicago: Bancroft Co., 1983). See esp. chap. 24, "The Midway Plaisance," 835.

16. Quoted in Lisa Krissoff Boehm, *Popular Culture and the Enduring Myth of Chicago, 1871–1968* (New York: Routledge, 2004), 45.

17. Quoted in James Gilbert, "A Contest of Cultures," *History Today*, July 1992, 38–39.

18. "The Opening of the World's Columbian Exposition," *Manufacturer and Builder* 25, no. 4 (April 1893): 89.

19. "Columbian Exposition: What It Will Do for America," *Century*, October 1892, 955.

20. Jacques Hermant, "L'art à l'exposition de Chicago," *Gazette des Beaux-Arts* 73 (November 1893): 425, quoted in Lewis, *Early Encounter*, 177.

21. Lewis, *Early Encounter*, 191.

22. Quoted in Graham Clarke, *The American City: Literary Sources and Documents* (New York: Routledge, 1997), 3:323.

23. Constance McLaughlin Green, *Washington: Capital City, 1879–1950* (Princeton, NJ: Princeton University Press, 1963), 154.

24. Arnold William Brunner, in *Proceedings of the Eighth National Conference on City Planning, Cleveland, June 5–7, 1916*, New York, National Conference on City Planning, 1916, 14–34; quotation is on p. 34.

25. Gray Brechin, "Sailing to Byzantium: The Architecture of the Panama-Pacific International Exposition," in *The Anthropology of World's Fairs*, edited by Burton Benedict (London and Berkeley: Lowie Museum of Anthropology and Scholar Press, 1983), 95.

26. Mario Manieri-Elia, "Toward an 'Imperial City': Daniel H. Burnham and the City Beautiful Movement," in *The American City: From the Civil War to the New Deal*, by Giorgio Ciucci, Francesco Dal Co, Mario Manieri-Elia, Manfredo Tafuri, and Barbara Luigi La Penta (Cambridge, MA: MIT Press, 1979), 89.

27. Carl Smith, *The Plan of Chicago: Daniel Burnham and the Remaking of the American City* (Chicago: University of Chicago Press, 2006), 108.

28. Daniel H. Burnham and Edward H. Bennett, *Plan of Chicago* (1909; Princeton, NJ: Princeton Architectural Series, 1993), 4.

29. Ibid., 117.

30. For an engaging account see Stephane Kirkland, *Paris Reborn: Napoleon III, Baron Haussmann, and the Quest to Build a Modern City* (New York: Picador, 2013).

31. Ibid., 18.

32. Ibid., 50.

33. This felicitous phrase comes from Larry Bennett, *The Third City: Chicago and American Urbanism* (Chicago: University of Chicago Press, 2010), 38.

34. Ibid., 161–62.

35. Dennis H. Cremin, *Grant Park: The Evolution of Chicago's Front Yard* (Carbondale: Southern Illinois University Press, 2013), 71.

36. Ibid., 94.

37. Ibid., 97–98.

38. Blair Kamin, "Reinventing the Lakefront," series published in the *Chicago Tribune*, October 26–November 5, 1998.

39. George Papajohn, "Challenge for a New Century—the City Needs a New Blueprint, a Vision That Draws on Its Strengths and Addresses Its Problems in a Vein Similar to Daniel H. Burnham's 1909 'Plan of Chicago,'" *Chicago Tribune*, February 7, 1999.

40. Lou Carlozo, "Expanding the Branch Operations," *Chicago Tribune*, August 29, 1993.

41. "Mayor Daley Presents New Museum Campus to Chicago," July 31, 1998, from the *US Conference of Mayors Archives* at http://usmayors.org.

42. Remarks from Mayor Richard M. Daley, Keynote Address to the Urban Parks Institute's "Great Parks / Great Cities" Conference, July 31, 2001, "Revitalizing Chicago through Parks and Public Spaces," http://www.pps.org/topics/whats_new/daley_speech.

43. Blair Kamin, "A Critic Weighs in a Park for the People," *Chicago Tribune*, April 5, 1998.

44. Chicago City Council, *Journal of the Proceedings*, Municipal Reference Collection, Chicago Public Library, May 21, 2007, 12–22.

2. Arresting Chicago's Long Slide

1. Jon C. Teaford, *The Rough Road to Renaissance: Urban Revitalization in America, 1940–1985* (Baltimore: Johns Hopkins University Press, 1990), 5.

2. Robert A. Beauregard, *Voices of Decline: The Postwar Fate of U.S. Cities* (New York: Blackwell, 1993), 174.

3. Andrew H. Malcolm, "Chicago," *New York Times*, April 10, 1983, A24.

4. U.S. Department of Commerce, Bureau of the Census, various reports, 1950, 1990.

5. Joel Rast, *Remaking Chicago: The Political Origins of Urban Industrial Change* (DeKalb: Northern Illinois University Press, 1989), 88.

6. Richard C. Longworth, "The American Millstone," in "Lost Jobs Leave Legacy of Despair" series, *Chicago Tribune*, September 29, 1985.

7. Quoted in Milton L. Rakove, *Don't Make No Waves—Don't Back No Losers: An Insider's Analysis of the Daley Machine* (Bloomington, IN: Indiana University Press, 1975), 80.

8. Quoted in Kim Phillips-Fein, "The Still-Industrial City: Why Cities Shouldn't Just Let Manufacturing Go," *American Prospect*, November 30, 2002.

9. Karen Plunkett-Powell, *Remembering Woolworth's: A Nostalgic History of the World's Most Famous Five-and-Dime* (New York: St. Martin's, 1999), 209.

10. David Beito, *Taxpayers in Revolt: Tax Resistance during the Great Depression* (Chapel Hill: University of North Carolina Press, 1989), 57.

11. Oscar Hewitt, "Seek 3 Million from Officials for Relief Fund," *Chicago Daily Tribune*, August 17, 1931.

12. "All Employed Folk Urged to Aid Relief Drive," *Chicago Daily Tribune*, August 28, 1932.

13. Katherine Kelley, "Camp Algonquin to Revive Poor Children," *Chicago Daily Tribune*, June 12, 1932.

14. Robert G. Spinney, *World War II in Nashville: Transformation of the Homefront* (Knoxville: University of Tennessee Press, 1998), 23, 25.

15. "In the Region of Chicago," Chicago Regional Planning Association, Chicago Historical Society, 1926 (ICHi-37497).

16. Chicago Plan Commission, *Building New Neighborhoods*, Chicago Historical Society, 1943 (ICHi-37496).

17. Richard A. Thompson, "DuPage Roots," DuPage County Historical Society, 1985, 82.

18. John F. McDonald, *Urban America: Growth, Crisis and Rebirth* (Armonk, NY: M. E. Sharp, 2008), 95–96.

19. Glen E. Holt and Dominic A. Pacyga, *Chicago: A Historical Guide to the Neighborhoods* (Chicago: Chicago Historical Society, 1979), 29–37.

20. Rast, *Remaking Chicago*, 47–48.

21. Paul F. Gehl, "Printing," in *Encyclopedia of Chicago* (Chicago: University of Chicago Press, 2004).

22. Holt and Pacyga, *Chicago*, 22.

23. McDonald, *Urban America*, 96.

24. Daniel P. McMillen, "Polycentric Urban Structure: The Case of Milwaukee," *Economic Perspectives* (Federal Reserve Bank of Chicago) 25, no. 2 (2nd quarter 2001): 16.

25. Ibid., 86–87.

26. Robert A. Beauregard, *When America Became Suburban* (Minneapolis: University of Minnesota Press, 2006), xi.

27. Daniel P. McMillen, "Employment Subcenters in Chicago: Past, Present, and Future," *Economic Perspectives* (Federal Reserve Bank of Chicago) 27, no. 2 (2nd quarter 2003): 2.

28. U.S. Bureau of the Census, City and County Data Book, 1974, 1994.

29. Janet L. Abu-Lughod, *New York, Chicago, Los Angeles: America's Global Cities* (Minneapolis: University of Minnesota Press, 2000), 326.

30. William Grimshaw, *Bitter Fruit: Black Politics and the Chicago Machine, 1931–1991* (Chicago: University of Chicago Press, 1992), 78.

31. Spinney, *World War II in Nashville*, 219.

32. Douglas Bukowski, *Big Bill Thompson, Chicago, and the Politics of Image* (Urbana: University of Illinois Press, 1998), 232.

33. Milton Rakove, *Don't Make No Waves... Don't Back No Losers: An Insider's Analysis of the Daley Machine* (Bloomington: Indiana University Press, 1975).

34. Rast, *Remaking Chicago*, 27.

35. Dick Simpson, *Rogues, Rebels and Rubberstamps: The Politics of the Chicago City Council from 1863 to the Present* (Boulder, CO: Westview, 2001), 249.

36. Roger Biles, *Richard J. Daley: Politics, Race, and the Governing of Chicago* (DeKalb: Northern Illinois University Press, 1996), 45.

37. Richard Flanagan, "Opportunities and Constraints on Mayoral Behavioral: A Historical-Institutional Approach," *Journal of Urban Affairs* 26, no. 1 (2004): 51.

38. Gregory D. Squires, Larry Bennett, Kathleen McCourt, and Philip Nyden, *Chicago: Race, Class, and the Response to Urban Decline* (Philadelphia: Temple University Press, 1987), 157.

39. Quoted in Adam Cohen and Elizabeth Taylor, *American Pharaoh: Richard J. Daley; His Battle for Chicago and the Nation* (Boston: Back Bay Books, 2001), 292.

40. "Chicago 21," *Time*, July 2, 1973.

41. Quoted in Lois Wille, *At Home in the Loop: How Clout and Community Built Chicago's Dearborn Park* (Carbondale: Southern Illinois University Press, 1997), 30.

42. "Chicago 21," *Time*, July 2, 1973.

43. Quoted in Cohen and Taylor, *American Pharaoh*, 293.

44. Quoted in Wille, *At Home in the Loop*, 13.

45. Ibid., 82.

46. David Emmons, *Dearborn Park / South Loop New Town Park: A Project in the Chicago 21 Plan*, Report to the Citizens Information Service of Illinois, January 1977, 16.

47. "Chicago 21," *Time*, July 2, 1973.

48. Ibid.

49. Cohen and Taylor, *American Pharaoh*, 11.

50. Larry Bennett, "Chicago's New Politics of Growth," in *The New Chicago: A Social and Cultural Analysis*, ed. John P. Koval, Larry Bennett, Michael I. J. Bennett, Fassil Demissie, Roberta Garner, and Kiljoong Kim (Philadelphia: Temple University Press), 45.

51. Steven P. Erie, *Rainbow's End: Irish-Americans and the Dilemmas of Urban Machine Politics, 1840–1985* (Berkeley: University of California Press, 1990), 65.

52. Thomas M. Guterbock, *Machine Politics in Transition: Party and Community in Chicago* (Chicago: University of Chicago Press, 1980), 236.

53. Paul Kleppner, *Chicago Divided: The Making of a Black Mayor* (DeKalb: Northern Illinois University Press, 1985), 74–75.

54. Ibid., 78.

55. Bennett, "Chicago's New Politics of Growth," 45.

56. Ibid., 45–46.

57. "Inaugural Address of Mayor Michael A. Bilandic," Chicago Municipal Reference Collection, June 22, 1977.

58. Ester R. Fuchs, *Mayors and Money: Fiscal Policy in New York and Chicago*, (Chicago: University of Chicago Press, 1992) 7.

59. Ibid., 8.

60. Rast, *Remaking Chicago*, 109–11.

61. Ibid., 99.

62. Costas Spirou and Larry Bennett, *It's Hardly Sportin': Stadiums, Neighborhoods, and the New Chicago* (DeKalb: Northern Illinois University Press, 2003), 195–201.

63. Barbara Ferman, *Challenging the Growth Machine: Neighborhood Politics in Chicago and Pittsburgh* (Lawrence: University Press of Kansas, 1996), 103–7.

64. Third Generation Chicago Native, blog posting, January 21, 2008.

65. Larry Bennett, "The Mayor among His Peers: Interpreting Richard M. Daley," in *The City, Revisited: Urban Theory from Chicago, Los Angeles, and New York*, ed. Dennis R. Judd and Dick Simpson (Minneapolis: University of Minnesota Press, 2011), 242–72.

3. Master Builder

1. Hilary Ballon and Kenneth T. Jackson, *Robert Moses and the Modern City: The Transformation of New York* (New York: W. W. Norton, 2007), 65.

2. R. Bruce Dold, "Daley Slates Top Aide for Pier Chief," *Chicago Tribune*, July 13, 1989.

3. James Ylisela Jr., "McPier Meltdown," *Crain's Chicago Business*, November 21, 2009.

4. "Richard M. Daley's 22 Years as Mayor," *Chicago Tribune*, April 30, 2011.

5. James Smith, "Re-stating Theories of Urban Development: The Politics of Authority Creation and Intergovernmental Triads in Postindustrial Chicago," *Journal of Urban Affairs* 32, no. 4 (2010): 425–48.

6. William Recktenwald and John McCarron, "Parks Group Wants Hiring Frozen at Top," *Chicago Tribune*, January 12, 1987.

7. Ben Joravsky and Mick Dumke, "Shedding Light on the Shadow Budget," *Chicago Reader*, December 10, 2009.

8. The Civic Federation, *Chicago Park District FY2011 Budget: Analysis and Recommendations*, December 1, 2010, https://www.civicfed.org/sites/default/files/CPDFY2011Analysis.pdf.

9. Smith, "Re-stating Theories of Urban Development."

10. George Papajohn, "Challenge for a New Century—the City Needs a New Blueprint, a Vision That Draws on Its Strengths and Addresses Its Problems in a Vein Similar to Daniel H. Burnham's 1909 'Plan of Chicago,'" *Chicago Tribune*, February 7, 1999.

11. Fred Bernstein, "Big Shoulders, Big Donors, Big Art," *New York Times*, July 18, 2004.

12. Ed Lowe, "Convention and Tourism Bureau Names Officers," *Inside Lincoln Park*, March 27–April 2, 2002.

13. Chicago City Council, *Journal of the Proceedings*, Municipal Reference Collection, Chicago Public Library, May 6, 1991, 13–19.

14. Gordon Wright, "Decaying Pier Gets a Life Preserver," *Building Design & Construction* 37, no. 2 (1996): 36.

15. Hedy Weiss, "Building for the Millennium: Theater Companies Playing Bigger Role in the Community," *Chicago Tribune*, September 12, 1999; Deborah Wilk, "At the Top of the Glass: Museum of Stained Glass Windows Is Making Its Debut at Navy Pier," *Chicago Tribune*, February 11, 2000.

16. "Crain's List Largest Tourist Attractions (Sightseeing): Ranked by 2007 Attendance," *Crain's Chicago Business*, June 23, 2008, 22.

17. "Navy Pier Sets Attendance Record," *Crain's Chicago Business*, January 24, 2013.

18. Robert L. Kaiser, "Blazing a Trail through Lost Chicago," *Chicago Tribune*, August 5, 1997; John McCarron, "Downtown Unchained? The Building Boom Is Back," *Chicago Tribune*, August 11, 1997; David Bernstein, "Just a Quiet Night at Home," *Crain's Chicago Business*, May 3, 2004.

19. "Forrec Develops Strategic Vision for Chicago's Navy Pier," Forrec Ltd. press release, February 25, 2006.

20. Blair Kamin, "Navy Pier's Cheesy Makeover Plan Is Full of Holes," *Chicago Tribune*, January 22, 2006, 12.

21. Kathy Bergen, "Second Crack at Navy Pier Upgrade," *Chicago Tribune*, November 11, 2010.

22. Ellen Jean Hirst, "Developers Sought for Navy Pier Hotel," *Chicago Tribune*, July 9, 2014.

23. John McCarron, "Nation's Mayors Find a New Daley and a New Era," *Chicago Tribune*, June 17, 1990.

24. Editorial, "Richard Daley for Mayor," *Chicago Tribune*, February 10, 1991.

25. Thomas Hardy, "With Election behind Him, Daley Set to Get Down to Business," *Chicago Tribune*, April 4, 1991.

26. Chicago City Council, *Journal of the Proceedings*, Municipal Reference Collection, Chicago Public Library, May 6, 1991, 13–19.

27. Chicago City Council, *Journal of the Proceedings*, Municipal Reference Collection, Chicago Public Library, May 5, 2003, 12–29.

28. Robert Muccigrosso, *Celebrating the New World: Chicago's Columbian Exposition of 1893* (Chicago: Ivan R. Dee, 1993).

29. Neil Harris, "Dream Making," *Chicago History* 23, no. 2 (1994): 52.

30. Diane Dillon, "Mapping Enterprise: Cartography and Commodification at the 1893 World's Columbian Exposition," in *Nineteenth Century Geographies: The Transformation of Space from the Victorian Age to the American Century*, ed. Helena Michie and Ronald R. Thomas (Brunswick, NJ: Rutgers University Press, 2003), 85.

31. See "History," McCormick Place Chicago, http://www.mccormickplace. com/about-us/history.php.

32. Chicago Mayor's Committee to Investigate McCormick Place Fire, *Report of the Investigation of the McCormick Place Fire of Jan. 16, 1967*, City of Chicago, 1967, Municipal Reference Collection, Chicago Public Library.

33. *KPMG Peat Marwick: Metropolitan Pier and Exposition Authority Long Range Marketing Study*, 1990, iv–7.

34. PricewaterhouseCoopers, *Metropolitan Pier and Exposition Authority: Long Range Strategic Plan for the McCormick Place Convention Complex*, March 2000, i.

35. Illinois Economic and Fiscal Commission, *McCormick Place Expansion and the Illinois Tourism Industry*, October 2002, Springfield.

36. Ibid, i.

37. Tom Hale, "McCormick Place West Expansion," *Construction Digest*, July 11, 2005.

38. See Choose Chicago, http://www.choosechicago.com, posted March 28, 2008.

39. Costas Spirou, "Infrastructure Development and the Tourism Industry in Chicago," in *Twenty-First Century Chicago*, ed. Dick Simpson and Connie Mixon (San Diego, CA: Cognella, 2012), 198. See Choose Chicago, http://www. choosechicago.com.

40. "Largest Shows at McCormick Place, Ranked by Attendance, List and Directories," *Crain's Chicago Business*, March 26, 2007.

41. Kathy Bergen, "Big Trade Shows Boost City: Regains No 2 Spot in Event Space Used," *Chicago Tribune*, May 1, 2007.

42. Kathy Bergen, "Mixed Results for McCormick Place: More Conventions, but Attendance, Space Use Drops," *Chicago Tribune*, April 18, 2012.

43. Kathy Bergen, "McPier Hires Planning Help," *Chicago Tribune*, September 10, 2008.

44. William Recktenwald, "Navy Pier Bill a Plum for Daley," *Chicago Tribune*, July 3, 1989.

45. Kathy Bergen, Robert Channick, and John Byrne, "Emanuel Launches $300M in Projects: Taxpayers to Fund New DePaul Arena," *Chicago Tribune*, May 17, 2013.

46. John McCarron, "Lake Shore Drive Shift Offered Plan for '92 Fair Would Move Lanes West," *Chicago Tribune*, January 22, 1985.

47. "Lake Shore Drive," *Planning* 61, no. 2 (1995): 42.

48. Blair Kamin, "Reinventing the Lakefront: To Shape the Shoreline," *Chicago Tribune*, October 26, 1998.

49. Blair Kamin, "Nature's Way in Making Room for a More Accessible Lakefront: The Lake Short Drive Rerouting Reflects a New Vision of Highways and Bolsters the Case for Making Meigs Field a Park," *Chicago Tribune*, November 1, 1996.

50. Blair Kamin, "Gem in the Making: The New Museum Campus Is Chicago's Latest Lakefront Jewel, but It Still Needs a Little Polishing," *Chicago Tribune*, June 4, 1998.

51. Sandra Jones, "Attendance at Top Museums Fell in '04," *Crain's Chicago Business*, January 31, 2005.

52. Ibid.

53. Ana Mendieta, "Planetarium Shines New," *Chicago Sun-Times*, September 30, 1999.

54. Gregory Meyer, "Attendance at Major Local Museums Up 2% in 2005," *Crain's Chicago Business*, January 19, 2006.

55. "Chicago's Most Popular Cultural Attractions, Ranked by Attendance, List and Directories," *Crain's Chicago Business*, March 26, 2007.

56. James Hill and Daniel Borsky, "City Lifts Veil on Hopes for Meigs Wetlands, Botanical Gardens Are Included," *Chicago Tribune*, July 2, 1996.

57. Kamin, "Nature's Way in Making Room for a More Accessible Lakefront."

58. City of Chicago, "Mayor Daley Announces Compromise Plan on Northerly Island; Meigs to Reopen for Five Years, Then Become Park," Office of the Mayor, January 6, 1997.

59. John W. Fountain, "Chicago Mayor Bulldozes a Small Downtown Airport," *New York Times*, April 1, 2003.

60. Greg Kot, "Stunning Skyline," *Chicago Tribune*, June 27, 2005.

61. Fran Spielman, "Northerly Island Upgrades Make Way for More Urban Campers to Pitch Their Tents," *Chicago Sun-Times*, August 15, 2012.

62. Robert A. Baade and Allen R. Sanderson, "Bearing Down in Chicago," in *Sports, Jobs and Taxes*, ed. Roger G. Noll and Andrew Zimbalist (Washington, DC: Brookings Institution, 2007), 330–31, as cited in Liam T. A. Ford, *Soldier Field: A Stadium and Its City* (Chicago: University of Chicago Press, 2009), 298.

63. Robert Davis and Daniel Egler, "Bears Owner Told to Cool Off before He Packs Bags," *Chicago Tribune*, November 29, 1990.

64. Costas Spirou and Larry Bennett, *It's Hardly Sportin': Stadiums, Neighborhoods, and the New Chicago* (DeKalb: Northern Illinois University Press, 2003), 139–44.

65. Evan Osnos and Rick Pearson, "Bears, City Say This May Be Real Deal for Soldier Field," *Chicago Tribune*, August 15, 2000.

66. Quoted in Ford, *Soldier Field*, 304.

67. Quoted ibid., 309.

68. Quoted ibid.

69. Liam Ford, "Soldier Field Landscaping Takes Shape," *Chicago Tribune*, April 26, 2004.

70. Quoted ibid., 314.

71. Timothy J. Gilfoyle, *Millennium Park: Creating a Chicago Landmark* (Chicago: University of Chicago Press, 2006), 341.

72. Ibid., 81.

73. Ibid., 81–82.

74. Ibid., 82–83.

75. Richard M. Daley, "A Letter to the People of Chicago," City of Chicago press release, August 1998.

76. Yvette Shields, "Chicago Plans Issue for Park Expansion," *Bond Buyer*, April 2, 1998, 324(30364): 3.

77. City of Chicago, "New Millennium Plans Unveiled to Chicago Plan Commission on March 11, 1999," Department of Transportation, March 1999.

78. City of Chicago, *Chicago's Millennium Park*, Office of Tourism, May 2003.

79. Tara Burghart, "Chicago Gets Millennium Park, 4 Years Late," Associated Press, May 15, 2004.

80. Gilfoyle, *Millennium Park*, 119–34.

81. Chris Jones, "A One-Man Fundraising Machine," *Chicago Tribune*, July 15, 2004.

82. Ibid.

83. Gilfoyle, *Millennium Park*, 123.

84. Blair Kamin, "Steel Appeal," *Chicago Tribune*, July 6, 2003.

85. "Crain's List Largest Tourist Attractions (Sightseeing): Ranked by 2007 Attendance," *Crain's Chicago Business*, June 23, 2008.

86. "Crain's List: Chicago's Largest Tourist Attractions (Sightseeing): Ranked by 2008 Attendance," *Crain's Chicago Business*, March 22, 2010.

87. City of Chicago, "Media Advisory: Millennium Park Celebrates Its First Birthday," July 12, 2005.

88. Edward K. Uhlir, "The Millennium Park Effect: Creating a Cultural Venue with an Economic Impact," *Economic Development Journal* 4, no. 2 (Spring 2005).

89. Kathy Bergen and John Handley, "High-Speed High-Rises Stagger Streeterville," *Chicago Tribune*, July 17, 2005.

90. Norm Fossmeyer, "Voice of the People: Waste of Money," *Chicago Tribune*, September 28, 2006.

91. City of Chicago, "Mayor Rahm Emanuel and Choose Chicago Announce Additional Tourism Records for 2012: Economic Impact, Tax Revenue, and Job Creation," September 16, 2013.

92. Costas Spirou, "Infrastructure Development and the Tourist Industry in Chicago," in *Chicago's Geographies: Metropolis for the 21st Century*, ed. Mark J. Bouman, Dennis Grammenos, and Richard Greene (Washington, DC: Association of American Geographers, 2006), 117.

4. Power Broker

1. Robert Caro, *The Power Broker: Robert Moses and the Fall of New York* (New York: Vintage Books, 1975). Caro used these phrases as the titles of two of the seven parts of his book.

2. "King Richard's Rivals," *Economist*, November 16, 2002, 28.

3. Thomas Hardy and R. Bruce Dold, "Chicago's 2nd Daley Era Begins," *Chicago Tribune*, April 25, 1989.

4. Robert K. Kieckhefer, "Mayor Richard M. Daley: The Adapter instead of Boss II," *Illinois Issues*, June 1989, 12.

5. Pam Belluck, "Daley, Ever Neutralizing Critics, Runs Again," *New York Times*, December 9, 1998.

6. R. Bruce Dold, "Campaigning in Chicago, Easier Said Than Done," *Chicago Tribune*, April 16, 1989.

7. Joel Kaplan and Thomas Hardy, "Daley's 1st 100 Days: Even Opponents Agree the Mayor Merits Passing Grade," *Chicago Tribune*, July 30, 1989.

8. Irving J. Rein, "The Transformation of a Candidate: Richard M. Daley," *American Communication Journal* 2, no. 1 (2000), http://ac-journal.org/journal/vol2/Iss1/articles/rein.html.

9. Dennis R. Judd and Dick Simpson, "Reconstructing the Local State: The Role of External Constituencies in Building Urban Tourism," *American Behavioral Scientist* 46, no. 8 (April 2003): 1060.

10. David Moberg, "The Fuel of a New Machine," *Chicago Reader*, March 30, 1989.

11. Dick Simpson and Tom M. Kelly, "The New Chicago School of Urbanism and the New Daley Machine," *Urban Affairs Review* 44, no. 2 (2008): 231.

12. "Regional Business Leaders Merge to Create Global Marketing Organization Chaired by Mayor Richard M. Daley," press release, *World Business Chicago*, September 5, 2000.

13. Ibid.

14. Moberg, "Fuel of a New Machine."

15. Aurie A. Pennick and Howard Stanback, "The Affordable Housing Crisis in the Chicago Region," in the *New Chicago: A Social and Cultural Analysis* (Philadelphia: Temple University Press, 2006), 231–38.

16. Rick Pearson, "Executives Say Daley Is a Mayor Who Works," *Chicago Tribune*, May 3, 1998.

17. Dirk Johnson, "With Black Support, Daley Seems Sure of Re-election," *New York Times*, February 23, 1999.

18. "Daley's Legacy: An Interview with the Honorable Richard M. Daley, Former Mayor of Chicago," *Leaders* 34, no. 3 (2011): 60.

19. Richard M. Daley, "Richard M. Daley: Reflections on Government and Career as Chicago Mayor," Wheaton College, Wheaton, IL, March 2, 2011.

20. Richard M. Daley with Richard Florida, "Advice for the Mega City," Aspen Ideas Festival, Aspen Institute, Aspen, CO, June 29, 2012.

21. Inaugural Address of Mayor Richard M. Daley, Chicago Public Library Municipal Reference Collection, April 24, 1989.

22. Ibid.

23. John McCarron, "Nation's Mayors Find a New Daley and a New Era," *Chicago Tribune*, June 17, 1990.

24. "Richard Daley Wins Chicago Mayoral Race; Blacks Fail to Unite behind Tim Evans," *Jet*, April 24, 1989, 8.

25. "Richard M. Daley Calls for 'Racial Harmony' at Inaugural," *Jet*, May 8, 1989, 12.

26. Alysia Tate, "The Hispanic Vote: Gutiérrez Alliance Made Daley the Latino Choice," *Chicago Reporter*, September 28, 2007.

27. Lori Rotenberk, "Daley Is First Mayor to Lead Gays' Parade," *Chicago Sun-Times*, June 26, 1989.

28. Christi Parsons, "Mayor of Few Words," *Chicago Tribune*, February 8, 1995.

29. Belluck, "Daley, Ever Neutralizing Critics."

30. Thomas Hardy, "Daley Keeps Minority Inroad: Mayor Gets About 20% of Black Vote, Is Big with Latinos," *Chicago Tribune*, April 7, 1995.

31. Debbie Howlett, "Donors' Cash Turns City Green," *USA Today*, July 15, 2004.

32. Robert Davis, "The Son Also Razes; Mayor's Meigs Ploy Pales Next to Some of Father's Projects," *Chicago Tribune*, April 2, 2003.

33. John Hilkevitch, "Poll Finds Little Support for Daley's Raid on Meigs," *Chicago Tribune*, June 16, 2003.

34. Phil Kadner, "Foes Shocked and Awed in Battle of Meigs Field," *Daily Southtown*, April 1, 2003.

35. Lynn Sweet and Fran Spielman, "Daley's Meigs Alibi Crumbles," *Chicago Sun-Times*, April 9, 2003.

36. Melissa Block, "Mayor Richard Daley Orders Destruction of a Chicago Airfield in the Middle of the Night Due to Fears of Attack," *All Things Considered*, National Public Radio, April 1, 2003.

37. John Barber, "A Chance to Make Daley Strides," *Globe and Mail*, May 24, 2005.

38. Gary Washburn and Jon Hilkevitch, "Daley Rips up Meigs Runways in Surprise Raid," *Chicago Tribune*, April 1, 2003.

39. Debbie Howlett, "Donor's Cash Turns City Green," *Chicago Tribune*, July 15, 2004.

40. Ben Joravsky, "Temper, Temper," *Chicago Reader*, September 19, 2007, http://www.chicagoreader.com/Bleader/archives/2007/09/19/temper-temper.

41. "Chicago's Postponed Olympic Bid," editorial, *Chicago Tribune*, April 11, 1997.

42. Gary Washburn, "Mayor Expands Olympic Dream: Daley Says Games Would Benefit Not Just City but Region," *Chicago Tribune*, January 5, 2006.

43. Kathy Bergen, "Chicago 2016's Final Fundraiser Nets $5 Million," *Chicago Tribune*, August 19, 2009.

44. John Pletz, "Daley Agrees to Olympics Financial Guarantee," *Crain's Chicago Business*, June 17, 2009.

45. Dan Mihalopoulos, "Chicago 2016: Mayor Daley Trumpets Upsides of Olympics," *Chicago Tribune*, September 23, 2009.

46. Monee Fields-White, "Chicago Lured 45M Tourists Who Dropped $11.8B Last Year," *Crain's Chicago Business*, September 22, 2009.

47. Fran Spielman, "Daley Answers Critics of Chicago 2016 Bid," *Chicago Sun-Times*, July 21, 2009.

48. Dan Mihalopoulos, "Mayor Richard Daley Sought Olympics to Solve Myriad Problems; Now What?," *Chicago Tribune*, October 4, 2009.

49. Mike Royko, *Boss: Richard J. Daley of Chicago* (New York: Plume, 1988), 5.

50. Pennsylvania Economy League, *Greater Philadelphia Regional Review* (Philadelphia: Valley Press, 2006), 9.

51. Belluck, "Daley, Ever Neutralizing Critics."

5. Richard M. Daley's Ambiguous Legacy

1. Richard M. Daley, "No Pain, No Gain—or How New York Can Resolve This Crisis and Avert Another; Privatization," *New York Times*, June 16, 1991.

2. Richard M. Daley, "Chicago City Government: Smaller in Size but Greater in Performance," *Business Forum* 19, no. 2 (1994): 4.

3. Michael Barone, "The Last Gasp of Liberalism," *U.S. News & World Report*, September 27, 1993, 53.

4. "Uncoupling Chicago's Gravy Train," *Newsweek*, March 3, 1991, 53.

5. "Richard Daley for Mayor," editorial, *Chicago Tribune*, February 10, 1991.

6. Ibid.

7. Ben Bradley, "Poll: 37 Percent Approval Rating for Mayor Daley," WLS News, July 17, 2010, http://abclocal.go.com/wls/story?id=7560657.

8. Natasha Korecki, "Poll: Name Hurts Daley," *Southtown Star*, July 1, 2013.

9. Dick Simpson, James Nowlan, Thomas J. Gradel, Melissa Mouritsen Zmuda, David Sterrett, and Douglas Cantor, *Chicago and Illinois, Leading the Pack in Corruption*, Anti-corruption Report Number 5, Department of Political Science, University of Illinois at Chicago, and Institute for Government and Public Affairs, February 15, 2012.

10. Ibid.

11. Fran Spielman, "Scandals, Cronyism Cloud Daley's Legacy," *Chicago Sun-Times*, May 8, 2011.

12. Thomas J. Gradel, Dick Simpson, et al., *Patronage, Cronyism and Criminality in Chicago Government Agencies*, Anti-corruption Report Number 4, Department of Political Science, University of Illinois at Chicago, February 2011, 2.

13. Evan Osnos, "The Daley Show," Letter from Chicago, *New Yorker*, March 8, 2010, 49.

14. Mark Guarino, "Chicago Area Called Most Corrupt in US: Why Rahm Emanuel Is Under Fire," *Christian Science Monitor*, February 15, 2012.

15. Mark Brown, "Millennium Park Trial and the Paradoxes of Daley's Chicago," *Chicago Sun-Times*, April 29, 2014.

16. Richard C. Longworth, "Daley: A Falling Star in Chicago," *Chicago Sun-Times*, July 16, 2014.

17. Hal Dardick, "Millennium Park Built 'the Chicago Way,'" *Chicago Tribune*, July 13, 2014.

18. Mark Brown, "Daley's Legacy Takes Another Turn with Ex-Cab Official's Arrest," *Chicago Sun-Times*, September 29, 2014.

19. John Conroy, "The Police Torture Scandals: A Who's Who," *Chicago Reader*, June 15, 2006.

20. Flint Taylor, "Jon Burge, Torturer of Over 100 Black Men, Is Out of Prison after Less Than Four Years," *Chicago Tribune*, October 2, 2014.

21. Charles Nicodemus, "City Mum on if It'll Pay to Defend Cop in Suit," *In These Times*, November 29, 1991.

22. Flint Taylor, "Racism, Torture and Impunity in Chicago," *Nation*, February 20, 2013.

23. John Hagedorn, Bart Kmiecik, Dick Simpson, Thomas J. Gradel, Melissa Mouritsen Zmuda, David Sterrett, et al., *Crime Corruption and Cover-ups in the Chicago Police Department*, Anti-corruption Report Number 7, Department of Political Science, University of Illinois at Chicago, January 17, 2013.

24. Ibid.

25. Craig B. Futterman, H. Melissa Mather, and Melanie Miles, "The Use of Statistical Evidence to Address Police Supervisory and Disciplinary Practices: The

Chicago Police Department's Broken System," *Civil Rights Litigation Annual Handbook 5*, vol. 23, 2007, Thomson West.

26. Jason Meisner, "Judge Assigned to Vanecko Case Has Daley Ties," *Chicago Tribune*, December 11, 2012.

27. Tim Novak and Chris Fusco, "Daley Nephew Vanecko out of Jail," *Chicago Sun-Times*, April 14, 2014.

28. Mark Guarino, "Homicide Rate Jumps in Chicago, Daley Pushes for More Gun Control," *Christian Science Monitor*, April 27, 2010; Mark Guarino, "Chicago Erupts in Gun Violence," *Christian Science Monitor*, July 8, 2013.

29. Monica Davey and Mitch Smith, "Mayor Rahm Emanuel Fires Chicago Police Superintendent," *New York Times*, December 1, 2015.

30. Mark Berman, "Chicago Police 'Have No Regard' for Lives of Minorities, Report Says," *Washington Post*, April 13, 2016.

31. Mark Berman, "Chicago Will Make Some Changes to Its Police Department as a 'Down Payment' on Reform," *Washington Post*, April 21, 2016.

32. D. Bradford Hunt, "What Went Wrong with Public Housing in Chicago? A History of the Robert Taylor Homes," *Journal of the Illinois State Historical Society* 94, no. 1 (2001): n.p.

33. Marshall Kaplan and Franklin James, eds., *The Future of National Urban Policy* (Durham, NC: Duke University Press, 1990), 65.

34. Edward Walsh, "U.S. to Take Over Control of Troubled Chicago Public Housing Authority," *Washington Post*, May 28, 1995.

35. Jeff Glasser, "From Big and Ugly to Small and Promising," *U.S. News & World Report*, September 11, 2000.

36. Sarah Downey and John McCormick, "Razing the Vertical Ghettos," *Newsweek*, May 15, 2000, 36.

37. Amanda Paulson, "Chicago Raises the Bar for Living in Public Housing," *Christian Science Monitor*, October 5, 2004, 3.

38. Larry Bennett, *The Third City: Chicago and American Urbanism* (Chicago: University of Chicago Press, 2010), 176.

39. Erin M. Graves and Lawrence J. Vale, "Planning Note: The Chicago Housing Authority's Plan for Transformation: Assessing the First Ten Years," *Journal of the American Planning Association* 78, no. 4 (2012): 464.

40. Susan J. Popkin, *Long Term Outcomes for CHA Residents: How Chicago's Public Housing Transformation Can Inform Federal Policy*, Urban Institute, Brief 01, 2013.

41. Natalie Moore, "Daley's Legacy on Chicago Public Housing: Cabrini Green and Altgeld Gardens Try to Fit within Larger Communities," WBEZ91.5, January 21, 2011.

42. Michael Martinez, "Go-Ahead Expected for 8 Charter Schools in City," *Chicago Tribune*, January 22, 1997.

43. "Reform before the Storm: A Timeline of the Chicago Public Schools," *Chicago Magazine*, October 2, 2012.

44. Stephanie Banchero, "Daley School Plan Fails to Make the Grade," *Chicago Tribune*, January 17, 2010.

45. Ibid.

46. Stuart Luppescu, Elaine M. Allensworth, Paul Moore, Marisa de la Torre, James Murphy, and Sanja Jagesic, *Trends in Chicago's Schools across Three Eras of Reform: Summary of Key Findings* (Chicago: University of Chicago Urban Education Institute, 2011), 1.

47. Pauline Lipman, "Chicago School Reform: Advancing the Global City Agenda," in *The New Chicago: A Social and Cultural Analysis*, ed. John P. Koval, Larry Bennett, Michael Bennett, Fassil Demissie, Roberta Garner, and Kiljoong Kim (Philadelphia: Temple University Press, 2006), 248–58.

48. Richard M. Daley, Welcoming Remarks, National Chinese Language Conference, Chicago, April 30–May 2, 2009.

49. Ibid.

50. Fran Spielman, "Daley's Unique Legacy Secured," *Chicago Sun-Times*, May 14, 2011.

51. Jason Grotto, Heather Gillers, and Patricia Callahan, "City's Debt Splurge: 'It's Like a Cancer,'" *Chicago Tribune*, November 1, 2013.

52. Matt Taibbi, *Griftopia: A Story of Bankers, Politicians, and the Most Audacious Power Grab in American History* (New York: Spiegel & Grau, 2011), 167–69.

53. Fran Spielman, "City of Chicago's Cash Cushion Plummets, Debt Triples, Arrests Drop, Water Use Rises," *Chicago Sun-Times*, July 26, 2013.

54. Hal Dardick, "Daley Took Out Loans to Run Millennium Park," *Chicago Tribune*, November 4, 2013.

55. Grotto, Gillers, and Callahan, "City's Debt Splurge."

56. Civic Federation, *Financial Challenges for the New Mayor of Chicago: Analysis and Recommendations*, February 14, 2011, 2.

57. Caroline Cournoyer, "Moody's Cites Pension Problems as Reason for Downgrading Chicago's Bond Rating," *Governing*, July 19, 2013.

58. Mark Guarino, "Chicago's Credit Rating Downgraded: How Its Woes Differ from Detroit's," *Christian Science Monitor*, March 5, 2014.

59. Greg Hinz and Thomas Corfman, "Moody's Cuts Chicago's Credit Rating to Junk," *Crain's Chicago Business*, May 12, 2015.

60. Fran Spielman, "Poll: Rahm Re-election on Ropes; Voters Say No Better Than Daley," *Chicago Sun-Times*, May 10, 2014.

61. Hal Dardick, "Tribune Poll: Daley Gets Blame for City's Financial Condition," *Chicago Tribune*, August 14, 2014.

62. "Mayor Emanuel Outlines Vision for Continued Expansion and Growth of Tourism in Chicago," press release, City of Chicago, January 22, 2014.

63. Costas Spirou, *Urban Tourism and Urban Change: Cities in a Global Economy* (New York: Routledge, 2011), 41.

64. Lynn Sweet, "Rahm Emanuel's Inauguration Speech," *Chicago Sun-Times*, May 16, 2011.

65. John Hilkevitch, "Chicago Riverwalk Extension No Cakewalk," *Chicago Tribune*, August 25, 2014.

66. Fran Spielman, "City Unveils Riverwalk Concept, Asks Feds for Help Building It," *Chicago Sun-Times*, October 8, 2012.

67. Blair Kamin and Ryan Haggerty, "Children's Museum's Move to Grant Park Scuttled," *Chicago Tribune*, October 27, 2011.

68. Chicago Plan Commission, *The Chicago Central Area Plan: Preparing the Central City for the 21st Century*, City of Chicago, 2003, 128–29.

69. Ibid.

70. Greg Hinz and Thomas Corfman, "Measuring the Mayor," *Crain's Chicago Business*, November 10, 2014.

Epilogue

1. Bernard J. Frieden and Lynn B. Sagalyn, *Downtown, Inc.: How America Builds Cities* (Cambridge, MA: MIT Press, 1989), 43; also, Dennis R. Judd, "Constructing the Tourist Bubble," in *The Tourist City*, ed. Dennis R. Judd and Susan S. Fainstein (New Haven, CT: Yale University Press, 1999).

2. David Harvey, *Spaces of Capital: Towards a Critical Geography* (New York: Routledge, 2001), 143–44.

3. Quoted in Tony Hiss, "Reinventing Baltimore," Annals of Place, *New Yorker*, April 29, 1991, 41.

4. Mike Davis, *City of Quartz: Excavating the Future in Los Angeles* (New York: Verso, 1990), 78.

5. Peter Eisenger, "The Politics of Bread and Circuses: Building the City for the Visitor Class," *Urban Affairs Review* 35, no. 3 (2000): 316–33.

6. Elie Parker, "Priority Problem," *Chicago Tribune*, August 15, 1995.

7. Kathleen Smith, "Mixed-Up Priorities: Whole New Meaning," *Chicago Sun-Times*, April 28, 2002.

8. Henry Blake Fuller, *With the Procession: A Novel* (New York: Harper & Bros., 1894), 86–87.

9. Ray Stannard Baker, *American Chronicle: The Autobiography of Ray Stannard Baker* (New York: Charles Scribner's Son, 1945), 2.

10. Robert Herrick, *The Web of Life* (New York: Macmillan, 1900), 135.

11. U.S. Department of the Interior, Ninth Census (July 1, 1870), vol. 1, Population and Social Statistics (Washington, DC: Government Printing Office, 1872), 386; U.S. Department of Commerce, Bureau of the Census, Thirteenth Census of the United State Taken in the Year 1910, vol. 1, Population 1910 (Washington, DC: Government Printing Office, 1913), 178.

12. Joseph Kirkland, "Among the Poor of Chicago," *Scribner's Magazine*, July 1892, 19.

13. P. J. O'Keefe, "The Chicago Stockyards," *New England Magazine*, May 1892, 358.

14. As quoted in Louis C. Wade, *Graham Taylor: Pioneer for Social Justice, 1851–1938* (Chicago: University of Chicago Press, 1964), 76.

15. Richard T. Ely, "Pullman: A Social Study," *Harper's Magazine*, February 1885, 463.

16. Stanley Buder, *Pullman: An Experiment in Industrial Order and Community Planning, 1880–1930* (New York: Oxford University Press, 1967), provides an excellent analysis of the social structure at Pullman; and Almont Lindsey, *The Pullman Strike* (Chicago: University of Chicago Press, 1942), closely details the strike.

17. James Gilbert, *Perfect Cities: Chicago's Utopias of 1893* (Chicago: University of Chicago Press, 1991), 165.

18. Frederic L. Ford, "The Scope of City Planning in the United States," in City Planning, Hearing before the Committee on the District of Columbia, United States Senate, on the Subject of City Planning, 61st Congress, 2nd Session, Senate Document No. 422 (Washington, DC: Government Printing Office, 1910), 70–73.

19. "Demands for the City Beautiful," *Municipal Journal and Engineer* 21 (September 5, 1906): 243 (editorial).

20. Quoted in Robert W. Rydell, *All the World's a Fair: Visions of Empire at American International Expositions, 1876–1916* (Chicago: University of Chicago Press, 1984), 8.

21. Quoted in Alan Trachtenberg, *The Incorporation of America: Culture and Society in the Gilded Age* (New York: Hill & Wang, 1982), 215.

22. Louis H. Sullivan, *The Autobiography of an Idea* (New York: Press of the American Institute of Architects, 1924), 324.

23. Lewis Mumford, *The City in History: Its Origins, Its Transformations, and Its Prospects* (New York: Harcourt Brace & Co., 1961), 401.

24. William Cronon, *Nature's Metropolis: Chicago and the Great West* (New York: W. W. Norton, 1991), 351.

25. Ibid., 358.

26. Jane Jacobs, *The Death and Life of Great American Cities* (New York: Vintage, 1961), 24.

27. Peter Hall, *Cities in Civilization* (New York: Pantheon Books, 1998), 784, 937.

28. Michael Sorkin, ed., *Variations on a Theme Park: The New American City and the End of Public Space* (New York: Hill & Wang, 1992), 208, 211.

29. Leonard Nevarez, *New Money, Nice Town: How Capital Works in the New Urban Economy* (New York: Routledge, 2003), 182.

30. Janet L. Abu-Lughod, *Race, Space, and Riots in Chicago, New York, and Los Angeles* (New York: Oxford University Press, 2007), 53 (first quotation); 276. We argue that what Abu-Lughod calls the "backstage" is actually a complex geography that defies easy description, but clearly it is racially and ethnically diverse, and the wards and neighborhoods are thoroughly incorporated into the politics and cultural life of the city. Things were different a century ago. At the time of the Columbian Exposition, the conditions in the immigrant neighborhoods were shocking, a fact often noted by the progressive reformers of the time and by historians ever since. Scarcely had Burnham's White City been built as the centerpiece of the World's Fair than allusions to the "black city," with its immigrant wards and staggering social problems, began to appear. It does not add much to our understanding of Chicago, or probably of any big city in America, to describe it in such language today.

31. Ibid., 278.

32. Heywood Sanders, "Building the Convention City: Politics, Finance, and Public Investment in Urban America," *Journal of Urban Affairs* 14, no. 2 (1992): 135–60.

33. Heywood Sanders, *Flawed Forecasts: A Critical Look at Convention Center Feasibility Studies*, White Paper Number 9, Pioneer Institute for Public Policy Research (Boston: Pioneer Institute, 1999).

34. David Harvey, *The Condition of Postmodernity* (New York: Blackwell, 1989), 92.

35. Mark Douglas Lowes, *Indy Dreams and Urban Nightmares: Speed Merchants, Spectacle, and the Struggle over Public Space in the World-Class City* (Toronto: University of Toronto Press, 2002), 116.

36. Michael A. Pagano and Ann Bowman, *Cityscapes and Capital: The Politics of Urban Development* (Baltimore: Johns Hopkins University Press, 1995), 74.

37. Heywood Sanders, *Convention Center Follies: Politics, Power, and Public Investment in American Cities* (Philadelphia: University of Pennsylvania Press, 2014), 150–208.

38. All data from Heywood Sanders, Space Available: The Realities of Convention Centers as Economic Development Strategy (Washington, DC: Brookings Institution Press, 2005), 1; also see Sanders, *Convention Center Follies*.

39. "State of the Industry," Successful Meetings, July 1993, 32–33.

40. Data provided by Heywood Sanders, April 25, 2015.

41. Tim Chapin, "Beyond the Entrepreneurial City: Municipal Capitalism in San Diego," *Journal of Urban Affairs* 24, no. 5 (1993): 567–68.

42. Josh Goodman, "Skybox Skeptics," *Governing* 19, no. 6 (2006): 41–42.

43. "Forbes: Mets' Value Drops 13 Percent; Yankees Top List," CBS New York, March 24, 2011.

44. Richard Sandomir, "New Stadiums: Prices, and Outrage, Escalate," *New York Times*, August 28, 2008, www.nytimes.com/2008/08/26/sports/26tickets.html.

45. Ibid.

46. Ibid.

47. Tim Tucker, "Falcons' PSL Plan: $10,000 to $45,000 for Club Seats," *Atlanta Journal-Constitution*, January 7, 2015.

48. Yvette Shields, "Missouri Touts Progress on Rams Stadium Site," *Bond Buyer*, February 13, 2015.

49. David Hunn, "Chamber Study Calls New Stadium 'Critical,'" *St. Louis Post-Dispatch*, November 14, 2015, A11. The quotation is from the newspaper source.

50. Sam Farmer and Nathan Fenno, "NFL Will Return to Los Angeles for 2016 Season," *Los Angeles Times*, January 12, 2016.

51. Erik Hare, "Stadium Frenzy Ignores Economics," *Mintpress News*, May 8, 2014, http://www.mintpressnews.com/stadium-frenzy-ignores-economics/190351/.

52. Ibid.

53. Jon Teaford, *The Unheralded Triumph: City Government in America, 1870–1900* (Baltimore: Johns Hopkins University Press, 1984), 247.

54. Stanley K. Schultz, *Constructing Urban Culture: American Cities and City Planning, 1800–1920* (Philadelphia: Temple University Press, 1989), 174.

55. Ibid., 246.

56. Blake McKelvey, *The Urbanization of America, 1860–1915* (New Brunswick, NJ: Rutgers University Press, 1963), 90.

57. President's Commission for a National Agenda for the Eighties, *A National Agenda for the Eighties* (Washington, DC: Government Printing Office, 1980), 66.

58. Quoted in David Halle and Elizabeth Tiso, *New York's Edge: Contemporary Art, the High Line, and Urban Megaprojects on the Far West Side* (Chicago: University of Chicago Press, 2014), 387. The original source is Julian Brash, *Bloomberg's New York: Class and Governance in the Luxury City* (Athens: University of Georgia Press, 2011), 252.

59. Halle and Tiso, *New York's Edge*, 387.

60. Matt Taibbi, *Divide: American Injustice in the Age of the Wealth Gap* (New York: Spiegel & Grau, 2014), 3–52.

61. Robert Caro, *The Power Broker: Robert Moses and the Fall of New York* (New York: Vintage, 1975), 21.

62. Bill Ruthhart, "Emanuel: Charge Downtown Developers More, Spend Money in Struggling Neighborhoods," *Chicago Tribune*, February 18, 2016.

Index

Page numbers in italics refer to figures.